Mur
at the
Villa Madeira

Murder at the Villa Madeira

The Rattenbury Affair

by Sir David Napley

Weidenfeld and Nicolson
London

First published in Great Britain in 1988 by
George Weidenfeld & Nicolson Limited
91 Clapham High Street, London SW4 7TA

This paperback edition published by
George Weidenfeld & Nicolson Limited 1990

ISBN 0 297 79208 3 (Cased)
      0 297 81036 7 (Paperback)

Printed and bound in Great Britain by
The Guernsey Press Co. Ltd., Guernsey, Channel Islands

Contents

Illustrations

Foreword

The sensation of the year 1935 was the trial at the Old Bailey on charges of murder of Alma Rattenbury, an attractive woman of, perhaps, thirty-nine or forty, and her lover, George Stoner, who had been employed in her house as a chauffeur/handyman.

The crime of murder was then a capital offence. The story which unfolds involves all the shades of high drama. A highly sensuous woman had seduced her very young servant, despite the marked differences in their status and their lives: she a talented musician, acclaimed as a concert pianist and violinist, and a writer of romantic songs, sung by famous tenors; he a callow youth of barely eighteen, from a humble background, with little more than three years' schooling, in the aggregate, to his credit. Her husband, an erstwhile architect of great note, had fashioned some of the most famous buildings in Canada; thirty years his wife's senior, impotent, depressed and an alcoholic, he was found in the sitting-room of the Villa Madeira with his head fractured by blows from a mallet. And then there was the preparation for the trial, hampered initially by the determination of both of the accused to protect the other from hanging, until the woman, ostensibly to preserve the good name of her children, submitted to putting the blame on her young lover.

It is hardly surprising that the tragedy has formed the subject of many books, many articles and at least one play. But it is hoped that this book requires no apology for its appearance, since it aims, in a number of important respects, to differ from anything which has gone before. In the first place I have endeavoured as I did with the Camden Town Murder case, while adhering strictly to the essential facts in their entirety, to draw on my imagination to reconstruct the linking episodes necessary to turn the events into a coherent story. Secondly, and perhaps just as importantly, I have subjected the preparations for the trial, and the trial itself, to a degree of analysis, investigation and dissection which inevitably results in the question 'Was justice really done?'

It will be seen, and accepted I believe, although this proposition has never before been suggested or even canvassed, that unhappily the trial, in a number of respects, did not meet those high standards which have come to be expected of British justice. The prosecution case was inadequately investigated, poorly conducted, forensically inadequate from a medical and scientific viewpoint, and tried under conditions such that, had more attention been paid to the forensic realities and less to the passing of narrow moral strictures, the result may well have been different. But different in what way? It is for the book to explain, and the reader to determine, the answer to that vital question.

I wish to record my grateful thanks to all those who permitted me to refer to, and quote from, previous publications, including Butterworth Ltd in respect of the *Trial of Rattenbury and Stoner* in the Notable British Trials series; Sono Nis Press of British Columbia in respect of *Rattenbury* by Terry Reksten; William Kimber Ltd in relation to *Tragedy in Three Voices* by Sir Michael Havers, Peter Shankland and Anthony Barrett; Harrap Ltd for *A Lance for Liberty* by J. D. Casswell.

I have also had recourse to the *Dictionary of National Biography*, *Criminal Days* by Travers Humphreys, and *Sir Travers Humphreys* by Douglas G. Brown. I also record my thanks to the former Director of Public Prosecutions for making the transcript of the trial available to me.

I am especially indebted to Elizabeth Murray for her tenacious, painstaking and always helpful research on my behalf; to my Editor, Alex MacCormick at Weidenfeld & Nicolson, for her useful suggestions; to my secretary Dianne Potts for her copious typing; and to my daughters for having read the original script and giving me their comments.

DAVID NAPLEY

CHAPTER 1

Fateful Encounter

With the approach of the 1930s, Francis and Alma Rattenbury took up residence in the Villa Madeira. The very name inevitably brings to mind a long, winding drive between an avenue of stately elms, enlivened by the radiance of massed poinsettia, and the distant vision of an imposing white colonial-style residence, its magnificent colonnades resplendent against the azure blue of the sky.

Alas, that was not the way of it. The Villa Madeira was a more modern 'bijou' dwelling, remarkably small, in Manor Road, Bournemouth, on the south coast of England, a resort long renowned for its sunshine and balmy air, richly prized by members of the middle class seeking a place for retirement. Indeed, it was so much sought out by the aged that on the distant Kent road, connecting London with Dover, an unkindly wag wrote under one of the many signs which read 'Dover for the Continent' the words 'and Bournemouth for the incontinent'.

Some may have regarded the Rattenburys as an ill-assorted pair: he a man of over sixty years of age, someone of whom the years may have excessively taken their toll; his wife some thirty years his junior, whom no one saw as unattractive and many regarded as beautiful. Fate or, as some might have it, a designing relative or friend having brought them together when they were both in Canada, they married in British Columbia in 1928.

A great deal was written about them over the years which followed. The picture which sometimes emerged was one which presented him as a quiet, generally easy-going man, capable of charm but with a quick temper, and, if his wife was to be believed, somewhat mean with money. Alma was generally presented as a kindly, highly sexed, attractive woman who had

1

a way with men, but was unreservedly devoted to her children.

Some believe that our course through life is predetermined at the moment of birth; others believe we are, and do, whatever we make or determine for ourselves. What is, however, incontestable is that no one who has played a central part in a criminal trial would have done so were it not for his or her background, history and the special features of his or her character. Yet, as one delves into the earlier lives of Alma and Francis Rattenbury, one comes to question whether previous assessments reached a correct determination, and whether with more penetrating research one might not have found their lives and personalities, in the words of Winston Churchill when speaking of Russia, 'a riddle wrapped in a mystery inside an enigma'.

Francis Mawson Rattenbury came from Devon stock, but was born in Leeds on 11 October 1867. Just as many a fond parent has set his offspring on the path of the law because he was loquacious and argumentative, Rattenbury was steered into the profession of architect because he displayed some talent for drawing. It proved to be a wise choice. An ambitious and enterprising young man, restless and energetic, he soon decided that Yorkshire, where he started his career, offered insufficient challenge for him and he took himself across the Atlantic to Canada. Within a year of his arrival in British Columbia he was chosen from a field of sixty-eight competitors to provide the design for the Parliament Buildings in Victoria, from which he netted a substantial fee. By the age of thirty, still thirsting for adventure, he journeyed to the Klondike, where he engaged in some successful but highly speculative enterprises. He constructed three boats, the *Ora*, *Nova* and *Flora*, to bring back gold from the Klondike gold rush; and when Dawson City was snowed up and starving, he drove a small herd of cattle into the city and saved its inhabitants.

By 1898 he was well established, certainly prospering, and he married his first wife, Eleanor Florence Nunn, known as Florrie, the daughter of an army captain. He took her to Victoria for the opening of the Parliament Buildings. The Prince of Wales, later to become King Edward VII, remarked when he performed the opening that they and the Ottawa Parliament Buildings were the finest he had seen in Canada.

Rattenbury then decided to take things easier, although he was still only thirty-one. Two high points of his life were the births of a son and a daughter, upon both of whom he lavished affection. He had built himself a grand house, which was sumptuously furnished. He called it 'Ichineel', which he said meant 'a place where a good thing happened'. It could have been better named, for some singularly bad things would happen there as well.

Ability such as he clearly possessed could not, however, be that easily put aside and it was not long before he was thoroughly engrossed once again in his architectural activities. There may have been additional reasons for this new burst of creative energy. By then, his marriage was not, perhaps, fulfilling its early promise, and dedication to his work may have been a solace as much as a spur.

One of the buildings which he designed and saw erected in Victoria was the Empress Hotel. It has been written that 'there is no armour against fate', and little did Rattenbury realize as the Empress rose from the ground – a consequence of his own endeavours – that it would later play such a significant part in the ultimate tragedy of his life.

By the time he reached his early fifties, although not a person who easily made friends, he was highly regarded and indeed a famous Canadian architect with many fine buildings to his credit. He was 'tall, some six feet two inches in height, he had dark reddish hair and a clipped moustache and was broad-shouldered, powerful, rubicund', with a strong chin and a sullen temper. A stolid man, somewhat unintellectual, and, despite his ability to play the piano and his architect's skill, one who had little imagination or artistic sense.

He began to display symptoms which were to recur throughout the rest of his life. He became ill; his drive and enthusiasm waned and were replaced with sadness and despair. His wife had, by then, lost what little enthusiasm for his work she ever had. It should have been otherwise, since he was still acclaimed throughout Canada. Indeed, in 1923, when he was fifty-six, a banquet was given in his honour in the Empress Hotel. At the conclusion of the proceedings, he walked slowly out of the dining-room and into the lounge, where, for the first time, he encountered Alma.

She has been described as 'beautiful, with a lovely oval face, deep hauntingly sad eyes and full lips which easily settled into a pout, at once fashionable and sensuous'. Her voice had 'a warm vibrant quality, pitched very low, musically slow and distinct'. In speech she used her hands expressively and extensively. She was in many ways a remarkable character. A certain obscurity surrounds her birth. One account asserts that she was the daughter of a German immigrant to Canada who became a mining prospector, and that because she was born in a remote prospecting area her birth was not recorded. Another account, probably more reliable, asserts that she was born in 1895 or 1896 to Walter and Elizabeth Clarke of Kamloops, British Columbia. Her father, it is said, was co-owner of the *Kamloops Standard*, which he printed himself, and for which he also gathered the news – indeed, he generally ran its affairs. Her mother, according to the first source, was English, a member of the same family as W.G.Grace, the great English batsman, and therefore someone of good background; she taught the piano and the violin, and quickly detected a special talent for music in her daughter – indeed, she soon believed that Alma possessed a quite exceptional talent, as was indeed the case. Her teacher, at a school called St Ann's, described her as 'brilliantly clever . . . a vivid little thing full of happiness and music, with a special attraction of her own'.

Terry Reksten, in an excellent book about Rattenbury, carefully researched his and Alma's early life, discovering that her father sold the *Kamloops Standard* and became a travelling journalist, whatever that may be. By 1902, when Alma would have been six or seven years of age, she was to be found in Havergal School, Toronto, where one of the pupils at the time was Raymond Massey, who later became a famous actor. Terry Reksten recorded Alma as a little girl with blonde curls, 'a tiny little thing whose feet could barely reach the pedals', playing for the enjoyment of the Victoria musical circles on one of her family's sojourns there. Alma was also an accomplished violinist, and understandably she received much praise and minor acclaim, which ensured that bad behaviour and petulance were attributed to her 'artistic temperament'.

By 1912, when she was seventeen or so, she appeared at a concert with the Toronto Symphony Orchestra, playing two concertos, one for the piano and the other for the violin. She had become an exceedingly attractive young woman, with small, bright grey eyes, and the sort of charm usually associated with an Irish colleen, including the retroussé nose, thick, long hair and the overall appearance of sweetness and simplicity masking a passionate nature. She had a special attraction for the opposite sex and fully reciprocated their interest. In the Canadian field of music, she was something of a star, and that brought her many admirers. Above all, she was undoubtedly a romantic, with highly emotional overtones, which enabled her mentally

4

to project herself into romantic fantasy. She had, in addition to her musical ability, a facility with words, which enabled her to put to music the romantic lyrics which she would jot on the back of envelopes and other odd scraps of paper. It was not great poetry, but it sufficed.

Her father, accompanied by the family, next took up employment with the *Sun* newspaper in Vancouver, when an event occurred which doubtless had a significant effect on Alma's future and which may have left her inwardly scarred for life. She met and fell head over heels in love with Caledon Dolling, a distant relative of the Earl of Caledon, of whose family in later years Field Marshal Earl Alexander of Tunis would become the most famous member. It is probable that Alma was never to love anyone again – certainly not with the same intensity – other than her children, whom she adored. Caledon Dolling had been intended for Sandhurst and the army but when, as a result of his eyesight, he failed the medical, he made for Vancouver, where in 1910 he opened an estate agency.

He married Alma in 1914, and, immediately on the outbreak of war, when medical requirements were slightly relaxed, he joined the army, was commissioned, posted to the 2nd Battalion Royal Welch Fusiliers and thence to France. Alma took herself to England, where she found employment at the War Office so as to be with him whenever possible.

In 1916 Dolling was wounded and awarded the Military Cross, but in August of the same year he was killed by a shell. Alma was devastated. She at once joined a Scottish nursing unit, having decided to go to France to discover his grave, and to this end was engaged with a field ambulance as an orderly. This was probably an indication both of her sense of desolation and of her courage; iron determination was present behind her simple, sweet and youthful beauty.

She carried out her duties with exemplary courage, assisting at operations and amputations of limbs and enduring bombardments. Later, as the war drew to its close, she became a transport driver. She was twice wounded and ultimately awarded the Croix de Guerre with Star and Palm by the French government for her war work. It is perhaps possible to imagine the emotions which must have assailed her at that time: an inconsolable grief at the loss of her beloved Caledon; an intense desire to lose herself in her work, partly in rage and partly in grief; and, throughout, the questioning within her mind whether she could ever again recapture the contentment and sexual enjoyment which she had known over the short time she spent with her husband. Certainly she complained that she spent all her time with the French and was homesick for the sight of English officers.

At the end of the war, Alma returned to London, where she made the acquaintance of Captain Compton Pakenham. He seemed, no doubt, a likely candidate to replace Caledon Dolling. He was an officer; he had been awarded the Military Cross for courage; he was charming; he shared Alma's love of music; and, although it may not have counted with her, he came of good aristocratic background. He was one of the Pakenhams who made up the family of the earldom cf Longford. He secured an appointment as a professor at an American university, and they lived for a part of their married life in the United States.

He suffered, however, one tiresome disadvantage: he was already married. When he secured his divorce, Alma was the woman named in the suit. After they had married in 1921 it began to appear that he also had other disadvantages. In the first place he seems to have had little or no money; he claimed to have been educated at Harrow, but had never been there; and he appropriated to himself an Oxford D.Phil., which he did not possess – indeed, he had never been up at Oxford. He had, in fact, been educated at the Mission School in Che Foo, China, where his father was a member of the Diplomatic Service. The greatest disadvantage of all, though, was that he did not make Alma happy; indeed, he made her so very unhappy that in 1923 she sent an sos to her mother, who travelled to the Far East, where they were then living, and took her and her small son Christopher, who had meanwhile been born, back to Vancouver.

Alma was now about twenty-eight and a woman of some experience. She had travelled Canada, lived in England, France, America and the Far East. She had been twice married; she had been named in a divorce suit; she had lived under all sorts of conditions, including those of war in close proximity to French army officers. She had known happiness and despair, and throughout it all a constant consolation had been her music. So she turned to it again, giving concerts in Vancouver and later in Victoria, to which city she had removed, staying there with Mrs Crittall, her aunt. Her circle of friends was growing, and so it came about that she was sitting in the lounge of the Empress Hotel, which Francis Rattenbury had designed, when he walked out of the dining-room and into her life.

Alma had, however, seen him quite shortly before that. He

had played a significant part in the promotion of an amusement centre, the buildings for which he was to design. The scheme, involving hundreds of thousands of Canadian dollars, had just been approved and the dinner at the Empress Hotel, at which Rattenbury was the principal guest, was in celebration of that success.

Alma had, that evening, taken part in a recital and was sitting in the hotel lounge with a friend when she heard the enthusiastic singing of 'For he's a jolly good fellow' coming from the dining-room. 'I wonder who that's for?' she said to her friend.

'Heaven only knows,' the friend replied, 'must be someone of some importance, for it sounds as though the room is filled to bursting point, and as if some of the guests are as well.'

'Do you think we dare peep?' asked Alma, her face alight with devilment.

'Why not?' said her companion, getting to her feet. 'It's a free country.'

Alma followed her friend to the dining-room doors, which they pushed open sufficiently to enable them to see inside. The guests were on their feet singing vociferously, so the pair moved inside to see who was the recipient of such great enthusiasm. The figure sitting at the top table, beaming at the assembled throng, meant nothing to Alma, except that he looked quite distinguished.

'Who is he?' she asked her friend.

'Oh,' replied the other, 'I know him slightly. I've met him. He's Francis Rattenbury, the famous architect. Would you like to meet him?'

'I'd love to,' said Alma, always eager to meet people of note.

'Well,' said the friend, 'if we sit at this table he'll have to pass us when they leave; hopefully he'll remember me.'

They took up position as close to the door as possible, ordered themselves another drink and waited for the exodus of the dinner company and the great man. In due course the guests began to leave and Francis Rattenbury strolled out with a number of the top-table dignitaries. When he happened to glance in their direction, Alma's friend seized the opportunity to say, 'Good evening, Mr Rattenbury.'

Rattenbury paused, always having an eye for a pretty face, and said, 'Good evening.'

'Of course,' said the friend, 'you won't remember me.' She mentioned where she had been introduced to him.

Rattenbury, aglow with his recent success and well wined,

replied, probably more out of courtesy than truth, that he remembered her very well. Then turning to Alma, whose unrestrained pleasure at meeting such a tall, elegant and successful man, shone from her face, Rattenbury said, 'And I know who you are. I had the great pleasure to attend one of your concerts and I was enthralled by your wonderful talent.'

Alma beamed. By then his companions had walked along the lounge, so Francis Rattenbury, indicating an empty chair at the table and undoubtedly entranced by Alma, enquired whether he might sit with them for a moment.

There is a saying which Rattenbury might have heard in his native Yorkshire that 'Many a mickle makes a muckle', but from that chance meeting, and a second which followed when Alma invited him to another of her recitals, there grew what both of them soon believed to be the love that would endure for ever.

At the conclusion of the recital, when it was Alma's turn to be flushed with pleasure at the rapturous reception she had just received, Francis Rattenbury asked her if she would accompany him to a dance which was taking place in a big house owned by one of the prominent citizens. She readily agreed. Francis proudly danced her round the floor – she apparently entranced by the mature and handsome man in whose arms she now found herself, he enthused by the realization that his companion was the belle of the dance.

'You know,' she whispered as they glided around together, 'you really do have a lovely face.'

'Great Scott,' said Francis, 'have I? I'm going right home to have a look at it. I never thought it worth looking at before.'

'I'm not joking,' said Alma, 'you really have almost the kindest face I ever saw.'

8

CHAPTER 2

The Road to the Villa Madeira

It was soon noticed that Francis Rattenbury was a frequent visitor to the Crittalls' home, and that he was paying great attention to their niece.

Because Francis Rattenbury was living in Victoria, Alma was anxious to remain there, but staying with her aunt was only a temporary arrangement. She was by now involved in a passionate affair with Francis, and the constant presence of Mrs Crittall raised problems which were difficult to overcome. She decided she would be able to provide for Christopher and herself by giving piano lessons, so she leased a small house in Niagara Street, in James Bay.

There she was soon ensconced, admired for her musical ability, the subject of sympathy because of the difficulties she had encountered in her life, and respected for the brave and discreet way in which she managed. Her friends and neighbours who, in a small parochial community, included many who knew Florrie, Rattenbury's wife, little realized that the small dwelling was also a convenient love nest for the two lovers – until the wife of another prominent architect, Sam McClure, was given some information by a young lady, herself a singer, who lived close to Alma. Mrs McClure had shown great kindness to Alma, sending her food when she was ill and entertaining her in her home. Mrs McClure asked the exchange for Alma's telephone number and, when Alma answered, she began the conversation quietly, trying to hide her annoyance and indignation. 'There is something, Alma,' she said, 'which I feel you should know.'

'Oh yes,' said Alma, quite unsuspecting of what was to follow.

'People, I am afraid, are talking.'

Alma was on the alert. 'Oh, indeed. About what?'

'You and Francis Rattenbury,' came the reply.

'That', said Alma firmly, 'is my business.'

'No doubt,' replied Mrs McClure, 'but it is also Florrie's; she *is* his wife, you know.'

'She causes him great distress and unhappiness,' said Alma. 'He needs someone to whom he can turn for a little kindness, and if people want to talk they can do so, as far as I'm concerned.' Rats, as she now called him, would soon sort them out, she thought to herself.

'Well,' continued Mrs McClure, 'they are saying some pretty unpleasant things about you.'

'Good!' was the retort.

'Unfortunately,' rejoined Mrs McClure, 'it sounds as though they are right. Goodbye,' and she put down the receiver.

When Rats arrived that evening, Alma told him of the conversation. Whether or not he then realized how matters would develop is far from clear. Until then he had been well accepted and appreciated in local society. He played the piano, was good at sports, in which he regularly indulged, was interesting company and a figure of importance in the community. If he thought he could ride out the situation, he was to be disappointed. In any case the die for him was cast. He was hopelessly in love with Alma, returning her affection with the intensity of a man approaching sixty, responding to the devotion of someone thirty years his junior, whom he saw as beautiful and bewitching, whose very presence had revived his waning zeal for life and whose experience and highly sensuous nature was such as he had never before encountered. Francis was on the hook and nothing was likely to extricate him from it.

He asked Florrie for a divorce, but she would not hear of it. His relationship with Alma was now public knowledge and he resolved to bluff it out. In Canada and the North American continent in general, charming as its people are, the communities have always been highly parochial and inward-looking. And when they did look, they tended to look closely and narrowly. Francis soon discovered he was no longer accepted where hitherto he had been most warmly welcomed. He tried to ignore it. He was seen in all the best places with Alma at his side – at the theatre, at concerts, at the Empress – and when invited to parties, although invitations were fewer, Alma was his constant companion.

Florrie was not seen at all. There were, however, other ugly rumours. About those, Terry Reksten has much to say, and it provides such an interesting sidelight on the ultimate Old Bailey trial that it is worth quoting at length:

> There were those ... who said Alma was addicted to drugs and hinted that Rattenbury had become a changed man under their influence.
>
> Probably no one will ever know for a certainty if this was the case. Alma may well have developed a drug dependency during the years she spent with the ambulance corps during the war. In battlefield hospitals both morphia and cocaine were used as anaesthetics and while morphia was known to be addictive, the properties of cocaine were not fully understood. ... Alma may have begun to use it to keep her going for long hours of unaccustomed hardship and labour. ... Other Victoria girls, serving as nurses or drivers during the war, had returned home with an addiction to morphia or a dependency on cocaine, but most, surrounded by the soothing presence of family and friends in peaceful post-war Victoria, had overcome their drug habit. Perhaps Alma had not – for Alma certainly had an addictive personality. Self-denial was alien to her. One drink, more often than not, led to two or three more. She was a chain-smoker who found it difficult to finish a meal without pausing between courses to smoke a cigarette.
>
> Rattenbury's children, Frank and Mary, who were twenty and twenty-five at the time l'affaire Rattenbury became the talk of Victoria, remain convinced and take some comfort from their conviction that 'dope' played a role in their father's entrapment, and they may be right. Cocaine may have brought back his youthful virility and may have induced in him a state of excitement and euphoria that encouraged his recklessly indiscreet behaviour.

Florrie was unflinching in her determination not to give him a divorce. The sympathy of local society was with her. So Rats and Alma embarked upon a course of conduct to compel Florrie to change her mind which may be highly relevant when later evaluating the real character and the true personality of Alma Rattenbury. Certainly there was nothing simple or sweet in her behaviour at this time, nor – although this is less material – was there in his.

Rattenbury's first action was to move out of the family house, taking in the process the best of the furniture. When the removers were not looking, Florrie and her maid managed to retrieve and hide in a locked room some of the choicer pieces, together with her husband's stock of champagne. Thus forestalled, and infuriated by Florrie's stubborn resistance, he turned to disconnecting the light and heat. Florrie, by now a dumpy little woman, was beside herself with worry, without light or heat and with inadequate food. Mrs McClure, anxious no doubt to demonstrate where her sympathies lay, supplied her with hampers of food. Florrie retaliated on 28 July 1924 by applying to the local court for a declaration of her right to remain unmolested in the property, and no doubt for an injunction to restrain her husband from his cruel and intemperate conduct. It was some indication of the extent to which he was besotted with and, it is to be suspected, encouraged by Alma that he allowed himself to behave so abominably.

Discouraged, he took Alma on a Mediterranean cruise. On their return, fortified by sunshine and good living, he began a new campaign, taking Alma to his family home, royally entertaining her there and driving Florrie to remain upstairs.

Florrie, distressed beyond endurable measure, became ill. What next happened provides a special insight into the real Alma Rattenbury, since people are often better judged by incidents and behaviour small in themselves, when compared with the great events of life, because they reflect spontaneous and uncalculated action stemming from the real character.

On this occasion Florrie had taken to her bed. Alma, in the sitting-room with Rattenbury, was playing the piano with much the same volume as she would have produced in a large concert hall. Rattenbury's daughter Mary came downstairs and politely asked them to reduce the noise as it was disturbing her mother. Alma listened to the complaint and then resumed her playing, with still greater intensity, pointedly selecting the funeral march as an indication of her contempt for the complainer and her displeasure with the subject of it.

Eventually, Rattenbury won; Florrie conceded victory; they were divorced in January 1925, Rattenbury agreeing to provide her with a house and 225 Canadian dollars per month as maintenance, worth at the time about £45 sterling. Alma for the second time in her career achieved the distinction of being 'the woman named' in the divorce proceedings.

As Florrie moved out of 'the house where a good thing happened' Alma, considered to be another good thing, was moved in. Rattenbury designed, and had erected, a splendid music room, and envisaged an existence in which they would live happily ever after, as the fairy stories always have us believe. He was, indeed, blissfully happy, flattered by his young and lovely companion, who filled the house with dogs, cats, birds and joy. It is certain that Rats and Alma were married, but precisely when and where remain doubtful. One account fixes the marriage as April 1925, three months after his divorce. Were this so, there is little reason to doubt – particularly in the face of the disapproval they were engendering in Victoria – that Rattenbury would have been at some pains to ensure that the nuptials received the widest circulation. This was certainly not the case – hence the mystery surrounding it.

Indeed, in 1927, two years after the divorce, Alma, perhaps unwisely, picked up the telephone to renew her acquaintance with Mrs McClure.

'Who is calling?' asked that lady.

'Mrs Rattenbury,' replied Alma gaily.

'Which Mrs Rattenbury?' came the question in stentorian tones.

'Why,' said Alma, 'it's me, my dear, Alma.'

'I know only one Mrs Rattenbury,' said Mrs McClure, 'and that's Mrs Rattenbury of Prospect Place,' and once again she replaced the receiver.

By the time their son John was born on 27 December 1928, the Rattenburys' intense happiness at the event was overshadowed by the bitter feelings exhibited towards them. Rattenbury was accused of paying an inadequate reward to another architect, who claimed that the design for the Crystal Garden Amusement Centre, an important development which Rats had been commissioned to create, had been principally his work. This Rattenbury vehemently denied. The truth was never determined, but there were many whose sympathy was not with Rattenbury. One thing was certain; it soured his relationship with his professional colleagues, who were already disenchanted by his personal life.

His situation was described by Terry Reksten, as a result of her careful research, as one in which 'he was avoided on the street, cold-shouldered in the Union Club and shunned by his former clients and business associates. ... Now people found just how easy it was to despise him. To divorce and remarry was bad enough, but to have left his wife for Alma who was seen as an immoral woman – a man-eating tigress – was quite beyond the pale.'

By late 1929 the unfortunate and wretched Florrie had died. The cause of her death has been nowhere described, but somewhere amongst the causes may well have been a broken heart.

'Rats, darling,' Alma said to him when they were sitting together one evening in their home, 'what are we going to do? You seem to be getting more and more depressed and low.'

'I'm sorry, darling,' he replied, 'but things have not worked out as we planned, have they?'

'But Rats, we're happy enough together, and we have John. What more do you need?'

'There is nothing for me any more outside of this home. These bloody people do not see how hard I have always tried to do the right thing. My work has suffered – such as I am now getting. I am being viciously and deliberately ostracized wherever I appear. I'm sick of the lot of them, and would be happy to see the back of the place.'

'Where would we go?' asked Alma.

'God knows,' he replied.

'What about going back to England? Your skill would be appreciated there.'

'Come now, darling, you know that's not true. I'm unheard of there. No. I'm sixty-two after all. That's too late for fresh starts, but I might give it all up and find somewhere where we could retire.'

So the germ of the idea that they would leave Canada was formed, and it began to take more shape when he came to realize not only that he was estranged from his friends and professional colleagues but that he had, or more correctly Alma had, destroyed his relationship with his own children, whom he dearly loved. The final decision was soon taken and they left Canada – Alma, he and John – seen off only by his son Frank, whose recollection of Alma was that 'She was in a stupor from booze or something else.'

Rattenbury was in no hurry to reach England. They made their way first to Cuba. After a period there they went on to New York, where Rattenbury seems to have incurred large debts gambling with crooks, which necessitated that he, Alma and John take off surreptitiously under cover of night for Monte Carlo and then Venice. They spent some time in Northern France before going on to England, and understandably Rattenbury's first choice was Devon, the home of his forbears. In September 1930, so it was reported in the local paper, their son was baptized in the parish church. Okehampton was delightful, sleepy, rural and peaceful; it was wholly unsuited to the requirements of a fun-loving romantic with musical ambitions such as Alma.

In that regard Bournemouth had no greater claim as the answer to what Alma secretly wanted of life, but it had many of the attractions and attributes of Victoria in Canada, and, to keep Rats happy, they settled themselves there, taking a tenancy of 5 Manor Road, a house owned by a Mrs Price and rejoicing in the name of the Villa Madeira.

CHAPTER 3

Alma the Songwriter

In England, the General Election of 1929 had seen the coming of the first Labour Government, under the premiership of Ramsay MacDonald. The Communists, at that time generally referred to as the Bolsheviks, regarded him as more Conservative than the Tory leader Stanley Baldwin. The Liberals, under Lloyd George, were very much at the bottom of the poll. As a sign of the times, however, women having just been enfranchised, it was the first election in which the whole of the adult population had been entitled to vote, and there were those who were heard to say, in those very different days, that the result of the election was exactly what you deserved if you allowed women to vote.

Others were complaining of the high cost of living, when twenty-one shillings was the price demanded for a mackintosh, fifty shillings was being extracted for a man's suit, cigarettes were just over a shilling for twenty, and a man's shirt with two collars to match was ten shillings and sixpence.

It soon became evident that life in the Villa Madeira was not such as to satisfy either Rats or Alma. He was getting old, and was already older than his years; he was becoming deaf; he was drinking quite heavily, which had begun to show on his countenance. And he had become virtually impotent, so that there had been no sexual intercourse between them since the birth of John at the end of 1928. Alma had been diagnosed as suffering from pulmonary tuberculosis, for which she was prescribed, in the then state of medical knowledge, fresh air. Always a highly sexed romantic, her frustration was the greater because one of the curious results of the disease from which she suffered is that it intensifies the sexual drive.

That Alma could be a kind, most affectionate, warm and outgoing person there is no doubt at all, but she found herself wholly starved of the sort of companionship which her nature so desperately needed. She had staff working in the house. This generally included a male servant who did the cooking, until an advertisement which she had inserted locally brought to her door Irene Riggs. A locally born girl, she was then about twenty-two years of age. The daughter of a gravedigger, who lived on the other side of Bournemouth, she had entered employment as a domestic servant at the age of fourteen. Alma was willing to pay her twenty-five shillings and 'all found', as the expression went, and Irene took up residence in the Villa Madeira.

She soon came under Alma's influence and charm. A simple girl of limited education, she could hardly do otherwise than respond to the kindness and affection which Alma extended to her; although never engaged as such, she became, as time passed, as much a companion as a maid. Alma confided in her, took her about with her, bought her presents and showed her a relationship and a way of life which she would never have imagined available to her. It was a commendable facet of Alma's character that status and position were not matters of importance to her. If she liked someone it did not matter who to her they were or what their position in society, and although her two earlier marriages had secured her two entries in Debrett and Burke's Peerage, that would have carried no weight with her. What did matter was that she could share her romantic and sentimental fantasies and ambitions with someone who appreciated the lovelorn messages which she inscribed in the lyrics of the songs she was always jotting down.

Of the value of money Alma had little understanding.

'I'm very worried about money,' Rats said one evening.

'You always are,' she replied. 'We have everything we need, don't we?'

'You seem to think that we are still as well off as when I had a thriving business in Canada,' Rattenbury said. 'It simply isn't so. As I keep reminding you, I have never got over the expense of the case I brought against the Government in Canada, when I tried to get rid of those bloody taxes they were after. The expense was punishing, especially when we lost the case. We really have to look after the pennies.'

Alma turned away, having not the slightest belief in the truth of his constant assertions of shortage of money. When he had wanted to travel the world en route to England, she remembered, she had heard nothing of it then. Rattenbury, on the other hand, would become, each time he reminded himself of his position, increasingly depressed.

'Everything will be fine,' Alma said, 'when I have established myself once again in the musical world. Once I can get my songs published, I shall be famous and the royalties will pour in.'

Rattenbury sat pondering this. 'That could well be the answer,' he said, after a while. 'No one has ever said otherwise than that you have the musical talent. Why don't we really start about it in a more businesslike way?'

'I've got masses of songs running through my head,' Alma said, 'and if I can find them, masses more jotted about the place.'

Enthused by Rats' new interest in the possibilities, Alma began putting together the material she had noted over the years and recording the melodies which came into her mind when she sat at the piano. When she was satisfied with a composition, she passed it on to Rats, who with his wide and successful business career was more likely than she to secure a suitable publisher.

Armed with several manuscripts Rattenbury journeyed to London where he called on the well-known music publishers Boosey & Co. In his days as an architect, one of the qualities for which he was noted was his persuasive power and his ability to ensure that any request which he made did not go unanswered. He was not, however, the man he had been and he was now moving in a sphere in which he had no experience. Although he succeeded in securing an interview with the right man at Booseys, they were not even prepared to consider Alma's work. They had, of course, never heard of her, and anyhow music was not selling well; indeed, they were not even prepared to look at the manuscripts. Rats returned to Bournemouth rather disconsolate to relate the disappointing result.

'They were quite unreasonable, darling,' he said to Alma. 'It is not as if they heard what you had written and disliked it or considered that it lacked merit. They simply were not prepared even to look at it. What we need is someone with influence whose opinion they cannot ignore. Just leave it to me.'

He set about finding such a person. He had learned long ago that success in life often depended not so much upon what you knew or did, but whom you knew. After ferreting around he secured an introduction to Sir Dan Godfrey, who conducted the Bournemouth Symphony Orchestra. He saw Sir Dan and gave him a run-down on Alma's high-powered Canadian musical career, showing him some of her work. The talent which they revealed spoke for itself. The conductor assured him he would lend his support and pointed him in the right direction to secure additional influential introductions to Keith Prowse & Co. in London, whom he recommended as the best publishers for music of the ballad variety which was Alma's musical style. The company had for years been famous not only as publishers of music but also as theatrical booking agents with the house caption 'You want the best seats; we have them.' Rattenbury secured, with the help of the introductions he had obtained, an interview with the head of the company, a man named Van Lier, and he and Alma made their way to London to see him.

They were shown into the important man's presence, Alma at once displaying all the charm and vivacity which bubbled over when she encountered anyone of the opposite sex.

'Let me see what you have brought us,' Van Lier said after they had chatted about her Canadian experience. She handed him several hand-written scripts, which he glanced over. 'Would you like to play them for me?' he asked Alma, indicating a piano on the far side of the room.

Alma walked across to the instrument, sat down and asked Van Lier, 'Which one would you like to hear?'

'They all look quite good to me,' he said, 'but you choose the one you think best.'

Alma began to play a piece, a sentimental love ballad which she had called 'Avelette'. Such was her skill that she had the ability, it was said, to make the most indifferent melody sound quite splendid. Her composition had the advantage of being a lilting, attractive ballad in its own right. She then played some more. Van Lier was delighted on every count: the pleasing tunes, the superb playing and the exciting and attractive player.

Alma, flushed with excitement, finished the piece, and turned towards Van Lier. 'Well,' she asked, 'what do you think?'

'I am greatly impressed. I will publish them.'

For one moment it seemed as though Alma was going to rush to him, put her arms around him and kiss him. She jumped to her feet. 'You will,' she said, 'you really will? Oh, how splendid, isn't it, Rats? Oh Mr Van Lier, you are a darling.'

'Yes,' said Van Lier, 'I will publish three of the numbers. The first I will have orchestrated, so that it can be broadcast and publicized; the other two we will reserve for the piano for the present.'

Rats almost danced for joy, throwing his arms around Alma and kissing her. They discussed the royalties the company would be paying, and a clerk was dispatched for a copy of the firm's usual contract for Alma to sign. Van Lier, having ascertained that they would be staying in London for the next few days, invited them to join him for dinner the next night at the Mayfair Hotel.

Visions of a new and exciting life were opening before Alma's eyes; Rats was equally excited both for the pleasure which it had given Alma and for the financial possibilities it offered for the future.

The following morning Rats – in excellent spirits – took Alma shopping, so that she might buy a new gown for their visit to the Mayfair. When they arrived at the hotel, she looked resplendent, her eyes shining and her thoughts centred on the belief that she was now on her way to becoming truly famous. She had decided for the new musical career on which she was about to be launched that she would call herself Lozanne, which she speedily imparted to Van Lier when they met him in the foyer. He introduced them to his fiancée Yvette Darnac, and Rats seemed to be as enchanted with her as Van Lier seemed to be intrigued by Alma. Together they made their way into the ballroom where they were to dine. Some couples were already dancing to the music of Ambrose and his Orchestra. Alma had frequently heard this famous band on the radio and had some of Ambrose's records. Like so many others, she adored dance-band conductors, and Ambrose was one of the most famous of all. Her excitement was intense when, in one of the breaks in the dancing, Ambrose – noticing Van Lier at the table – stepped off the dais and made his way to the table.

'Good evening, Van,' he said to the host, 'I had been meaning to come in and see you, as I am anxious to get some new numbers. Have you got any coming along?'

'I have a few which I believe might please you, Bert,' he replied. 'Why don't you get your secretary to ring mine and come and have lunch with me?'

'I'll certainly do that,' Ambrose replied.

'May I introduce you', said Van Lier, 'to Mr and Mrs Rattenbury. Alma – Mrs Rattenbury that is – is going to be a fabulous composer. She has written some music which is quite a delight.'

Alma visibly blushed. 'You are much too kind, Mr Van Lier.'

'I'm not at all,' he said.

'Am I going to hear them?' asked Ambrose. 'Tell me about them.'

'Of course you will,' said Van Lier, 'and you will soon be

20

playing them. They are delightful romantic ballads and ideal for Elsie Carlyle's vocals.'

'Wonderful,' commented Ambrose. 'If they are as good as you say, I'll include them in my radio repertoire.' And turning to Alma he added, 'That will soon get them known, won't it?'

'Oh, Mr Ambrose. That would be truly stunning,' said Alma excitedly. 'Everything your orchestra plays always sounds so splendid.'

'Not tonight,' responded Ambrose. 'This is one of our off nights. One or two of my fellows are doing gigs tonight. I'm sorry you're not hearing us as I like it to be. Anyhow, it has been a great pleasure to meet you both. I look forward to playing your music.'

As Ambrose bid them good-night and walked away, Van Lier said, 'There you are, the great man himself.'

'Oh, I am so thrilled to have met him,' babbled Alma, obviously swept along with the intoxication of the setting and the company. 'Do you really mean you will let him hear my music and that he might play it on the radio?'

'But of course,' said Van Lier. 'You're marvellous. I've travelled the world searching for suitable tunes. Good ones are very rare and you are teeming with exquisite melodies.'

'He's right,' said Yvette. 'Just think of it. You do realize that when you come into a ballroom, the band will stop whatever it's playing, and change to one of your tunes.'

'Go along with you,' said Alma. 'You're pulling my leg now.'

When they returned to Bournemouth, Alma recounted to Irene Riggs all that had occurred.

'What is so splendid,' she told her, 'is that Rats is as excited as I am. On our last day in London we went to a record shop to buy some records to bring back with us. I listened to one by Frank Titterton. Oh, Irene, he has the most beautiful tenor voice, and the moment I heard it I said to Rats, "That's the voice that must sing my songs." So, Irene, what do you think he said?'

'I don't know,' replied Irene.

'He at once decided that he would get Frank Titterton's address from Mr Van Lier, and would write to him. And what do you think, Irene? Oh, you're never going to believe this. He has heard from him and he has accepted our invitation to have lunch with us in London. Can you believe it?'

Alma was in her seventh heaven – the excitement of the fashionable spots in London; the company of famous and wealthy people; everyone lavishing praise on her musical ability and responding to her charm. This, indeed, was the life for her, and it was only just beginning.

CHAPTER 4

Disappointment

Since Van Lier had taken them to the Mayfair Hotel, and they had so much enjoyed it, they arranged for the luncheon with Frank Titterton to be at the same venue. Titterton brought his secretary with him, a Miss Esmond. Alma had decked herself out in a smart suit, had paid a visit to the hairdresser and had spent a long time in front of the mirror ensuring that she looked her best. Frank Titterton was duly impressed. 'It was exceedingly kind of you to invite us to lunch,' he said.

'Well,' replied Francis Rattenbury, 'we are delighted to have the pleasure of your company, and Alma is thrilled to meet you because the moment she first heard your voice she decided there was no one else she would want to introduce her songs.'

'That's so,' said Alma. 'I'd be over the moon if I could hear you singing something I had written.'

'I had better try them out then,' said Frank Titterton. 'Have you written many?'

'I have jotted many down, over the years, on scraps of paper as they have come into my head, but I have only actually completed a smaller number. Keith Prowse are going to publish three of them and one of those they are having orchestrated. Ambrose has said he will include it in his repertoire.'

That was to be only the first of many such meetings. Titterton and the Rattenburys were to become close friends, and Titterton would both sing and record some of Alma's songs.

As Frank Titterton was later to remark, he was at once impressed with her conversation as that of 'a well-travelled, cultured woman with keen powers of observation'. From their first meeting he sensed her to be very emotional. 'At one moment she would be wildly gay. She would fling her arms in the air to emphasize her voluble flow of words. The next moment she would be silent and subdued.' Her eyes, as he observed, were 'grey and magnetic and compelled attention to everything she said'. Particularly noticeable was the intense way in which she looked into the face of the person she was addressing, her eyes becoming large with emotion or excitement. To Frank Titterton she presented a picture of great charm and attractiveness, but the more discerning might well have questioned whether what he described did not carry the signs of an underlying instability.

There were also other indications of excessive emotional conduct on Alma's part. She was in most respects enjoying the happiest period of her life. Devoted to her children, Christopher and John, there was nothing which was too good or too much for them, and they gave her great joy. She took them on frequent outings into the surrounding country, to early-morning swimming in the sea, and lavished on them, in addition, all the undoubted affection which she felt for them and which flowed from her warm and indeed torrid nature, a nature that yearned to give and receive real love.

There was, however, a labile side to her character, which, without realizing its true significance, Frank Titterton had noticed. She could suddenly become as quiet and morose as she had been wild and hysterically happy a few moments before. Irene Riggs had by now become her closest confidante and companion for most of the time. They called one another 'darling' and there seems little reason to doubt that Irene Riggs also held her in very great affection, and may perhaps have loved her. She would stay up with her through the night, when Alma, as sometimes occurred, would choose to sit listening to music on the gramophone rather than sleeping in bed. One wonders what outlet Alma found for her excessively high sexual drive, since there was no indication of her having alliances with any men in Bournemouth or elsewhere; clearly she had no sexual relations with Rats, and the emotion which she injected into her music could never have been enough to satisfy the innermost desires of someone such as Alma.

It was her invariable habit while in the house to wear throughout the day the same pyjamas as she used for sleeping at night. They consisted of trousers and a top over which went a long, loose coat, and she very much liked the pretty colours in which they could be procured. During the day she wore a vest and brassiere underneath, which she removed at night before dressing again in the pyjamas she had worn that day. So attired she would sometimes spend hours at night wandering about the garden during the warm months of the year.

When she felt herself getting low she would mix herself a cocktail, a form of drink which doubtless seemed more in keeping with the bohemian style of living which she believed best suited her artistic temperament. Certainly, it did not appear in the first years of her return to England that she was drinking excessively, or that, being content with her life (apart from the sexual frustration, which she probably hoped would be easier to satisfy once her fame was established), she had a particular desire for drink.

Although the music publishers fulfilled their promise to publish her songs and although from time to time selected compositions were issued by the gramophone record company, the music did not take off so as to carry Alma to the dizzy heights of success for which she was hoping and waiting. It also followed that the financial rewards did not supplement their fortune in the way which Francis Rattenbury regarded as essential. Rattenbury began again to apply his mind to other means of resuscitating his wealth, and as each idea fell on stony ground, his former depression returned. It was not cocktails for him but good Scotch whisky and he was increasingly turning to the bottle.

His interest in Alma's musical career diminished as his own personal concerns increased, and Alma would from time to time entertain her publisher and the artists interested in her work in London, without Rats. The friendship with Frank Titterton stil flourished and Alma welcomed the opportunities which occurred for her to journey to London. One of her songs which Frank Titterton recorded, 'You Brought My Heart the Sunshine', gave her especial pleasure because she played the accompaniment to it herself. Not always without difficulty, she was still able on occasion to persuade Rats to go with her when she visited her new-found friends. Once, Frank Titterton gave a party and she was pleased when Rats agreed to go with her. He liked Titterton and found his company amusing.

The lyrics which Alma wrote for her songs were in no sense of the quality of her musical compositions. They had too much of the character of verses found in birthday and anniversary cards. Some of the lyrics were in fact written by others, and when, at the party at Titterton's, the subject of lyrics arose, Rattenbury himself felt he had a contribution to make. 'You may be surprised to hear', he said to Titterton and his friends, 'that I have had a stab at lyric-writing myself.'

'Really,' said Titterton. 'I thought your artistic ability lay in the drawing and painting field.'

'I cannot pretend that my lyrics quite have the flair of Shakespeare's sonnets, but I hoped Alma might be able to put one of them to music.'

'We must hear them some time,' said Titterton.

'It so happens', Rattenbury replied, to Alma's surprise, as he searched in his pocket, 'I have one with me. Would you really like to hear it?'

The flush on Rats' face and the unusual exhilaration which he exhibited made Alma think he must have had a good many tots before they had their meal and a considerable amount of wine during it.

With great expression he began to recite his great work. As he proceeded the company looked at him with incredulity bordering on horror. The verses were excruciatingly bad, the worst of doggerel. When he reached the end, there was a pregnant pause. No one quite knew what to say or quite where to look. After a few moments' intense silence, one of them began to laugh. Before long, everyone, including Rats, joined in. He took it in good part, observing, 'Well, perhaps you're right. I'd better stick to architecture and not try to become a poet.'

Titterton greatly valued the friendship of the Rattenburys. He was anxious to give Alma as much help as he was able, but he soon began to understand that Rats, as he also now called him, was losing, and perhaps had already lost, interest in Alma's musical prowess. He invited her to lunch when one of her songs was shortly to be published, because he thought he could give her a few tips to ensure that she got the maximum publicity. During the meal he asked her to tell him something of her earlier life.

'Really,' said Alma, 'it can all be summed up very quickly.' She picked up the menu, turned it over, took a pencil from her handbag and wrote for him: 'Born in Victoria, BC. Played Phil. and Toronto Symphony Orc. – youthful romance – elopement – died, first year, end of war – quick marriage – death in war – 3rd marriage S. America. Hobby – jotting airs on backs of menus – back of envs.' And passing it across to Frank Titterton she commented, with evident sadness, 'That's about it.'

On the train on the return journey to Bournemouth, she sat gazing out of the window, thinking over the lunch, and the summary of her life which she had written on the menu came into her thoughts. Where, she asked herself, had she gone wrong? Everyone agreed she should have had a life full of the excitement, love and success which she so desired. Yet here she was, quite unable to make things happen as they should; approaching forty years of age, she would return home to an old man, who was incapable of showing her the love she longed for, and the future would be no less bleak, unless – unless – she repeated to herself, she could really get to the top of the musical world and make her life in London.

On arrival at the Villa Madeira, she mixed herself some cocktails, and asked Irene what time dinner would be ready.

'I'm cooking it tonight,' said Irene, 'so I am afraid, darling, it will be a little late.'

'Why is that?' asked Alma. 'What's wrong with Gregory?'

'It appears he has left for good,' said Irene.

'But why?'

'I'm sorry about this,' was the reply, 'but he says you keep making up to him and he thinks he would be better out of the way.'

'Such nonsense,' said Alma. 'As if I would be interested in anything like him. He's got an infernal cheek.'

Irene was not impressed; she knew that after her good lady had taken cocktails, and when her passions were aroused, she would make for the nearest male. She did not know that before she entered Alma Rattenbury's service a chef named Davis had left in not dissimilar circumstances. She contented herself with handing Alma another cocktail and leaving for the kitchen, remarking that she would try and speed up the meal.

From 1932 Alma's health became a matter of ever increasing worry, and, on the recommendation of friends, the Rattenburys sought the assistance of a Bournemouth general practitioner, Dr William O'Donnell. He was clearly concerned at the increased pulmonary tuberculosis from which Alma was suffering and he arranged for her to enter a nursing home for two weeks for observation and for her to undergo x-rays of her chest and lungs. He became far more concerned when she developed suppurating tubercular glands, and from this time he would generally visit the Villa Madeira weekly.

Rats had worked out a scheme for a local property development of blocks of flats, but he had been unable to find anyone willing to finance it. He had the site, the design and the bills of quantity available; all that eluded him was the money. In a mood of growing frustration he had increased his input of whisky and was consuming a bottle a night. His hearing was getting worse and the total absence of mental stimulus was speedily putting years on him. Seeing that she was tied to him, with no longer any real prospect of being freed from the boredom of it by musical success, only increased the stress to which Alma found herself subjected, and the additional stress, as is always the case, was inimical to any improvement in her physical condition.

William O'Donnell was typical of the old-style family doctor, and he became something of a family friend. He would on occasions visit the house socially, and was available, on call, for any problem which arose, where he might intervene as counsellor and friend. Indeed, he became, as far more doctors did in the thirties than today, the first port of call in an emergency. His patients would, when they telephoned, speak to his wife, whom they knew well, rather than to a secretary whose main pursuit in life was to guard him from his patients, and they did not have to make appointments in advance when they wanted to be ill. It was to become a matter for debate later, when she faced what appeared to be insurmountable problems, whether he might act on the highly commendable desire to protect her which he so zealously displayed throughout the time he was her doctor, mentor and friend.

CHAPTER 5

Drugs and Sex

Bournemouth, 'the Queen of the South', owed its reputation to a Dr Granville, who, some hundred years before the Rattenburys arrived there, had strongly recommended its mild, sunny climate to those in delicate health. In addition to the heart of the poet Shelley, deposited in St Peter's Church, a considerable number of doctors and an even greater number of undertakers, it also possessed a phrenologist.

Phrenology is the scientific study of the mental faculties, and those who practise it claim that by examination of the external conformation of the cranium they can evaluate the mental powers of the subject under investigation. In September 1932, Alma had decided that it would be an excellent thing for herself and her husband to see W. G. Clarke, the phrenologist in question, and have their heads examined. Whilst Rats considered there were a number of facets of his present situation which clearly indicated the need for his head to be examined, he declined the invitation but agreed to accompany Alma. She saw Clarke twice; he seemed extremely interested in her bumps. At the end of the second interview he told her he would write his report and send it to her.

'Please, Mr Clarke,' said Alma, 'do tell me now. I would love to know what you have discovered about me.'

Clarke was far from eager to reveal his findings. 'I make it a rule never to discuss these matters until the written report has been sent to the subject. It can be exceedingly embarrassing.'

'You'll find it impossible to embarrass me,' replied Alma. 'What's more, I'm one of those who simply love breaking rules; didn't my bumps tell you that?'

'I shall have to consider my notes in depth,' explained Clarke,

29

who took himself exceedingly seriously. 'It's far too soon to express opinions now.'

Alma was not to be thwarted. 'You must have formed some views, even at this stage. Come along, do tell me. I shan't be upset, I assure you.'

Clarke was anxious to bring the discussion to a close, but, if she wanted to hear something, he decided, she could jolly well hear it. 'Very well,' he said after a moment's further hesitation, 'but this is totally in breach of all my usual practice. I find your brain is small in size; you're weak-willed, you lack grit and you've no backbone.' Although Alma looked anything but pleased, he went on: 'You have very little fight in you and you need to guard against emotional excitement.'

'That part, at least,' said Alma, 'I know to be true. I have always thought that my emotional condition was due to being over-worked when I was young, especially when my mother kept me at my musical studies, to the exclusion of so many things which the young like to do.'

'One of the troubles', interposed Francis Rattenbury, 'was that she appeared before large audiences in Canada at the age of eight, and the strain and excitement was too much for a child of that age.'

'Perhaps so,' commented Clarke, by no means convinced, 'perhaps so.'

'Is there anything good to be found in my bumps?' pleaded Alma.

'Oh! Indeed there is,' said Clarke, who had now had quite enough, 'but for that you will have to await my full written report.'

Whether the phrenologist's diagnosis was right or wrong, it was not the characteristics which he described that created the greatest difficulties for Irene Riggs. Those were occasioned by what were known in the Villa Madeira as Alma's 'attacks'. When she had them, she would become very excited, and would run about the house behaving in a highly elated fashion. This would continue for some time; then she would gradually be overcome by drowsiness, which left her in a condition akin to drunkenness. She would then, with Irene's assistance, make her way to her bed, where she would fall into a deep sleep for several hours. The condition was inexplicable in relation to any of the symptoms of her illness. It had nothing to do with tuberculosis or with any other known condition to which she might be subject; and if Irene Riggs ever discovered the cause, such was her adoration for, and loyalty to, Alma that she was never prepared to say. The furthest she would go was to observe that it was just as if Alma had taken something. Even if she did not know the actual cause – as she may well have done – and had she had any medical knowledge and known of the strong rumours which were associated with Alma over the period before her departure from Canada, she might have attributed her condition to drugs, since the symptoms were wholly consistent with those experienced after taking cocaine or even heroin.

The sudden onset of these symptoms made that suspicion more likely. From time to time Mrs Price, who owned both the Villa Madeira and a shop which sold cigarettes, tobacco and accessories, would be invited to lunch. She arrived for such a visit in October 1933. After a pleasant lunch followed by afternoon tea in the garden, Alma suggested that Mrs Price might like to stay on for dinner. Mrs Price at first declined, explaining that there were a number of things which she had to do, and that as much as she would have liked to stay she would be unable to do so. Alma was not to be put off. Why did Mrs Price not go home and return later, for her home was only a short distance away, and join them for dinner? In the face of Alma's insistence, Mrs Price agreed, and shortly afterwards left for home.

Alma went to her bedroom for a nap, while Irene began to make preparations for dinner. When, within a short while, she came out of the kitchen she was surprised to find Alma pacing agitatedly round the house, in the full throes of an 'attack'. It was not the result of the cocktails she had taken before lunch or the wine she had with it, because that was far too long before to have produced such a delayed effect. Words were gushing from Alma's mouth; and she was frantically wringing her hands, as she made her way to the cabinet in the sitting-room in which the ready-made cocktail bottles were kept. Indeed, so frenetic and excitable was her condition and so high did she appear to be that Irene became extremely concerned, and begged Francis to do something for her.

'What in the name of Hades do you expect me to do?' asked Rattenbury, who disliked Irene Riggs and considered he had little reason to do otherwise.

'But *something* must be done,' said Irene, having seen Alma dashing back to her bedroom.

'I suppose,' said Rattenbury, 'she's taken a bloody sight too much drink. You know she can never hold her liquor.'

31

He was himself in an intoxicated and semi-drowsy state.

'It's not that,' replied Irene Riggs, 'it's some hours since she had lunch and she's had nothing since then – at least until now. I'm sure she is going to harm herself.'

'Well, ring the sawbones,' was Rattenbury's only contribution. 'He spends enough time here. Another call won't worry him.'

Irene duly called Dr O'Donnell. By the time he arrived Alma was lying on her bed soundly asleep. Having attended to her in the bedroom O'Donnell made his way to the sitting-room to tell Rattenbury that he had given her something which would ensure she had a good night's rest.

'She's invited Mrs Price for dinner,' Rattenbury told him. 'We've already had her for lunch and tea, if you please. Now for dinner. I really can't take any more. For God's sake, Bill, stay and have dinner in order to help me out.'

O'Donnell, having nothing better to do, agreed, settled himself down with a drink, and explained his presence to Mrs Price on her return by saying that Alma had suddenly been taken quite ill so that he had decided to put her to bed. Mrs Price pointed out how well Alma had seemed at both lunch and tea, but O'Donnell assured her that in her condition the onset of something like this could be quite sudden – as indeed was the case, but not because of tuberculosis.

By 1934 the visits of Dr O'Donnell had become far more frequent, whilst Alma's 'attacks' got no less. She was still writing her music as an outlet for her romanticism but the rewards she sought continued to elude her. 'You Brought My Heart the Sunshine', as the title of one of her songs proclaimed, was not the real reflection of her situation, and when Edward Lockton, a lyricist, wrote the words of 'Dark-Haired Marie' to Alma's music he was certainly not thinking of the back of the Villa Madeira, the English Channel or Alma herself when he wrote,

> Are you waiting in your garden
> By the deep wide azure sea?
> Are you waiting for your loveship,
> Dark-haired Marie?
>
> I shall come to claim you someday,
> In my arms you'll be,
> I shall kiss your lips and love you,
> Dark-haired Marie.

Nevertheless, the words reflected the inner hopes and wishes of Alma Rattenbury. It was otherwise with her husband. For him life seemed to have little to offer in the future. His hearing was worse; his hopes of launching his property development were no further advanced; his wife, whom he thought extended too much of her affection to her maid, as a result had none for him. Life often lay heavily on him.

By 1934, 9 July to be precise, the full measure of his depression became apparent and he expressed himself, in a semi-drunken state, to Alma. 'Wouldn't I be better dead?' he said.

'You're always moaning and complaining,' she rejoined.

'It's all right for you. You live in a world of fantasy. I have to live with reality. I know I cannot keep spending at the rate you wish; I know I've got nothing to which I can happily look forward. You gallivant off with that bloody woman; you dote on her. Never a thought about how I manage. If I had the courage I'd end it all.'

'Oh, my God,' exclaimed Alma, 'that's all I ever hear, but you do nothing about it. Instead of threatening to kill yourself why, in the name of charity, don't you bloody well get on with it? At least with you gone I could get myself a real man. Go on, kill yourself, instead of continually promising to do so.'

Aghast at her words, Rattenbury struck Alma in the face with his closed fist. She reeled back and fell into a chair, nursing her face.

'You bloody coward! You drink-sodden bastard!' she cried. 'That's the end. I'm finished with you.' And she burst into tears, throwing herself into Irene's arms and sobbing convulsively.

As Irene led Alma up to her bedroom, Rattenbury gulped down the remainder of the whisky in his glass and walked into the hall, saying, 'You'll see if I'm such a coward. I'll do it. I've had enough.' He disappeared out of the front door, adding as he went, 'I'll go over the East Cliff; that'll teach you a lesson.'

Irene had the greatest difficulty in controlling Alma. She would not lie down in the bedroom. She rushed around the house, screaming, crying and uttering imprecations. At last, at her wits' end, Francis Rattenbury having failed to return, she telephoned for Dr O'Donnell. He arrived around midnight, examined Alma, dressed her eye and administered a quarter of a grain of morphia, saying it would calm her. After he had elicited the story from Irene, they waited to see whether Rattenbury would return. By 1.30 a.m. he was not back, so they reported it to the police by telephone and they took off for the East Cliff to see whether they could find him. They had not been long gone when Rattenbury, looking morose and disconsolate, came in to the house and made for his bedroom on the ground floor.

Alma slept for a full eight hours before she awoke peaceful, calm, clear-headed and with nothing to show for her previous night's experience but a very shiny black eye.

Whilst Rattenbury convinced himself that his rage and temper had been fully justified by reason of Alma's brutal words, he was exceedingly remorseful when he saw her black eye. He told her that he should not have struck her, apologized and handed her a cheque for £100. Money to spend as she wished had always proved a great solace to Alma. In fact, although she never ceased to complain of his meanness, and constantly upbraided him for it, he treated her in a most generous fashion, the more so since, compared with his best days in Canada, his fortune was so reduced. She had £50 a month for housekeeping and other sums from time to time. In all she received something of the order of £1,000 to £1,200 each year, which in 1934 was a not inconsiderable sum.

On her good days, Alma could talk herself into contentment with her lot. She enjoyed the occasional fillip when a new song was published, convinced, on each new publication, that this would be the big breakthrough. She obtained, as ever, the greatest pleasure from her children. Christopher was away at school, but returned for the weekends permitted him, when he would sleep in the small spare room on the upper floor. John was at a local school and she would take him and collect him each day.

Having to be at the school for a particular time was something she found both tiresome and restricting, and she began to consider employing someone who could drive, who might take this chore off her hands and act as a handyman about the house. No lyricist had yet written the words for Peggy Lee to sing – 'It's so nice to have a man about the house' – but whatever the age of the 'man', it expressed sentiments in which Alma could always happily concur. She put the idea to Irene.

'No, darling,' was her reply, 'we can manage as we are, I'm sure.'

'But, Irene,' protested Alma, 'it would relieve you as well as me of so many things.'

'It might be a means of giving you too much relief,' said Irene. 'Another man in the house would be a menace.'

'I do believe you're jealous, darling,' laughed Alma. 'You'd rather do all the work than not have me to yourself.'

'P'raps so,' said Irene, 'but don't forget how tricky it became when we had the chef living here last time.'

'You're impossible,' said Alma. She sat thinking for a while before she spoke again. 'I've thought of a compromise. Why don't we get a very young fellow? Then all the problems you suggest would be avoided.'

'What's "young"?' enquired Irene.

'Ooh,' said Alma, thinking aloud, 'suppose we say – ah – fourteen to eighteen? We could soon train him then into our ways.'

Irene was not enthusiastic. 'That's just what worries me,' she said.

The longer Alma thought about her idea, the more attractive it seemed, and on 23 September 1934 there appeared, as a result, an advertisement in the *Bournemouth Daily Echo*, which read:

Daily willing lad, 14–18, for housework; Scout-trained preferred. Apply between 11–12, 8–9, 5 Manor Road, Bournemouth.

The first applicant to arrive at the Villa Madeira was a young man named Bert Parsons. He was in the higher level of the age parameters, and was a likely looking lad. Alma ensured that she looked her best when she interviewed him, wearing, as was her usual practice, her all-purpose pyjamas. He, in turn, thought she looked very much like Madeleine Carroll, a popular and beautiful actress of the period. He seemed to meet all the requirements.

'You can drive a car?' Alma asked him.

'No, I'm afraid I can't,' he replied.

His reply did nothing to dampen Alma's enthusiasm. 'We'll soon teach you,' Alma at once reassuringly told him. 'The job's yours if you want it.'

'Thanks,' said Bert Parsons. 'I'd like to think it over. Is it all right if I let you know?'

'Yes,' said Alma, 'as long as it is soon.'

Bert Parsons gave his sister a full account of the interview. With that inherent intuition which most women possess, she thought it sounded 'a little bit dicey'. Bert Parsons declined the offer.

'All human things', wrote Dryden, 'are subject to decay. And when Fate summons, monarchs must obey.' George Percy Stoner was no monarch, but it was the oddest and most unfortunate quirk of fate which drew his attention to Alma's advertisement, and took him to the Villa Madeira, as applicant for the job on offer.

Seventeen years of age, approaching his eighteenth birthday, he was a short, stocky youth, with slightly bowed legs. He had been born during the war, when Alma was already a widow, to Olive Stoner, the wife of a private in the Machine-Gun Corps, and had been an ailing child during his early years. He was her only child. He had not walked until he was three and was very backward in many respects. His father, after leaving the services, had become a bricklayer, and as his work took him and his wife to different parts of the country, George Stoner had spent most of his family life with his grandmother.

He had been prone in his early life to fainting fits and probably had no more than three years' schooling in the aggregate, when he finally left school at the age of fourteen. He lived 'over the tracks' in the least salubrious outskirts of Bournemouth, and such work as he had done had been with his father as a carpenter's help.

'He never wanted to go out in the road to play with other children. He would always stay in and mess about with his old bicycle doing repairs or making up things to try and get electricity.' His grandmother had never known him to go about with a girl, and he was very prejudiced against drink and never took alcohol. His uncle, Richard Stevens, a general dealer, described him as 'a good, honest boy, and the best boy that I have ever seen in my life'. He, too, had never known George have anything to do with girls – or, for that matter, with boys. In short, George Stoner's grandmother may not have been exaggerating when she summed him up as 'a good lad, an extraordinary good boy'. He was of a kindly disposition and, being somewhat backward, he tended, as is so often the case with such people, to choose friends younger than himself, whom he would protect and champion when they got into scrapes.

When he parked his bicycle and first confronted Alma Rattenbury he might not have been regarded as handsome. He was, however, far from ugly, having a pleasant, somewhat coarse, boyish, open countenance, and an engaging smile. He had one decided advantage over Bert Parsons in that he could drive a car. Anyone could then obtain a licence to drive a vehicle, the need to pass a test not being introduced until the Road Traffic Act 1935 came into effect, in June of that year, and even then it did not apply to those who already had sufficient driving experience. Nevertheless, Alma's advertisement was odd in one respect. In seeking a chauffeur one would be unlikely to look for a boy of fourteen or fifteen, but nor would he be a woman's choice, it is assumed, if she were advertising for a lover.

George Stoner was in high spirits when he told his grandmother, with whom he continued to live, that he had got the job at £1 a week. To him the Rattenburys must have seemed people of some importance, and to have a car to drive was a special bonus. That he would be working for a glamorous, attractive, easy-going lady of around forty probably never entered his head.

It entered Irene Riggs' head, however, and the more she thought about it the less she liked it. Her reaction was not propitious for the advent of George Stoner. His tasks were not great; in addition to doing jobs around the house, he would deliver little John to school and collect him later, he would take Alma, and usually Irene with her, on shopping expeditions. He would drive Alma and Rattenbury when they wished to go about. Apart from Irene's latent hostility, he counted himself lucky in his employment.

How the relationship between Alma and George Stoner developed is by no means clear; suffice it to say that few people could ever have anticipated it would move to intimacy with the rapidity it did. He was a shy and inexperienced youth. His reaction to a woman who was old enough to be his mother may well, as she displayed great kindness towards him, have caused him to see her as a mother-figure.

In November, about a month after Stoner had commenced employment, Alma decided the time had come to take off on one of her jaunts, which she occasionally took with Irene. Two problems, as usual, presented themselves; the first was to satisfy Francis and secure his agreement; the second – a necessary corollary to the first – was to extract money from him to defray the expense.

Alma discussed with Irene which story might sound best, and decided to tell him she was proposing to visit relatives in Sunderland. She had, in truth, set her heart on a visit to Oxford, where she and Irene could stay at the Randolph Hotel and visit the shops.

Alma was lucky in her approach to her husband. He had enjoyed his lunch, and had taken sufficient drink to be happy, yet not enough to have become morbid.

'Of course,' he said, 'you must go to Sunderland, though who would want to go there from choice, I can't imagine.'

'Well, I would not go, of course, if I didn't feel I have a duty to go and see them,' commented Alma.

'No, darling, I'm sure,' he laconically observed.

'Are you sure, darling, you'll be able to manage when I'm away?' she asked hopefully. 'I intended taking Irene with me. She enjoys it so much, you know, and she has so few pleasures in life.'

'I've managed before,' said Francis, 'and I can manage again. Don't worry about it, and yes, for God's sake take Irene with you. On no account leave her here, although she'd be safe enough, so far as I'm concerned.'

'Really, darling,' said Alma, 'you spend more time thinking about the things you can't do, than you spend time employing yourself on the things you can.'

'I don't have any illusions any more. I know exactly where I stand. I'm no use to man or beast. You are still young; you must enjoy yourself whenever and wherever you can. You must lead your own life and find your own pleasures. It's no use looking to me for them.'

'Does that include all the pleasures I feel necessary?' she enquired.

'The whole bloody lot,' was the reply. 'Lead your life as if I had already gone. That can't be long delayed in any event.'

For Alma enough had been said, and having told him how much money she needed for the trip and obtained a cheque to cover it, she went to the kitchen to tell Irene she was about to make the necessary arrangements.

History does not record the fashion in which Alma succeeded in seducing George Stoner at Oxford. Whether she made her first advances in the car, when Irene was not there; whether she contrived to find herself in his bedroom, whilst Irene was asleep, or whether she induced him to join her in her own room, may never be known. Certainly, she achieved it without the knowledge of Irene, since she had an adjoining bedroom, with a communicating door, next to Alma's, and Stoner's bedroom was opposite on the same corridor.

However it began, it was destined to continue; Alma had found a ready means of satisfying her needs, and was already devising ways and means of ensuring the ready availability of Stoner. Somehow, she reasoned, she must get him ensconced in the house. So, within a short while of their return from Oxford, it was arranged that he should 'live in' – thus, as she explained, having him more accessible as a chauffeur/handyman.

The upstairs portion of the Villa Madeira consisted of four bedrooms, a bathroom and lavatory. Alma occupied the largest bedroom, at the back of the house, above the drawing-room or sitting-room John slept in a bed in his mother's room. Irene slept in the adjoining room going towards the front of the house, which was over the small kitchen. There was a spare room, at the side of the house, in which Christopher stayed when he returned from school, which was over Francis Rattenbury's bed-room on the lower floor; this left an unoccupied front bedroom, over the dining-room, in which, it was decided, Stoner would henceforth sleep.

Stoner, with all his inexperience and the joys of his introduction to sex by a highly sophisticated and attractive woman with three husbands to her credit, was still far from happy with the situation in which he found himself. He was bright enough to see the dangers which might come from sexual intercourse with the wife of the man in whose employment he earned not only his keep but his bed and board as well. When he put these concerns to Alma, she brushed them aside; she had not had sex with her husband, she asserted, since John was conceived, over six years before; he was, in any event, quite beyond having sex with anyone, and the trump card was that he did not care and had himself told her she was to lead her own life, which included her sex life. In moments of doubt she knew the way to get Stoner's mind quickly on to other matters.

At first, they took their pleasures with some discretion, but since Stoner had to pass Irene's bedroom to reach Alma's it was not long before Irene was able to confirm what had previously been no more than a suspicion.

'I heard Stoner go into your room last night, darling,' she said to Alma. 'Don't you think you're taking a big risk?'

'A risk of what?' asked Alma.

'Of Mr Rattenbury finding out,' she replied.

'It doesn't matter if he does, but he won't because he won't enquire. He doesn't care. He knows he can't have it and doesn't worry any more who else may.'

'I think you're making a great mistake,' persisted Irene.

'Now, my darling, don't you be silly. You know how much this sort of thing means to me. I can't help it; it's the way I'm made. Please don't look so worried and concerned.' She put her arms round her. 'Stoner's presence will make no differences between you and me, I promise you. You are both necessary to me know.'

Irene could see that further remonstrance would be useless, but her dislike of Stoner was to grow as the relationship between him and Alma became more intense.

As Alma lay in bed over the ensuing weeks with Stoner beside her, she would tell herself how silly she had been not to have contrived such a situation before. All those years of frustration might have been avoided. She felt alive when she was with him and would take care to see that nothing happened to bring this idyllic arrangement to an end. Equally, she tried to divine what were Stoner's thoughts. That he enjoyed the sex as much as she, there was, she knew, no doubt. To him it was a new and wonderful experience. He was, however, so young; he had never been in love before and there was no doubt from all he said and did that he was hopelessly in love with her. She thought back to her own first love – Caledon Dolling – and, in many ways, she envied and pitied Stoner. Her one concern was the jealousy which from time to time he revealed. She had repeatedly assured him that she had no longer any feelings for her husband, and she told him, at least when they were in bed together, that she loved him as much as he loved her. The idea which, in a childish fashion he would sometimes entertain, that he alone could possess her, was so impracticable as to be absurd.

Francis Rattenbury seemed to be taking it all in his stride, always allowing for the fact that, by the end of each night, striding was the last thing it might enter his head to attempt. He, Alma, sometimes Irene and invariably Stoner would play cards together in the evening. Stoner would be offered a drink, and after dinner, when he returned to the sitting-room, Alma – having given Francis a cigar – would offer one to Stoner. Before long, whilst in the Villa Madeira, Stoner and his evening cigar became the established thing. He had come a long way from the home of his bricklayer father in Pine Vale Crescent, Ensbury Park.

CHAPTER 6

Affair with a Chauffeur/Handyman

Christmas 1934 had been a happy occasion for Alma. She had given Stoner £10, out of which he was to buy presents for the children, keeping the remainder for himself. Considering that the value of money has increased between twenty and twenty-five times since then, this was a most generous gift.

Alma used to leave on her dressing-table a heavy, gold man's watch, which Stoner believed she had given to him, but which she believed she had only lent to him. The ownership, as it happened, never fell to be resolved; other problems did.

In early February Irene Riggs was asleep in bed when, between 11.30 and midnight, she was awakened by considerable noise coming from Alma's bedroom. It was quite evident that she and Stoner were quarrelling violently. John was, as usual, asleep in the room, in confirmation of Alma's oft repeated assertion that he slept exceedingly well and, once asleep, was difficult to waken. Doubtless, however, there were limits even to the depth of his sleep, and Irene heard them, still quarrelling, move along the corridor on their way to Stoner's bedroom. There they continued their quarrel with greater volume and intensity; indeed, it became so noisy that she got out of bed and went to Stoner's room. When she opened the door she saw Alma dressed in a kimono, and Stoner, fully dressed, holding Alma, either by the throat or by the upper arm – which it was she could not clearly see. Irene was far from pleased with their behaviour at the best of times, but she was intensely put out and rather frightened by what she now saw. She separated them, told them that everyone would hear them unless they were quiet, and left in high dudgeon.

The following day Alma told Irene that the quarrel arose

because Alma had said their affair must come to an end, because of the disparity in their ages and because George was so very young. He said he could not live without her, so she had remained in his room and they made up the quarrel in bed.

Irene had her doubts about this version. She knew how important sex was to Alma and having it now on tap, after so few opportunities to be with a man over so many years, it was unlikely she would throw away the present chance. But she took some consolation from the fact that, whether true or false, it showed that Alma was at least contemplating that she might at some stage bring the relationship to an end.

The fact that two lovers had a quarrel was no occasion for surprise, but, if Dr O'Donnell and Alma were to be believed, certain events which they related as having occurred in the middle of February 1935 were not only surprising, but, when all the surrounding circumstances were considered, most improbable, almost to the point of being unbelievable.

It was said that Alma had telephoned the doctor to tell him she wished to see him, so he called upon her.

'I have something I must first tell you', she told him, 'that will shock you.'

'I doubt that very much, Alma,' replied the doctor. 'It isn't easy to shock doctors.'

'I am having an affair with my chauffeur/handyman. He is my lover.'

'Is that very wise?' he asked. 'Does Francis know?'

'I have not told him so, in so many words. But, as you know, we've had no sex for over six years, and he told me to live my own life. Shall you tell him?'

'No,' he said, 'of course not. It's not for me to do so. But what did you wish to consult me about in regard to that?'

'Well, Stoner tends to get very jealous,' she is said to have told him, 'and he has tried to strangle me – I believe he is taking drugs. He says he takes them for his head, and goes up to London to get them. Would you see him and see what you can find out, and, if he is taking them, warn him of the dangers?'

As a consequence Dr O'Donnell, according to his account, saw Stoner the following day. He told him he had been informed he was taking drugs and asked him what drug he was taking. Stoner was said to have replied that it was cocaine. The doctor then asked him where he had picked up the habit, and Stoner answered that he had found some cocaine at home, which he had sampled. He did not say if he meant his own home or the

Rattenburys'. It gave him pleasant sensations so he had carried on with it. Dr O'Donnell warned him that it was a dangerous thing to do, and offered to help him if he wished to give it up. Stoner did not accept the offer. According to Dr O'Donnell himself, he did not bother to look for any symptoms, but supposed the youth was telling the truth, and gathered that he had been up to London the previous day, when O'Donnell had called on Alma, to try and get some, but had failed to do so. The doctor was neither told nor did he ask where the money came from to buy the drug. He did no more than warn Stoner of the dangers, advice which he did not think would do much good.

Dr O'Donnell claimed to have reported his conversation to Mrs Rattenbury and to have told her he had warned the youth against drugs. Stoner, he told her, was taking cocaine.

Alma later purported to confirm this story, but said she did no more about it because Stoner seemed better from then on and she did not want to agitate him. She added that afterwards things went smoothly on and since he had stopped taking cocaine (although she never at any time said she had discussed the drug with him or mentioned his visit to the doctor) everything was all right.

Why is the whole of this account improbable to the point of being unbelievable? From first to last no one ever found any evidence of the existence of any cocaine. The idea that Stoner had first encountered cocaine in his father's house – a man who had never taken drugs in his life, an elderly, decent, upright bricklayer, who would be highly unlikely to have access to, or to desire, such a drug – was farcical, and it is unlikely that by temperament and upbringing he would have sought thus to blacken his father. It was even more unacceptable that he could have meant that he first found it in the home of his grandmother, where he also lived.

It is unlikely that Stoner would have known how to take cocaine, unless he had seen someone else doing it. If he had been in the habit of taking it in the Villa Madeira, as Alma was said to have suggested, it is unlikely that Irene would not have noticed that he was high, and she was always only too ready to say anything she could against him. In fact, she said that she had never seen anything about him which might suggest he was drunk or on drugs until one occasion very much later, by which time much had occurred to explain why – at a later date – he may have taken to drink.

If the doctor had told Stoner, as the doctor asserted he did, that he had been told Stoner was on drugs, Stoner would immediately have asked him who had said this, and the doctor is unlikely to have wanted to involve Alma; in any event Stoner would have guessed who had told the doctor, and would unquestionably have raised with her why she had thus gone behind his back. It would have been a singularly odd medical interrogation if it followed the course described by the doctor. It is highly unlikely, if Stoner had wanted cocaine, that he would have had the faintest idea of how to go about getting it, and perhaps the most significant thing of all was that much later, when he was being interrogated by another doctor and was asked to describe 'cocaine' – a substance so white in colour that it is known as 'snow' – he described it as 'brownish with black specks in it'.

There are two possibilities. The first is that the doctor's and Alma's accounts of this incident are true, however unlikely and despite their gross improbabilities, and that Stoner was telling Alma such a story to win sympathy for some purpose. The second is that it was untrue, in which case it becomes interesting, as the story unfolds, to consider why these two characters in this saga thought it necessary, together, thus to present it.

The Romans called the full moon 'the Ides', and in the month of March they fell on the 15th. Caesar was warned to beware of them and it was unfortunate that there was not a soothsayer about on that date in 1935 to warn Alma against the intrigue on which she now embarked.

She was, as usual, short of money. She knew if she asked her husband to pay off her bills and provide something on top she might ultimately succeed in getting it, but it would involve a gruelling argument and even a nasty row. She decided it was better, as she had done before, to arrange to go away for a few days and tell him she needed another operation. Occasionally, Dr O'Donnell would arrange for an operation on her tubercular glands at home, but Rattenbury had previously accepted her explanation that sometimes this was better done in a nursing home.

If she got the money she required she could this time make a trip to London rather than to Oxford, and she would take Stoner. He would enjoy that; they would be able to sleep together without any risk of interference from anyone and she would leave Irene at the Villa Madeira to look after Rats. Irene would, of course, be upset and disappointed, but it would be much more fun for Alma to be alone with Stoner. Alma made her way to the sitting-room, thinking that she would have to alert Dr O'Donnell to the truth, since Rats might send for him, although that was unlikely, or the doctor might make a social call on him; but, she reassured herself, dear old Bill would play the game. He liked her so much and, she felt sure, would never let her down.

'I am afraid I have some bad news,' she lied to Rats. 'I'm having more trouble with the glands, and, rather than let it get worse, I have agreed to go into a nursing home, and have it done there.'

'Oh!' said Rattenbury. 'That's a pity. Will it be a long job?'

'No,' replied Alma, 'not at all. Only a few days, but they can do it more effectively under the proper conditions.'

'Well, if you have to have it done, there is no alternative.'

'I shall leave Irene here to look after you,' she told him. 'I will get Stoner to drive me and he can stay in London and then bring me back, but I am sorry to say, darling, it will all be rather expensive.'

Rattenbury sat up at the mention of the expense. 'How much is expensive?' he asked.

Alma sat as if calculating, and then said, 'I would think at least two hundred and fifty pounds.'

'Christ,' said Rats, 'that's a hell of a lot of money. Are you sure it will cost all that?'

'Well,' said Alma, 'it isn't only the operation; there are the expenses as well.'

Rattenbury looked pensive and glum. 'Well! I will have to find it, if it is a question of your health, but we keep on having all these expenses to find out of a fixed income. It isn't easy, and the value of my securities has fallen of late. Still, if you tell me you must have it, then I suppose you must, but I hope this won't happen too often,' he said.

'So do I,' said Alma, already planning in her mind how she would spend the money.

She now had to await an opportunity when she could speak on the telephone without Rats overhearing, and when this came she booked two rooms at the Royal Palace Hotel, Kensington, for 19 March.

As soon as Alma got the cheque signed by Francis she paid it into her bank, eliminating her overdraft of £57 10s. She then sat down to write out cheques for the local shops to which she owed money – 'Bobbys' for dresses, Aish for electrical work, Wimborne for fruit, her dentist, Boots the Chemists, Tarrants and Plummers for more dresses, Williams & Tredgold for groceries, Sainsbury the Butcher and Parman the Baker. As she looked at the pile of bills which ate so heavily into the £250 she sighed at the prospect of all this lovely money disappearing so very quickly.

Alma was quite excited at the prospect of getting away for a few days with Stoner, and when Tuesday, 19 March arrived they took to the road for London. They got no further than Southampton, where the car spluttered to a stop and would not be persuaded to continue. With some difficulty they managed to get the car to a garage and, collecting together their luggage, made for the station where they took the train to London.

When they arrived in Kensington, Alma signed the register as 'Mrs Rattenbury and brother', and they were given rooms on the same corridor opposite each other. Alma realized that they would need some ready money, and that Stoner would have to be kitted out if he was to begin to look the part of her brother. She sent him to cash a cheque for £50, taking £25 of it from him when he returned and leaving the remainder for him.

That afternoon they went off on a shopping expedition. Harrods was close by, at Knightsbridge, and they made that their first port of call, heading for the shoe department, where they selected a pair of men's shoes. Alma, being in a generous mood, in holiday spirit and in anticipation of the delights, as she saw it, in store, decided that Stoner should have two pairs of shoes, and two pairs of shoe-trees to keep them in shape. The assistant, however, discovered that they had only one pair in stock, so Alma said they would take that pair, and gave instructions for the remaining pair to be ordered and dispatched to her, in due course, at the Villa Madeira.

The assistant wrote out in her name a sales card because she had told him they would be making other purchases in the store, and this bore her correct name and address. They next passed on to another department, where they selected three pairs of men's pyjamas, which Alma had asked to examine. The pyjamas were made of crêpe-de-chine, the like of which Stoner had never seen before; far less had he ever envisaged being the owner of such sophisticated night attire. Indeed, in face of Alma's sexual demands, he may well have been wondering when he would have the opportunity of wearing them. The cost was £9, which

46

today would be around £180, and was hardly the attire for a chauffeur/handyman earning £1 a week 'all found'. Indeed, Alma gave a new dimension to the expression 'all found' when it comprised bed, board, sex, *de luxe* clothes and the other metropolitan delights of high society. She chose in the same department three shirts, three ties and two handkerchiefs, all made of silk, and a dozen linen handkerchiefs; the cost in total £6 2s 6d, all of which she had debited to her Harrods charge account. The *sang froid* which Alma exhibited in having men's shoes sent to her at her home, and charging menswear to her account was typical of her. It was true that never in the whole of her relationship with her husband had he ever asked to see the counterfoils in her cheque book, or her passbook, or the statements from the shops, such as Harrods, where she maintained accounts. However, he would have had to become very forgetful, had he ever discovered them, to have forgotten when it was that she had bought him crêpe-de-chine pyjamas, silk shirts and ties and expensive shoes.

Having moved on to purchase for Stoner, in still another department, three pairs of socks, two pairs of gloves and three sets of underwear at a cost of £5 10s 6d, likewise charged to her account, it must have occurred to her that Stoner could not enter a fashionable restaurant with her over the next few days attired only in socks, underwear, shoes, shirt and tie, however beautifully made and however exquisite the quality, so she guided him to the outfitting department where they selected a grey suit, a blue suit and a mackintosh, at a cost of 7 guineas each for the suits and £1 17s 6d for the belted mac. Stoner told the assistant that he wanted to wear the grey suit right away, but since it required alteration the assistant promised to have this effected at once, and to have it delivered, on Alma's instructions, to the Royal Palace Hotel that very day.

Alma felt they had had a good day's shopping, but Stoner was sensitive to the fact that everything which had been bought had been for him, whilst Alma had nothing. He would like to purchase something for her, so they made their way from Harrods to Kirby & Bunn, the jewellers, in Old Bond Street, where Stoner selected a single-stone diamond ring with diamond shoulders, at a cost of £15 10s, for which he paid out of the money he had received from Alma, giving as his name and address, in answer to the enquiry from the assistant, George Rattenbury, 104 Redhill Drive, Bournemouth, which was the address neither of his parents, nor of his grandmother, nor, of course, of the

Villa Madeira. When Alma tried on the ring, which was size 'N', it was slightly too large, so the assistant said they would alter it at once and deliver it later that day to the Royal Palace Hotel. When it arrived, Stoner gave it with some pleasure to Alma.

It had been a felicitous excursion. It bore many of the characteristics of kitting Stoner out for a honeymoon, and the ring might well have been regarded by both of them as carrying some of the stamp of an engagement ring. Did this 'betrothal' carry with it more sinister connotations? In due course, others might so contend.

The next few days passed all too swiftly. For Alma it was a pleasant interlude of the kind she had enjoyed over the years with Francis, plus the opportunity for sex, which was, for her, far more than an added bonus. It is difficult to imagine the reaction of Stoner. He was experiencing a way of life wholly alien to anything he had ever known before. Shy by nature, barely educated, from a poor background, it must have seemed as if someone had rubbed Aladdin's ring for him, although from time to time, as they visited restaurants, the cinema and the London sights, he must also have felt unsure of himself and somewhat self-conscious. It was not to last for ever, and on Friday, 22 March they had, certainly with regret so far as he was concerned, and with resignation so far as Alma was concerned, made their way to the garage at Southampton where the car had been repaired, and back to the Villa Madeira.

By the time they arrived there, Rattenbury, having made good work of at least a bottle of Scotch, had gone to bed. Alma thought she ought to let him know she was back, and made her way to his bedroom.

'We're back,' she announced, in as light-hearted a manner as she felt able.

'So I see,' mumbled Rats.

'Did you manage all right?' she asked.

'As usual,' he said.

'There was nothing you wanted?' she asked.

'Really,' was his only comment, 'this is no time for funny riddles.'

'Well, good night then, darling,' she said as she left the bedroom, on her way to bed with Stoner.

'Good night,' grunted Rats, without any enquiry about whether the operation had been a success or anything else.

The following day, Saturday, 23 March, was quite a pleasant

day with some sun. In the morning Stoner drove Alma to John's school to pick him up and bring him back for lunch. In the afternoon, Stoner drove Alma and John to Christopher's school to watch him play football.

In the evening, when they had returned, life had assumed what for Alma, apart from when she got to bed with Stoner, was its usual monotonous ritual. She played cards with Rats in the evening, when John had been put to bed in her bedroom, and ultimately made her own way to bed, where Stoner soon joined her. A thoroughly normal scenario for the Villa Madeira, if not for the rest of Bournemouth. The cuckolded husband lay in a drink-assisted sleep in the bedroom on the ground floor, whilst his loving wife was upstairs in bed with her eighteen-year-old chauffeur/handyman, her six-year-old son sleeping peacefully in an adjoining bed in her bedroom.

CHAPTER 7

Confession : Battered by a Mallet

At 1.15 on the morning of Monday, 25 March 1935, Bournemouth Police Station could not have been described as a hive of constabulary activity: the Station Sergeant, resting back, with his tall chair leaning aginst the wall, a cigarette, inexpertly rolled, hanging from his lips, a not too clean mug of thick brown tea on his desk, and two drunks in the detention room – one of them spark out, noisily snoring and sleeping it off on the floor, the other singing 'I'll Take You Home Again, Kathleen' with such force that Kathleen, back in Dublin, must have been wondering, without the need of a telephone, where he intended taking her, since she was already home.

When the telephone rang, the Station Sergeant readjusted his chair and picked up the receiver. He searched for his pencil, made a few notes, said 'Thank you, Doctor, I will look into it at once,' and, as he replaced the receiver, yelled out in order to reach above the happy Irishman, 'Bagwell!'

Police Constable Arthur Ernest Bagwell, so appropriately named for a police officer, emerged from the inner recesses of the station. 'Yes, Sarge?' he enquired.

'Dr O'Donnell has just telephoned. A chap called Rattenbury has been taken to the Strathallen Nursing Home with head injuries and the doctor suspects foul play. Step round there, will you, and see what it's all about.'

Bagwell jerked his head, put on his mac, went through the door and clambered on his bicycle. He arrived at the nursing home at around 1.30 a.m., where he asked to see the doctor. O'Donnell soon appeared with another man, whom he introduced as Alfred Rooke, the surgeon.

'Thank you for coming so promptly, officer,' said the doctor.

'We have a patient of mine in here. We saw him earlier on at his home, where he had sustained a severe head injury. I thought he had fallen – he drinks quite a bit – and had hit his head on the piano. Because there was so much congealed blood and we could not examine him properly, we brought him here in an ambulance. Now we've examined him, we are sure he has been violently assaulted about the head, and it seems to be a job for you.'

Bagwell was already unbuttoning his left-hand jacket pocket and extracting the inevitable notebook.

'The blow which has caused the most injury', added Rooke, 'is above the ear on the left-hand side and is so severe that it must have been inflicted by some instrument with pretty considerable force.'

'Will he live?' asked Bagwell.

'We hope he might,' replied Rooke, 'but it is always difficult at this stage to be sure with this sort of injury.'

Bagwell took down the address of the Villa Madeira, which O'Donnell gave him, and, commenting that he had better go there at once to see what he could find, prepared to leave. 'I shall need to get some more information from you two gentlemen', he added, 'if there has been a criminal assault, but that can wait until later.' Then, as an afterthought, 'I suppose I had better have a word with the victim before I go,' he half enquired.

'You can come along and see him,' said Rooke, leading the way, 'but he's quite unconscious, I'm afraid. He can't tell you anything.'

'Well, I'd better take a look,' said Bagwell, and followed them into the operating theatre.

It was about 2.00 a.m. when Bagwell arrived at the Villa Madeira. In response to the bell, Alma answered the door, Irene accompanying her. Alma was wearing her customary pyjamas and long loose coatlet. Bagwell followed her with ponderous tread into the drawing-room, his helmet under his arm, as he reached again for his notebook, and in copybook fashion said, 'I have just come from Strathallen Nursing Home where your husband has been taken this evening, suffering from serious injuries. Can you furnish me with any particulars as to how he came by them?'

Alma seemed very excited; Bagwell thought she was probably under the influence of drink to a mild extent, when she replied, 'At about 9.00 p.m. I was playing cards with my husband in the drawing-room, and I went to my bedroom. About 10.30 p.m.

I heard a yell. I came downstairs into the drawing-room and saw my husband sitting in the chair.' She indicated an armchair across the room. It was a well-upholstered old chair, with fairly high, upholstered, rounded arms and a round upholstered back. Alma continued, 'I then sent for Dr O'Donnell, and he was taken away.' While Alma was talking Irene Riggs stood by her trying to comfort her.

Because the injuries were obviously serious, the Station Sergeant also alerted an officer senior to Bagwell and, shortly after Bagwell had arrived, he was followed into the house by Inspector Mills. He too thought that Alma seemed very excited and appeared to have been drinking. It is somewhat curious that both officers thought her excited, since that is not the first adjective police officers normally use when describing drunkenness.

Mills followed the same line as had Bagwell, although in a less traditional fashion. 'What's happened?' he asked.

Alma said, 'I was in bed when I heard someone groaning. I came downstairs and found my husband in the easy chair. He was unconscious and blood was flowing from his head.'

Mills glanced around the room. It was March and not a warm night, but he noticed that one of the french windows was open. It was the left-hand window as you looked out of the room. He turned to Alma again. 'Was this window open when you came down?'

'No,' said Alma, 'it was shut and locked.'

Mills, accompanied by Bagwell, then began to examine the room more closely. They saw a stain on the carpet, near the side of the chair, on the right-hand side as one looked at the chair; there were other marks on the back and the arm. The seat had slight stains, which appeared to have been washed, and the chair itself smelt of urine.

'Let's look in the bathroom,' Mills said to Bagwell.

They both went into the bathroom which adjoined Francis Rattenbury's bedroom on the same floor. There they found a man's coat and waistcoat, which were both sopping wet as if they had been washed and wrung out. Mills, followed by Bagwell, then decided to have a look outside, where he found a dustbin; Bagwell looked in it and recovered from it a man's collar soaked with blood.

'Some of the clothes', said Mills, when he returned to the drawing-room, 'seem to have been washed?'

'Yes,' replied Irene, 'I washed them. I found them in the bathroom, and as I had some water in the bath, I put the tops in to try and clean them.'

'Were you asked to do it?' asked Mills.

'It was my own idea.'

Mills also took possession of a cretonne cover, which had blood on it. Irene said she had taken it off the chair and put it on the floor of the drawing-room, near the door.

Mills found it difficult to understand exactly what had occurred, but he noticed that there was a small table in the room, with a book face downwards on it. He turned it over and, although he did not bother to read it, he noticed, as a good police officer, that it was open at page 296, and that it was a library book called *Stay of Execution* by Eliot Gayshaw-Williams. He replaced it where he had found it.

Then he decided that he had better go to the nursing home, and he left Bagwell in the house with Alma and Irene. Little John appears to have been asleep still upstairs.

Bagwell wandered round the room, somewhat casually looking for anything else which might be of interest. Soon, after Irene had left the room, Alma said, 'I know who done it [*sic*].'

Momentarily surprised, Bagwell hurriedly considered his position. 'Mrs Rattenbury, before you say anything more I feel I should tell you that you are not obliged to say anything, but if you do I shall take it down in writing and it may be used in evidence.'

Alma took little notice. 'I did it with a mallet,' she said. 'Rats has lived too long. I did it with a mallet.'

'Where is it?' asked Bagwell.

'It's hidden,' was her reply.

Bagwell wrote this into his notebook, but had not finished doing so when Alma said, 'No, my lover did it.' She paused and added, 'It is urine on the chair.' She continued all the time to wander round the room, and then to the concern of the redoubtable Bagwell blurted, 'I would like to give you ten pounds.' Then, as an afterthought, 'No, I won't bribe you.'

She seemed to be in a very high state and to the consternation of the unfortunate Bagwell, who had never before found himself in such a situation, she approached him and tried to kiss him.

'Here', he said, 'easy on,' raising his arms in front of his face as Irene, who had meanwhile returned to the room, sought to restrain her. Alma was, however, so persistent in her pursuit of the reluctant policeman that the miserable Bagwell, who was bursting to use the toilet, decided he would go out to the garden, where he could at least perform in peace. So he told Irene he would go outside for a short while and at once did so.

Alma, in great excitement, with no intention of allowing Bagwell to escape, careered around, trying to reach different doors in an endeavour to get outside, while Irene restrained her, locking each door in turn so that she could not do so. In sheer desperation, Irene finally pushed Alma into a chair and sat on top of her so that she could not escape.

Meanwhile, outside, Bagwell had come across another officer, patrolling on his beat. Whether he had been suspicious of the man standing in the shadows of the house, not realizing it was one of his colleagues relieving himself, is not known, but having identified Bagwell, he accompanied him back to the door, before continuing his dreary routine.

At around 2.45 a.m., Inspector Mills arrived at the nursing home. Outside he noticed a car with a man asleep in the passenger seat, whom he later identified as Stoner and whom he had not seen before. Inside he asked if he might see the doctors whom PC Bagwell had previously seen and was taken to O'Donnell and Rooke. He told them he had been down to Manor Road, adding, 'That woman's drunk.' Then, 'How's Mr Rattenbury now?' he asked them.

'His condition, I am afraid, is critical,' said Rooke.

'Will he survive?' enquired Mills.

'One cannot tell,' said Rooke. 'The odds seem to be against it, but he might.'

'If he doesn't,' said Mills, 'this is murder.'

'Yes,' replied Rooke, 'these blows could not have been self-inflicted.'

Other than that arrangements were made for the taking of statements from the doctors the following day, there is no record of what passed between them and Inspector Mills on that visit.

This fact gives rise to certain curious features which never seem at any time to have been questioned. Here were circumstances in which a very serious and vicious assault had been committed; it was potentially a case of murder. If Dr O'Donnell's account as previously related was accurate, he knew of the relationship between Alma and Stoner; he presumed and may even have believed that Stoner was on cocaine; he knew that Stoner was said to be so jealous and difficult about it that Alma had turned to him; yet, presumably, he gave not the slightest hint or suggestion to the police about any of this.

True, there was an ethical duty of confidentiality between doctor and patient, but both the Rattenburys were his patients and

Stoner was not. Stoner was, as the doctor knew, waiting outside for him in the car. That he said not a word is clear, because Stoner was not questioned by the police as a suspect for some days.

At the very least one would have expected him to say to the Inspector, 'By the way, have you questioned the Rattenburys' chauffeur/handyman?' Plainly, he gave no hint at all. Dr O'Donnell for some reason known only to himself played his cards very close to his chest.

At 3.30 a.m. Inspector Mills arrived back at the Villa Madeira to find Alma in the hall giving every appearance of being slightly more agitated and, as the Inspector believed, under the influence of drink.

'Your husband has been seriously wounded and is now in a critical condition,' he said to her.

'Will this be against me?' asked Alma, which sounded sufficiently ominous to Mills.

'Mrs Rattenbury,' he later said he told her, 'I caution you; you are not obliged to say anything unless you wish to do so, but whatever you do say will be taken down and may be used in evidence.'

If true, his words did not deter Alma, who went on, 'I did it; he gave me the book. He's lived too long. He said, "Dear, dear".' There was a pause, and then, 'I'll tell you where the mallet is in the morning.' Mills did not consider it wise to interrupt her, or comment. She added, 'I shall make a better job of it next time. Irene does not know. I made a proper muddle of it. I thought I was strong enough.'

Knowing nothing more could be done, Dr O'Donnell came out of the nursing home. He noticed the clock showed 3.15 a.m. Stoner was awake and, having opened the car door for him, drove him to the Villa Madeira, where he went in with Stoner. Whether he overheard what Alma had been saying to Mills is not known, but he found the house in a state of some confusion. The gramophone was playing, although Irene Riggs claimed she did not hear it. There were four police officers in the house, and Alma was running about amongst them from one room to another. He tried to explain her husband's condition to her, but he did not believe she could take it in. He took her upstairs at about 3.45 a.m., and injected by hypodermic syringe half a grain of morphia, at a time when, so he later asserted, he formed the view she was very intoxicated. It was also reasonable for him to have assumed that this would place her beyond risk of making any statements similar to those she had made to Mills.

Having given the injection, however, the doctor went downstairs to the kitchen, believing he had seen the last of Alma for that night, in order to talk to Irene Riggs and Stoner. En route, he saw Inspector Mills and told him she was quiet, as he had given her morphia. Meanwhile, Alma, having been given the morphia, was lying on the bed 'in her pyjamas and light dressing-gown', when PC Bagwell went into her bedroom and looked under her bed. What he was expecting to find is anybody's guess. Perhaps he was looking for a mallet.

When, five minutes later, the doctor returned to the sitting-room, he was surprised to find Alma there walking about, and Inspector Mills asking her, 'Do you suspect anybody?'

According to the doctor's recollection, she replied, 'Yes,' and, when Mills asked her, 'Whom do you suspect?' she replied, 'His son.'

Mills, on the other hand, preferred the view that, without any prompting from him, she volunteered, 'I know who did it – his son.'

Both, however, were agreed that Mills asked her how old the son was, and she replied, 'Thirty-two, but he is not here.' In fact he was in Canada, as she well knew.

Dr O'Donnell was far from happy about this questioning to which the Inspector was subjecting Alma. He decided he ought to intervene. 'Tell me, have you cautioned this lady?' he asked.

The Inspector replied, 'No.'

'Well, look at her condition,' continued O'Donnell. 'She's full of whisky, and I have given her a large dose of morphia. She's not in a fit state to make a statement to you or anybody else.'

Later, when the Inspector came to give evidence, he was to say nothing about the doctor's contention that he asked him about a caution, or his reply that one had not been administered. Moreover, no one ever saw fit to ask him about it, although if the doctor was right the Inspector could hardly have been telling the truth when he said he had previously cautioned Alma at the time she blurted out, 'Will this be against me?' Likewise, if the doctor is to be believed, it is strange that Inspector Mills did not tell the doctor he had previously cautioned her.

Police officers, including inspectors, have the habit in many cases, when they come to give evidence, of interposing the notion that they administered a caution, when they know they should have done so but have not in fact done so, because, without it, a suspect's confession or inculpatory statement may be rendered inadmissible.

Whatever the truth, O'Donnell considered Alma had had enough, and escorted her with some difficulty up the stairs of the Villa Madeira and back to her bedroom, where she remained.

CHAPTER 8

Alma Arrested

Once he was satisfied that Alma was soundly asleep, Dr O'Donnell, not unreasonably, decided he might get a little sleep himself and so left the house. There was no sleep that night for Irene and Stoner, however, and a disturbed night into the bargain for Detective-Inspector William Carter, who was put in charge of the enquiries. Inspector Mills had reported back to the police station that the victim seemed unlikely to live and this would involve a murder enquiry. The Criminal Investigation Department was alerted and Carter was given the case to handle. Carter had been a police officer for nearly thirty years, the last five as an inspector.

By tradition policemen who investigate crime, as distinct from preventing it, always wear plain clothes, although quite why this should be so is not readily evident. In any case, at 4.30 a.m. on the Monday morning Carter arrived at the Villa Madeira. He discussed the earlier events with Inspector Mills and, having learned that Alma had been put soundly to sleep, his immediate concern was to discover when she was likely to awake.

At that stage he made no attempt to question either Stoner or Irene Riggs, but contented himself with looking around the house and the gardens. This was rather odd since he was clearly impatient to get on with his enquiries, but it certainly indicates that so far as he was concerned Stoner was not then under suspicion.

Carter had learned that Alma had been given half a grain of morphia at 3.45 a.m., when she was believed already to be under the influence of alcohol, so he could hardly have anticipated the likelihood of her awakening naturally for a number of hours. Despite this, he and the other officers in the house repeatedly asked Irene whether Alma was yet awake, and at 6.00 a.m., when she had been asleep for only two and a quarter hours, Carter went to her bedroom to find out for himself. He succeeded in getting some sort of response from her, so he sent another officer to fetch Irene. Alma was saying something which was far from intelligible, but which sounded very much as if she were saying that she wanted to be sick.

Detective-Inspector Carter suggested she should get up as he wished to ask her some questions, but she, having pushed back the covers, said she did not wish to do so as she had not had her coffee. Carter told her he wanted to know exactly what had occurred. She said to Carter, 'I picked up the mallet, and he dared me to hit him. He said, "You have not got guts enough to do it." I hit him. Hid the mallet. He is not dead, is he? Are you the coroner?' Carter told Irene to make some coffee for her, which she did. Meanwhile, Carter had evidently telephoned for a police matron to be sent to the house, for she arrived at the same time as the coffee. Alma had difficulty in drinking it and was unable to hold the saucer as she did so. Whilst Carter was engaged with Alma, Bagwell, conscious that she had said she had struck her husband with a mallet and then hidden it, now decided to see whether he could find such an object. He had no success at the back of the house.

At the front of the house, he had no greater success until he bent down to get under an overhanging tree and, having squeezed through a narrow gap between the trellis work and the garden wall, found a mallet. When he took it inside, he and Detective-Inspector Carter examined it and saw that there was a piece of flesh and hair on it.

Not long elapsed before Carter looked at his watch and saw it was about 7.00 a.m. Being anxious to move matters along, he decided to try and get Alma out of bed. Alma, however, did not share his anxiety and was reluctant to get up; moreover, Irene showed no inclination to persuade her. Whenever Carter tried to induce her to get dressed, she kept saying she wanted to have a bath.

Since the police matron had arrived Carter was agreeable to her taking one. The bathroom on the upper floor was used by the staff so Alma was taken to the ground floor to bathe. She staggered down with Irene's help and, when she had taken her bath, told Irene and the police that she wanted to go back to sleep. This did not fit in with Carter's plans. He told her she must get dressed, and, leaving her with the police matron, he went downstairs.

He made his way to the kitchen at around 7.30 a.m. where he saw Stoner and asked him if he could tell him anything about how Mr Rattenbury had received his injuries. Stoner having indicated willingness to tell him what he knew, Carter took a statement from him.

It read:

I am a chauffeur/handyman employed by Mr Rattenbury of 5 Manor Road, Bournemouth. I retired to my bedroom about 8.05 p.m. on Sunday, 24 March 1935, leaving Mr and Mrs Rattenbury and the boy John in the drawing-room. About 10.30 p.m. I was aroused by Mrs Rattenbury shouting to me to come down. I came down into the drawing-room and saw Mr Rattenbury sitting in the armchair with blood running from his head. Mrs Rattenbury was crying and screaming and said to me, 'Help me to get Rats into bed, he has been hurt.' I then took the car and went to Dr O'Donnell's house. He had left before I got there. When I returned I cleaned the blood from the floor on the instructions of Mrs Rattenbury.

Carter then asked him if Mrs Rattenbury had been drinking, and Stoner said, 'She was sober as far as I know; she had not been drinking.'

'What was her condition', asked Carter, 'when you went to bed?'

'Normal,' replied Stoner.

'Have you even seen a mallet on the premises?'

'No,' replied Stoner.

'Before you were aroused by Mrs Rattenbury, did you hear sounds of a quarrel or a noise of any kind?'

'No.'

'How long have you been employed here?' continued Carter.

'Since September 1934.'

'What has been the relationship between Mr and Mrs Rattenbury during that time? Did they seem happy together?'

'Yes, they seemed to be on the best of terms,' replied Stoner.

'Did you ask Mrs Rattenbury how this happened?'

'Yes,' said Stoner, 'and she said she didn't know.'

'How was she dressed when you came down?'

'She had on pyjamas and bare feet,' replied Stoner.

All his answers were incorporated into the statement which Carter was preparing for him. Curiously enough, it later emerged that the date which was put on the statement was 30 March, which Carter explained was the date when it was copied.

By the time Carter had finished taking Stoner's statement, Alma, under pressure from the police matron and with the assistance of Irene, had dressed. When Carter re-entered her bedroom, it became evident why he had been so anxious to get her out of bed and dressed.

He had decided to charge her. He told her who he was, gave her the usual caution once again, and said to her, 'Alma Rattenbury, I charge you that you did, by wounding, do grievous bodily harm to one Francis Mawson Rattenbury in an attempt to murder him on Sunday, 24 March 1935.'

According to the account given by Carter, Alma then made another statement. He later said she made it with deliberation, clearly understanding exactly what she was saying, entirely on her own without any questions being put by him or anyone else, and as she spoke he wrote what she said down in his note-book.

What he wrote down was the following:

About 9.00 p.m. on Sunday, 24 March 1935, I was playing cards with my husband when he dared me to kill him as he wanted to die. I picked up the mallet. He then said, 'You have not got guts enough to do it.' I then hit him with the mallet. I hid the mallet outside the house. I would have shot him if I had a gun. Alma Rattenbury.

Carter contended that he read it over to her; she, in turn, then asked to read it herself, and did so aloud. The names at the end were her signature, which she appended sitting on the bed, holding the book in one hand and writing with the other.

It is one of the peculiarities of the English court procedure that experienced judges and lawyers will accept without question that a statement couched in such terms is totally the product of the person to whom it is attributed. Although Carter's account of the matter was rightly challenged when Alma came to trial, this aspect, as is virtually the custom, was not raised. It is interesting, however, for the non-lawyer to look at the structure of the statement attributed by the police officer to Alma, and to consider whether it bears the mark of someone with no previous experience of making a statement in such circumstances, or whether it is manifestly worded, phrased and constructed in exactly the fashion of an experienced police officer. No doubt, however, the statement conveyed the substance of what Alma said, with the help of the Inspector.

Carter told Alma that he would be taking her into custody and she would have to accompany him to the police station. She put on her hat and coat and went downstairs to the hall, where Irene and her small son were standing. When she was satisfied that Inspector Carter could not hear, she whispered to Irene – if Irene is to be believed – 'Tell Stoner he must give me the mallet.'

Stoner had by then joined the others in the hall. When Carter invited Alma to 'Come along,' she turned and said to Stoner and Irene, 'Don't make fools of yourselves,' to which Stoner replied, in a despairing manner, 'You've got yourself into this mess by talking too much.'

She kissed John and as she walked out of the door of the Villa Madeira she saw the little boy at the door waving, and, with her eyes full of tears, went to the car to be driven away. No police car was available, so, at the request of the Inspector, Stoner drove her away in the Rattenburys' car. Having seen Alma taken into the police station, he drove back to Manor Road.

Inside the station she was again cautioned and formally charged with the attempted murder of her husband, to which she replied, 'That's right. I did it deliberately and would do it again.'

Meanwhile, if Irene is to be believed, she started to pass on to Stoner Alma's message about the mallet, but she had no sooner begun to tell him than she realized how silly the message was, since the police had already found the mallet. So she did not pursue the conversation.

Before being taken to the police cells Alma asked if she might communicate with her solicitor, Mr Lewis Manning of the Bournemouth firm of Other Manning and Boileau-Tredinnick. He was typical of so many country solicitors. In addition to the sort of work which arises in a provincial town – conveyancing, wills, family problems and the like – he was also experienced in the work of the local magistrates' court, although he little realized when he made his way to see Alma at the police station that he was walking slap into a *cause célèbre*.

It would be fascinating to know what transpired in the conversation he had with his client, but such communications are known to the legal profession as 'privileged', and cannot be revealed without the permission of the client, and will thus never now be known. He visited her that Monday morning on two occasions, and it is at least reasonably certain that one of the matters they discussed was whether he could conduct the proceedings himself at that stage or whether a barrister should be retained. This was of some importance because, if counsel were to appear, the expense would be that much greater and the question of how the expense would be met might not be without its difficulties. Alma's bank account was overdrawn and she was virtually dependent on the finances and generosity of her husband. It was somewhat indelicate to contemplate obtaining access to her husband's finances in order to defray the cost of defending herself against having attempted to murder him by hitting him around the head with a mallet. It was not to be the only unusual feature of the cost of defence in this particular case.

As the law required, Alma was taken before the magistrates at eleven o'clock that morning. Her solicitor appeared on her behalf and she was remanded in custody until Tuesday, 2 April.

Around one o'clock Dr O'Donnell arrived at the police station and asked if he could see Alma. Doctors are not infrequently called to police stations when a prisoner is taken ill, but it is most unusual for a doctor to arrive of his own volition and even more unusual for someone charged with the serious crime of attempted murder to be allowed visitors other than close relatives. Alma was taken into a room for the interview. She was unable to walk without the support of a police matron and Inspector Carter. According to Dr O'Donnell she swayed about, tried to be sick and appeared dazed, and, he noticed, her eyes contracted when exposed to light. Carter and the matron remained within earshot whilst he spoke with her, although whether they heard everything that passed is not known. Alma's concern was for the future welfare of her children; she was anxious, since he was there, that the doctor should do something about it. To have taken such trouble to visit his patient was, of course, a wholly commendable action on his part, but it may indicate that the doctor's concern for her was somewhat special.

Around this time Alma wrote out two cheques, one in favour of Stoner and another for Irene, which were passed on to them. Then she was taken back to the cell; within the space of forty-eight hours, the life of Alma Rattenbury had fallen apart.

CHAPTER 9

Stoner Arrested

Without Alma, the Villa Madeira seemed to Irene like an empty shell. Detective-Inspector Carter had said very little to her on the dreadful night when it had all happened, but on the Monday afternoon he arrived, with another detective, and said that he wished to take a full statement from her. He said he would prefer her to come to the police station but he would, if necessary, take it at the house, and she said that would be more convenient.

He commenced by asking her to tell him all that she could remember of the Sunday, 24 March. She told him she had been employed as a companion/help with the Rattenburys for some four years, and that she did a great deal of the work in the house. She described the rooms which each of those who lived in the house occupied. She gave this information in answer to questions from Carter.

'Now tell me what happened on Sunday afternoon and onwards,' he asked.

'Sundays were the days when I had time off,' she said. 'Yesterday, I went out around four o'clock in the afternoon.'

'What time were you due back?'

'On my day and evening off,' she explained, 'it was left to me when I came back, but it was usually about ten o'clock. My parents live in the neighbourhood of Bournemouth and I spent the afternoon and evening with them.'

'What time, then, did you actually return yesterday?' persisted Carter.

'I got back at about 10.15. There is just one key to the house and we hide that in a place which we all know. I opened the front door with it and went straight to my bedroom.'

'Was there a light downstairs?'

'I don't remember it being on. I stayed in my bedroom for about five minutes, taking off my coat and putting it away and tidying up. I felt a bit peckish so I thought I would go to the kitchen to see if there was something I could eat. When I reached the hall, I heard some heavy breathing. I could not make out what it was, so I listened at both the drawing-room door and the door of Mr Rattenbury's bedroom.'

'Did you discover where it was coming from?' asked Carter.

'No, I couldn't, so I switched on the light in Mr Rattenbury's bedroom, but he was not in bed.'

'Did you go into the drawing-room?'

'No, I assumed he had fallen asleep in the armchair. I must have decided not to go to the kitchen, in case I awakened him, so I went back to my bedroom. Not long after, I wanted to go to the lavatory, so I came out of my bedroom again, and I saw Stoner, dressed in his pyjamas, leaning over the bannisters looking towards the hall.'

'Did you speak to him?'

'Yes, I said, "Hello, what's the matter?" He said, "Nothing, I was looking to see if the lights were out." This was a bit funny, because he was leaning over the bannisters and I could see the lights were out from where I was standing.'

'Then?'

'When I had been to the lavatory, I went to bed, but five to ten minutes later Mrs Rattenbury came into my room.'

'Can you put a time on that?' asked Inspector Carter.

'I would say around a quarter to eleven to eleven o'clock, but I'm really not sure of the time at all.'

'What did she want?'

'Well, she came in for a talk. She often did that.'

'What did she talk about?'

'She seemed excited because she said she had arranged to go to Bridport today, to see a friend of hers at Bridport, a Mr Jenks. He is, in fact, a business friend of Mr Rattenbury's.'

Mr Jenks was Shirley Hatton Jenks of Pilsdon Manor, Pilsdon, which is about six miles north of Bridport, an old rope-making town, the 'Port Bredy' of Thomas Hardy's novels, and it is about thirty miles west along the coast from Bournemouth. Shirley Jenks had been called to the Bar by the Middle Temple in 1905, although it seems unlikely that he had ever practised, since he was a man of considerable wealth. His home was a splendid property, a fine old English manor house, and he was the lord of the manor. How Rattenbury came to make his acquaintance is not known, but there is no doubt that Rattenbury had high hopes that some of the proposed property developments which so occupied his thoughts might interest Jenks – if, indeed, he had not already invested in any.

'She told me', continued Irene, 'that she had telephoned Mr Jenks that evening and that she would be going the next day with her husband, but she was not yet sure whether he or Stoner would be driving. She said she had had a rumpus with Stoner because he did not want her to go away, but it had blown over and she felt sure she would be able to persuade Stoner to change his mind and drive them there, despite the fact that he had said he was unwilling to do so.' Irene paused as if trying to remember what else had been said, or whether she should volunteer it. Carter must have sensed her thoughts.

'Was anything else said?' he asked.

'No,' replied Irene, as if still thinking about it, 'there may have been some more conversation, I cannot clearly recall, but nothing of any importance.'

'What happened next?'

'Mrs Rattenbury went to bed and I prepared to get to sleep, but five or ten minutes later I heard a noise of somebody hurrying downstairs, and almost immediately afterwards I heard Mrs Rattenbury call me. I rushed down in my night clothes to the drawing-room, where I saw Mr Rattenbury in his armchair as if he was asleep. He seemed to me to have a black eye, and there was blood on the floor. Mrs Rattenbury kept saying, "Oh! Poor Rats. Look at him, look at him, he's been hurt," and told me to ring for Dr O'Donnell, which I did at once.'

'How was Mrs Rattenbury dressed?' enquired Carter.

'The same as when she came into my room, in her pyjamas.'

'Had she anything on her feet?'

'No.'

'What happened next?'

'Well! Mrs Rattenbury seemed terrified. I fetched a bowl of water and a cloth from the bathroom and the kitchen and bathed Mr Rattenbury's eye. Mrs Rattenbury said we had better get Stoner.'

'Did she always call him that or "George"?' asked Carter.

'She always called him Stoner when I was there,' she replied, as if waiting for further questions. But when none were forthcoming she went on, 'We both called him, and he came down. He was wearing trousers and, I think, a shirt, but no coat, and we all three carried Mr Rattenbury into his bedroom and put him

66

on his bed. We managed to get his trousers off and almost immediately after we had done so, the doctor hadn't arrived, so Mrs Rattenbury told Stoner to get the car and fetch him. He had not left for very long when the doctor did arrive.'

'What was Mrs Rattenbury's condition', interposed Carter, 'while this was going on?'

'She was raving; she kept saying, "Poor Rats. Oh, poor Rats. What has happened? Can't somebody do something?"'

'Did she drink anything?'

'Yes, she kept going backwards and forwards for whisky and soda. She said she did not want her son John, who was still asleep upstairs, to see all the mess in the morning and asked me to try and clean it up.'

'Did you do so?'

'Yes. I tried to get the blood off the carpet and the chair. Shortly after Dr O'Donnell arrived, Stoner returned; he had missed him. The doctor, it seems, had left by the time Stoner got to his house.'

'What time did the doctor arrive?' asked the Inspector.

Irene thought for a moment and said, 'I think it was about 11.30 to 11.45. He examined Mr Rattenbury and then telephoned to Mr Rooke, who came shortly afterwards. Mr Rattenbury was taken away in an ambulance.'

Carter's younger colleague had been busily engaged writing down all that Irene had said, and, at this stage, he read it over to Irene, who agreed that it was correct. At Carter's invitation, she signed it.

The police officers then left the house to walk back to the police station, where Inspector Carter had an appointment to take a statement from Dr O'Donnell, who had said he was happy to give it there.

'What do you make of it all, Sir?' asked the young detective as they walked.

'Parts of it seem a bid odd to me,' Carter replied. 'Listening to the maid you'd think that drunken bitch knew nothing about it, and was surprised to find her old man in that state. Still, if he recovers we may get to know exactly what occurred; if he doesn't I think it'll be considered a true bill and, if he dies, she'll probably swing for it.'

When they arrived at the station the doctor was already in a room used for interviews. After apologizing for having kept him waiting, the Inspector, after his colleague had obtained some more paper for a witness statement, said, 'Well, we may as well get on and get it down, Doctor.' They drew chairs up to the table and the Inspector asked, 'What are your full names, Sir?'

'William O'Donnell.'

'Could you first of all tell me something about yourself. You know, your qualifications and experience?'

'Well,' said the doctor, 'I qualified in Dublin in 1893. The description of my qualification was changed many years ago, so that today I am a Licentiate of the Royal College of Physicians of Ireland, and a Member of the Royal College of Surgeons, Ireland. I practised in Dublin, and later, when I came over here, in Malvern, Fishguard and, since 1924, here in Bournemouth. Now, I practise and live at my address in Parkland. I have been the Rattenburys' doctor for about two and a half years – since about autumn of 1932.'

'And you were called to their house on the 24th?' asked Carter.

'Yes, I received a telephone call at 11.30. I went almost at once and I arrived there at 11.45.'

'How did you get in?' asked Carter. 'I mean, who admitted you?'

'The door was open,' replied the doctor, 'and I went straight to Mr Rattenbury's room. He was lying on his bed, and I believe his wife was with him. I'm not sure of that, and I do not think anyone else was there then. He was partially dressed and when I tried to undress him I found it difficult to cope on my own. I had come in a taxi, which was still waiting, so I called the driver into the house, and he helped me remove his coat and waistcoat; I found that his trousers had already been taken off him.'

Dr O'Donnell paused before continuing. 'There was a bloodstained towel wrapped around his head, and when I removed it I found his head was bathed in blood, which was clotted and clinging to his hair. It was quite impossible to make any useful examination. He was unconscious; his breathing was laboured. His left eye was very contused, purple and swollen, and his pulse slow and irregular. I could see I needed help and there might be need for surgery from what I could see of the wound so I telephoned for a local surgeon, Alfred Rooke, to come over and look at him.'

'What was Mrs Rattenbury's state and behaviour at the time?'

'Ghastly,' said O'Donnell. 'She was excited; she had a whisky and soda in a glass in her hand and seemed slightly intoxicated.'

'Did she offer any explanation?'

'Well, I, of course, asked her what had happened, and all she said was "Look at him; look at the blood, somebody has finished him."'

'Did you remain with your patient?' asked the Inspector.

'No. The drawing-room adjoins his bedroom, and while I was awaiting Alfred Rooke, I went into the drawing-room.'

'Who was in there, anyone?'

'Mrs Rattenbury followed me out of the bedroom and the maid and Stoner were already there. At least, as far as I can recall.'

'Was anything said?'

'The carpet looked as though someone had already tried to clean or wash it, but there were still stains visible and Mrs Rattenbury told the maid to clean it up. I asked Mrs Rattenbury what had happened during the evening. She said she and Rats, as she calls him, had had a happy evening and had arranged to go to Dorset the following day to stay with a Mr and Mrs Jenks. She said Rats was very happy about this. She said, however, that he had shown her a passage in a book to read about suicide, and pointed out the book which was on the piano in the room. She was anxious that I should read it, but I told her I did not wish to do so.'

The doctor sat thinking for a while.

'Do please go on,' said Carter.

'I asked her how she had discovered her husband in that state, and she said she had gone to bed early, but she had been aroused by a cry or a noise (I could not swear which) and she had run downstairs. She found her husband lying back in his chair, with a pool of blood on the carpet at the side of the chair and his artificial teeth, which appeared to have fallen out, on the carpet.'

'Anything else?' enquired Carter.

'No, I think not,' replied O'Donnell.

'Did Mr Rooke arrive then?'

'Yes, he got there about midnight or five minutes or so past. He agreed with me that it was impossible to make any sort of diagnosis. I told him, because I knew that Rattenbury liked his whisky, that he had probably fallen and hit his head on the piano, but we both agreed we had better get an ambulance and take him to a nursing home where we could examine him properly.'

'You got an ambulance?' asked the Inspector.

'Yes.'

'How long was it arriving after Mr Rooke had got there?'

'About half an hour. I went in the ambulance with the patient; Mr Rooke went to his home to get his instruments, and I suggested to Mrs Rattenbury and Stoner that he should follow the ambulance in the car, so as to bring me back to the house later.'

'Why could he not have come for you later?'

'Stoner said he was not sure where the nursing home was, so it was easier for him to follow the ambulance and wait for me.'

'What happened at the nursing home?'

'Mr Rooke shaved the patient's head. He had to cut a lot of the matted hair away to do so, and we found he had three distinct wounds, one on the left side, one on the median line and one further over to the right. Well, it was obvious that three wounds in those positions could not have been caused by a fall, so we decided we had to tell the police and I telephoned. When I had finished there Stoner drove me back. I got back there at about 3.30 a.m.'

The Inspector took the doctor through the rest of his account, and by the time it was finished it was well into evening. It occurred to the Inspector that he should, perhaps, have looked more closely at the book which he had seen on the small table, so he told his colleague to return to the house and bring it back. When he returned he looked more closely at it, and decided he would take it home that night and read it or, at least, try to see if it had any relevance.

He found it was a book in which a principal character was intent on suicide. Not unlike Rattenbury, he had been highly successful but was now spent and fearful of the perils of old age. On the brink of committing suicide he meets a girl who believes herself to be in love with him and wants him to marry her. He is convinced it will not be successful and, at the page at which the book lay open, he is seeking to convince her of this. It read as follows:

'What sort of a person do you think would stand you?' she asked.

'Oh – some elderly frump who couldn't get anything else. A staid motherly soul who'd treat me like a child . . .'

'You don't think marriages between young girls and – and men a good deal older than themselves are possible?'

'They're possible all right. For some reason elderly men have a peculiar attraction for young girls. That may be due, nowadays, to the quality of young men of the day; but I don't think it is. It's always been so. And – the old men like to marry young girls; and after a bit it's hell for both.'

'Why?'

'Because it's naturally annoying to a young girl to see her

70

husband mouldering while she still feels frisky. To see the bare patch on the back of his head growing bigger and shinier. To have the shock one day of coming across most of his teeth grinning at her out of a glass of water. And there are other things besides.'

'What things?'

'Well, if you want me to enter into physiological details – a woman, let's put it, always wants more than a man. And when a man's a good deal older, she wants a good deal more than him. A good deal more than he can give her. It takes all his time for a young man to keep pace with a young girl. And an old man hasn't a chance of doing it. And then – she usually goes somewhere else to make up the deficiency.'

Carter put down the book and picked up his glass of beer. Strange, he thought to himself, that Alma should at one point have said, 'My lover did it.' What was she getting at, and was the similarity between Rattenbury's situation and the character in the book something which required further investigation? He sat thinking; it puzzled him.

Elsewhere Alma was also thinking. She was now in the Women's Prison at Holloway in North London, and she was constantly thinking of her home and her children, and wondering what was happening there.

Irene and Stoner were at the Villa Madeira, and if all that has been revealed is true, little conversation seems to have passed between them. However, the following day, Tuesday, 26 March 1935, they drove in Mr Rattenbury's car to Wimborne, which is five to six miles from Bournemouth. It is strange that despite all that has been written about the events surrounding the Rattenburys and all the evidence adduced at the ultimate trial no one ever explained why they went there. It certainly was not to play on the golf course which it boasts, to visit the Minster, which was built in 1673, or to examine the earth works which are located there.

It was always plain that there was no love lost between them, and if Irene was willing to go joy-riding with him in their unfortunate employer's car, she could hardly have believed he had played any direct part in the plight of her beloved Alma. Otherwise, it ill accords with the statement which she later made concerning Stoner in the course of their journey.

Irene's statement was that on their return journey from Wimborne Stoner had pointed out a house where an ex-soldier or ex-policeman – she could not remember which – lived, and later the houses where his mother and grandmother lived, and he added that he could say that he was out that way – it was in the Ensbury district – at half-past eight on Sunday evening. He also said that it was from his grandfather's house that he had fetched the mallet. More to the point, she said he also made what could, on one construction, have been a damaging admission. She asked him whether there would have been fingerprints on the mallet and he replied, 'No, I wore gloves.' This was at best an equivocal statement, since it might have referred to the time when he collected the mallet or later.

Irene's mother and sister moved into the Villa Madeira to keep her company. Certainly, her mother had moved in by the following day and it has been suggested by one writer, Terry Teksten, that the purpose of the journey to Wimborne may have been to collect her mother. This, however, seems more than unlikely since her mother lived in Holdenhurst Road in Bournemouth. The same author also suggested that 'Irene was in a terrible quandary. Alma was in prison charged with wounding her husband, but so far her relationship with Stoner had remained a secret, a secret which Alma had trusted Irene to keep. If the police were to direct their attention to Stoner, all the details of Alma's adultery would become public.'

Those assumptions are not, however, necessarily acceptable. Irene had no more evidence of any direct involvement by Stoner than she had possessed from the outset. It seems evident that she must always have known he had fetched the mallet, and his statement about the fingerprints evidently related to that occasion. Moreover, her adultery was not a secret; it had been disclosed to the doctor by Alma, and it is highly improbable that Alma had not ultimately disclosed this fact to Irene, who was her close confidante. In addition, Alma had at one stage told PC Bagwell that 'her lover' did it. It is true the police officer said later that Irene was not present at the time, but on Irene's account and despite the muddle surrounding this part of the evidence at the trial it seems probable that she was present when it was said.

Wednesday was the day on which Irene had an evening off and on 27 March, which was a Wednesday, she did not return to the house until 10.30 p.m. Her mother met her at the door and told her that Stoner was very drunk. This must have surprised Irene because she had never seen Stoner in that state and he had been strongly against drink. Her mother told her he had returned earlier when a taxi driver found him wandering the street, and she told Irene she had better go and see him. He was in his bedroom, lying on the bed, and he had vomited on the floor. Irene later said that he told her he wished to tell her something and then said that Mrs Rattenbury was in jail and he had put her there, that he was going up to London the following morning to see Alma and then to give himself up. He asked Irene to be sure to wake him early and not to let him oversleep.

That night a call was received by the police from the Villa Madeira; whether it was made by Irene or her mother, and whether it was before or after Irene had returned, is not known. It may have been made by the taxi driver when he returned Stoner into the care of a woman who may have given signs of being unable to cope.

In any case, Detective-Constable George Gates was deputed to go there. He found that Stoner was indeed drunk; that he was indeed in bed; that he had indeed vomited on the floor. There was nothing Gates proposed to do about that, so he left.

According to Terry Reksten, Irene, in her assumed dilemma, and although not a Catholic, had consulted a priest, which it is further presumed led to her going to the police. The source of this information was not disclosed but it does not really fit with the facts, since if Irene had seen a priest it must have been before she returned home, and Stoner did not make the statement she attributed to him until after she had got there. Terry Reksten finally, in regard to this aspect, records that the reason for Stoner's condition was that he had 'received a letter from Alma that day, and, perhaps, for the first time understood the seriousness of her situation'. She goes on to quote the contents of the letter. It bore the postmark of 27 March, and demonstrates the deterioration of postal services over the ensuing years, since it is evident that in 1935 a letter posted during the morning in London had been delivered in Bournemouth the same day. Stoner may well have been concerned, intent on helping the woman whom he believed he loved and with whom he was no doubt besotted. This could have occasioned him great anxiety and stress and perhaps guilt at his failure to protect her.

This apart, Alma had written to him twice before, as the letter revealed. It was headed 'No. 880: Name A. V. Rattenbury. Holloway Prison, 27.3.1935'. It was in her own handwriting, but it was not like her usual hand, and it was addressed to 'Mr George Stoner, Villa Madeira, 5 Manor Road, Bournemouth'. It read:

I am trying to have the lawyer's letter I received today sent to you, darling, so that you can make arrangements to come up with him, or make arrangements yourself with the Governor. But I must see you, darling. Please write to me. This is the third letter I have written. Hope you receive this. I hardly know how to write now. Let me know how Rats is getting along. No more now. God bless you. My love be with you always. Lozanne.

It then continued:

Have you talked with Dr O'Donnell about how Rats is? Goodness, there is so much I want to know. Please ask Irene to give you a few bobbing pins for my hair. I think they would be allowed.

On Thursday, 28 March, Stoner got up, as he had intended, at 6.30 a.m., so that when Irene, as she had promised, went to wake him she found he was already dressed. He left the house but returned about ten minutes later and then left again. That he went to London there is no doubt, but whether he succeeded in seeing Alma has never been fully established. Probably he did.

It is likely, although there is no evidence to support it, that whilst Stoner was in London Irene, having given the matter thought, and having possibly consulted a priest, decided to see Inspector Carter. She may then have told him for the first time that Stoner on the Monday had told her, 'I suppose you know who did it,' and that on Tuesday when they visited Wimborne he had remarked that Mrs R. was in jail and he had put her there. She may well have gone on to tell him that Stoner pointed out where he had got the mallet and that he had said there would be no fingerprints on it as he wore gloves. Carter may well have attached more importance to this latter statement than was justified. If these suppositions are right, and Irene had decided to do all she could to implicate Stoner, there may also have been some discussion between her and Carter during that day about the real relationship between Alma and Stoner.

It was, therefore, of little moment whether Stoner did or did not see Alma in prison that day, because whilst Stoner was in London Rattenbury had died, and when the train from London arrived at Bournemouth station at 6.30 that evening, Detective-Inspector Carter was waiting for Stoner on the platform. He went up to Stoner as he left the train and said, 'You know me to be a police officer?'

'Yes,' replied Stoner, whereupon Carter cautioned him.

'I must tell you that Francis Rattenbury died this morning,' said Carter. 'This officer with me is Superintendent Deacon and I am arresting you and taking you to Bournemouth Police Station.'

At the police station Stoner was charged 'with the murder of Francis Mawson Rattenbury, at Bournemouth on Sunday, 24 March 1935', although it could not have become murder until Rattenbury died on 28 March.

Stoner, looking shaken, replied, 'I understand.'

During the usual formalities at the police station Carter searched him, and took possession of the large man's watch which he carried. As Carter handled it Stoner said, 'Be careful of that watch. It was given me by Mrs Rattenbury and is worth £20.' The letter which Alma had written to him and which had been delivered the previous day, on the same day as she wrote it, was found in his pocket, as were two photographs of Alma.

'A Sensational East Cliff Tragedy Development' was how the *Bournemouth Daily Echo* described the appearance before the magistrates of Stoner, on the following day, 29 March.

Stoner could hardly have foreseen when he and Alma selected the smart grey striped suit with blue tie and shirt with blue striped soft collar at Harrods that he would be wearing them to face the magistrates on a charge of murder. He recognized one or two people in the court and smiled at them, but he looked pale when the charge was read to him. Stoner said nothing in reply, but someone at the back of the court, in an audible whisper, said, 'It's a lie.' He was remanded to the following Tuesday, the day to which Alma had previously been remanded. Shortly afterwards he was brought back into court and he made an application for legal aid, which was granted to him.

That application, simple in itself, probably gave a greater insight into the true relationship between Alma and Stoner than many factors which might have seemed of more importance. In 1935 legal aid was not administered in the way it has been for the last quarter-century. At that time it was available, and not extensively, under the Poor Prisoners' Defence Act which, when it was introduced in 1930, was regarded as a great step forward. Hitherto, and indeed for many years after, legal representation was provided as a social duty and an act of charity by the legal profession. In the great advance of 1930, even by the very low standards of the time, the fees paid by the state were derisory. The maximum payable even in a murder case, which was a capital offence, was 6 guineas to a solicitor, 11 guineas to junior counsel and 15 guineas to leading counsel. In magistrates' court hearings, solicitors were paid at the rate of 3 guineas for the first day, and an extra half-guinea for every subsequent day. There was no fear of anyone waxing rich on remuneration of that order, and it followed that such work was undertaken only by the very young or the less successful, and rarely by the well-established practitioners.

By the law of England a person is precluded from benefiting from the estate of a person he or she has unlawfully killed. Therefore, were Alma to be convicted of murdering her husband she could not benefit from his estate. But she had not yet been tried, far less convicted, so she did not turn to legal aid. Her solicitors were free, therefore, to choose, and pay, the best available counsel, and they chose, in the event, wisely and well.

Stoner, however, on legal aid, had a very limited and poor choice by comparison, and in many respects this became evident at the trial.

What then did this reveal about their relationship? If Alma Rattenbury was so deeply in love with Stoner, as some would have had others believe, would she not in securing the best-paid representation for herself have insisted that the same level of legal ability be made available for her lover? Indeed, some might consider that the object of such great devotion would have been her first care, even before herself. Yet Alma did nothing, and from first to last Stoner was represented only by a junior counsel who was willing to act under the Poor Prisoners' Defence Act. It may be that it was her wish to provide funds for his defence, but that she was advised that it would be unwise to do so because it might suggest they had acted in concert or that she was not displeased that her husband was dead. This is, however, highly improbable.

The question of legal representation arose at the very outset of the proceedings. She had been advised to retract her acceptance of guilt and to put the blame on Stoner. At that point she was resolute in her determination not to do so. Since she was then accepting the responsibility, nothing was more consistent than that she should see he was adequately defended. When she later changed her mind and decided to blame Stoner, different considerations might have obtained, but by then he was already committed to the Poor Prisoners' Defence Act and its inadequate provision of resources.

Whilst Stoner was at the magistrates' court that morning, he had been put into the custody of Detective-Constable Gates, the officer who had been sent to the Villa Madeira the night before when Stoner had been drunk. As they were waiting together Stoner said to Gates, 'You know Mrs Rattenbury, don't you?'

'Yes,' replied the detective, 'I do.'

'Do you know Mrs Rattenbury had nothing to do with this affair?'

Gates, very sensibly anticipating a confession, cautioned Stoner and took a piece of paper to write down what he had said and anything more he chose to say.

'When I did the job,' Stoner continued, 'I believed he was asleep. I hit him and then came upstairs and told Mrs Rattenbury. She rushed down then. You see, I watched through the french windows and saw her kiss him good-night, then leave the room. I waited and crept in through the french window, which was unlocked. I think he must have been asleep when I hit him. Still, it ain't much use saying anything. I don't suppose they will let her out yet. You know there should be a doctor with her when they tell her I'm arrested, because she'll go out of her mind.' And, after a pause, 'My parents did not stop long, did they?' This last comment probably meant that his parents had returned home soon after the remand hearing.

Many questions must arise in evaluating the worth and reliability of that confession by Stoner: questions to which he needed to be subjected in the investigation and preparation of his defence; questions which one would have expected to have arisen at his trial, but which never surfaced.

This statement appears to have emerged in a casual and matter-of-fact way, as if Stoner had no desire to make any secret of his guilt. Yet some five days had elapsed since the attack on Rattenbury during which Stoner had been in the presence of police officers on a number of occasions and had never taken the opportunity of telling this story to them. Why? Could it be that throughout that time Rattenbury was still alive and might recover, in which case he might have disproved the truth of Stoner's confession? It followed Stoner's visit to Holloway Jail. Was it the reflection of the desire of a youth of limited education and experience, in the throes of his first love affair, trying to protect his loved one? Was it significant that it came after the first opportunity for Alma to have told him what she had told the police? And did the words 'Still, it ain't much use saying anything. I don't suppose they will let her out yet' indicate the real motivation behind his statement, as being a desire, on his part and hers, to move the blame from herself to him? Finally, why, against that background of questions, was this statement so very different from the statement he had made to Carter on the very night of the attack? If these questions were ever pursued it certainly never came to notice from first to last.

CHAPTER 10

The Road to the Old Bailey

The inquest on Francis Rattenbury was opened by the coroner on 1 April. Because charges were pending, the coroner directed the jury to limit their enquiry to the identity of the deceased and the cause of death. Dr Harold Simmons, a police surgeon, said the cause of death was laceration of the brain, which was produced by some form of violent injury to the skull, behind an imaginary line drawn across the head from one ear to the other. The inquest was then adjourned until 27 June.

Thursday, 11 April 1935 saw the opening of the preliminary or committal proceedings at Bournemouth law courts. The purpose of such proceedings was to enable the magistrates, in this instance all laymen, to decide whether there was sufficient evidence to amount to a *prima facie* case so as to justify committing the accused for trial by a judge and jury. The test which they have to apply is whether the evidence adduced by the prosecution is such that a reasonable-minded jury, if properly directed by the judge, might convict. Lay magistrates, over the years, then and today, have tended to approach such proceedings in a somewhat cavalier fashion, not because they are unwilling or anxious to avoid the need to perform their duties, but because as laymen, they lack the legal training and experience of the laws of evidence and the practice of the higher courts which is essential if a proper decision is to be reached. This is regrettable since the proceedings provide an important protection for accused persons, they save time in the higher courts, and they enable the evidence to be tested by the defence for the first time. In this particular case it was of less importance since the outcome could hardly have been in doubt.

The justices comprised an alderman, the Mayor of Bournemouth and five other laymen; the presence of the Mayor, who sits only in an honorary capacity for his year of office, was an indication of the interest which the case had generated, not least in Bournemouth. Long before the doors of the court opened at 10.00 a.m. there were so many people queueing in the hope of gaining access that a sergeant and four police officers had to be employed in regulating them. There were in addition at least twenty-five journalists from the national and local press.

G. R. Paling, a senior barrister from the office of the Director of Public Prosecutions, appeared to prosecute, but before he opened the case, Lewis Manning, Alma's solicitor, made an application for the register to be altered to show Stoner rather than Alma Rattenbury as the first defendant. He said that he made this application 'on certain advice' he had received that 'certain advantages accrued to the order in which persons were charged'. No doubt the alderman in the chair, the remaining laymen on the bench and certainly the Mayor must have been mystified and bemused by the purpose of this application. What on earth, they must have wondered, was he getting at? In fact, the order in which the defendants appear in the register in the lower court, and generally as a consequence in the higher court, affects the order in which the prosecution witnesses are cross-examined by the defence advocates, and the order in which they address the jury. In this case, and given that Manning did not disclose the nature of the advice he had received, the application shows an even more significant purpose. If Stoner's name appeared first on the indictment, he would be the first to be called into the witness box and Alma's legal representatives could see whether he was attacking Alma, by giving evidence which incriminated her, and adjust their tactics accordingly.

The basis of his application was that, although Mrs Rattenbury had been first charged with attempted murder, since the death had occurred that charge would no longer proceed, and in regard to the actual charge of murder before the Court, Stoner had been charged before Mrs Rattenbury. Marshall Harvey, who appeared as solicitor for Stoner, opposed the application, and the chairman, with perhaps even greater honesty than he intended, said the Bench could see no reason for changing the order of appearance.

Paling then outlined the evidence, explaining to the Court at length the circumstances which brought the accused before them. He concluded, 'Part of the evidence, in the submission of the prosecution, would clearly show that the relationship between the accused was not confined to that usually expected between a servant and the wife of his master. . . .' This, as an exercise in understatement, was, of course, masterly, and was the first of a series of platitudinous observations which this case was to produce.

He went on to present a proposition which was to recur throughout the trial and which revealed the lack of direction and air of uncertainty which permeated the case for the Crown throughout. He said, '. . . the Bench may think the statement which she [Mrs Rattenbury] made as to having struck the blows was not perhaps strictly accurate, but that the statement made by Stoner that he struck the blows may possibly be a little more accurate account.' Since Stoner had not made his statement when Alma was first arrested and charged and since Alma's statement must then have been regarded as accurate, it is difficult to see why Alma's statement was necessarily less accurate because Stoner's statement later differed from it. The prosecution had not the slightest idea which of them was telling the truth in this connection.

There was little or no cross-examination of the witnesses until Marshall Harvey, appearing for Stoner, put a series of questions to Dr O'Donnell. 'While you have been her medical adviser, for what purpose have you treated her?' he asked.

O'Donnell turned to the Bench. 'Am I bound to reply to that question?' he asked.

'It is a matter for your own judgment,' Alderman C.H.Cartwright, the chairman, inaccurately replied.

The Clerk thought it wise to intervene and point out that a doctor is not entitled to any privileges in court.

Dr O'Donnell, undeterred, said, 'What illnesses I have attended Mrs Rattenbury for is irrelevant.'

'That', said the Clerk, 'is not the question.'

Marshall Harvey tried again: 'For what have you been treating her?'

'I refuse to answer.'

'Well,' said the advocate, 'I will leave it for another court.' But Marshall Harvey was not finished. 'Why did you not summon the police as soon as you saw the injuries?' he asked.

'I thought the first thing to do was to get Mr Rattenbury into a safe place – a nursing home – to see the extent of his injuries,' was the answer.

'You had time enough to summon the police, as well as getting the patient away?'

O'Donnell tried to hedge. 'The police never entered my mind,' he said.

The Clerk was getting rather disturbed by the doctor. 'Answer the question,' he said.

'Had you time?' repeated Harvey.

'Yes,' was the reply.

'Did you see any evidence, apart from his own statement, that Stoner was a taker of cocaine?'

'No.'

'Is Mrs Rattenbury, from your own knowledge, a drug addict?'

'No,' said O'Donnell, 'emphatically no.'

'You have treated her for years?'

'Yes.'

'If anyone knew, you would?'

'Yes.'

Unlike stipendiary magistrates, who are qualified barristers and solicitors, permanently employed to sit in magistrates' courts, lay justices rarely sit day by day to conclude their cases. Unpaid and untutored in the law, with occupational tasks to perform, homes to run, shops to keep or jobs to hold down, it is scarcely possible for them to be available to sit in court for long periods of time. As a result there were several adjournments of the proceedings at intervals of a week each time. There was a hearing on 16 April, at which Alma, with the help of the local police, had the opportunity of seeing Irene and Irene's parents.

At the end of each hearing, Alma and Stoner each went their different ways, he to Dorchester Prison, she to Holloway. Only those who have visited a prison know that depressing and terrifying feeling when the great heavy entrance doors swing shut with a resounding thud and the bolts are shot home. As a remand prisoner, Alma would not suffer all the restrictions imposed on the guilty. She was, by law, presumed innocent until convicted, but this is not all that evident in HM Prisons. With her lifestyle and background, the most distressing aspects would be the sense of isolation from her normal surroundings; the claustrophobic atmosphere of living in a cell; the dreadful unhygienic conditions which have always prevailed, and continue to do so; the inability to take a bath, except with difficulty, once a week; and, often, above all, the utter loss of dignity which comes from the inability to present a clean and tidy appearance.

On the morning of 18 April, Alma sat in her cell writing to Irene:

No. 880. Name A. Rattenbury. Holloway Prison. Darling. Was glad to see you looking so nice, also your M. and F. I wrote you dozens of letters in my mind last night, and have nothing but an empty box on top this morning. Will you hand to Mrs Grieg [wardress at Bournemouth Police Station] to give me before I go to Court a pair of tweezers, Yvette's rouge, things to do my nails with, and liquid polish, light colour. I think the perfume in small bottles would last longer, also that grey or fawn pair of slippers (same colour you were wearing), in case the brown shoes are not O.K. and I can in that case change over. The brown shoes with laces would be best. You might tell Mrs Grieg how much I appreciate her kindness, which has been most considerate. Oh, darling, I hardly know how to write. My mind is frozen. When Manning advised me to write about nothing but clothes it almost made one smile. I can hardly concentrate on even them. I think my mackintosh would help. Also that red woollen dress the skirt needs a hook on or something, and if I haven't a red belt, you might get a wide one. Oh, Lord and tomorrow Good Friday and I dare not think of the children. I even pretend I haven't any here. If one thought for five minutes they'd [sic] go mad. I saw nothing in the papers yesterday except what was cut out; I seem to see nothing but the missing parts. Darling, will one ever be happy again? Friday will be like Sunday here. Of all days in the week Sunday is the worst. I have to control my mind like the devil to not think of little John. Yes, take him out on Sundays darling. C. was awfully pleased to hear from you. I cannot understand my M. not doing anything, can you? Messages of love are not much use to me now, when I want her help with Long & [sic]. However, if I feel awfully sad, being separated in such a ghastly way from everything one loves, S.'s feeling must take some weighing up, but he'll be the same and not allow himself to think.

Then came the part of the letter on which the prosecution were to rely in, as will be seen, a somewhat unfair manner. She continued:

Should think his remorse at what he's brought down on my head, the children's & [sic] – smashed lives – would drive him a raging lunatic – a frightful responsibility to hold in one person's hands. God deliver me from such a hellish responsibility. I couldn't have courage to bear *that pain*; my own is more than enough in a hundred lifetimes as it is. Two times have found my feelings very hard and bitter – Oh, my God, appallingly so – but have managed to drown these feelings and get one's heart soft again. Darling, God Bless you, bless us all and get us out of this nightmare. My love to your M. and F. My love be with you always. Lozanne.

On the first day of May 1935 the preliminary hearing was concluded in no more than half a minute, and Alma and Stoner were committed for trial by judge and jury at the Central Criminal Court. As he left the dock, Stoner looked back and smiled at somebody in the public seats, before he was transported to Dorchester Jail, where he remained until he was transferred to Brixton Prison on 14 May.

Alma, unrestricted, as has been seen, by the limited resources which legal aid would have provided, had, with the help of her solicitors, collected together a strong and skilled team of barristers to defend her. Her solicitor, Lewis Manning, had briefed T.J. O'Connor KC to lead, and there were to be two juniors, the Hon. Ewen Montagu and a younger man, who has only come down through history as Mr Midford.

Terence James O'Connor was born at Bridgnorth in Shropshire in 1891, so at the time of the trial he was forty-four. The First World War had broken out before he could embark on his professional career. He enlisted and saw service with the Highland Light Infantry and the West African Frontier Force. At the conclusion of hostilities he continued his studies and was called to the Bar in 1919, entering the chambers of Cotes-Preedy, who later became a County Court judge. A man of great charm, wit and ambition, O'Connor dedicated himself to every task in hand, which is an essential for the success of any lawyer. His energy and intense application soon began to bear fruit, and as Cotes-Preedy was later to write, 'Though Terence O'Connor would have been the last to claim to be a strikingly erudite lawyer, by his industry he paved the way to a presentation of his case, which conveyed all that was necessary for a tribunal to consider.' He performed no less a task for Alma Rattenbury, who had every reason, if her case was to be skilfully put, to appreciate the wisdom of her solicitor in his choice of advocate.

In 1924, O'Connor became the Member of Parliament for Luton, and – polite and forceful – soon made his name in Parliament as a man of independent mind. He was defeated at the 1929 Election but was at once selected for the Central Nottingham constituency as the Conservative candidate, and was returned at a bye-election with a very substantial majority. He held that seat when he was instructed to represent Alma's interest.

He was a popular man, devoted to horses (he kept some at his country home in Oxfordshire), kind, thoughtful about others and regarded by all who knew him as a good and loyal friend. Indeed, he reaped the rewards which those qualities deserved. After Alma's trial he was appointed Solicitor-General, in 1936, and in the same year became a bencher of the Inner Temple and the Deputy Chairman of Oxfordshire County Sessions.

His style of advocacy was greatly assisted by a mellifluous voice, but his love of and enthusiasm for hunting became restricted when he suffered a fall in the field, which resulted in a strained heart and an anxious time for his wife, to whom he was happily married, and his two daughters. That fall was in due course to have tragic results because he died in 1940, shortly after the start of the Second World War, at the very early age of forty-nine. As one reviews his conduct of Alma's case there is little to fault his advocacy at the trial.

He was ably assisted by Ewen Montagu, the second son of Lord Swaythling. Ewen Edward Samuel Montagu was born on 29 March 1901; when instructed to assist in presenting Alma's case as junior counsel he was thirty-four years of age. Although his leader's scholastic qualifications are not recorded, Ewen Montagu had no lack of schooling. From Westminster School, he went to Harvard University and from there to Trinity College, Cambridge. He was called to the Bar in 1924. Meanwhile, he had served in the Royal Naval Volunteer Reserve and had a most distinguished naval career: whilst serving with Naval Intelligence he had played a leading part in a major deception of German Intelligence when the body of a serviceman was, as a result of the machinations of British Intelligence, washed ashore, in order to mislead the enemy into believing that the information found on the body was vital and secret. Later, Ewen Montagu wrote the story in book form under the title *The Man Who Never Was*.

Ewen Montagu, like his leader Terence O'Connor, was a man of infinite charm, with an excellent brain and a fine, commanding presence. For his naval service he received the OBE and for his many other services the CBE. In due course, he presided over Middlesex Sessions as its chairman, where he was generally regarded as a difficult judge before whom to appear, since his great charm and kindness, which brought him so many friends, seemed sometimes to disappear when he sat on the bench, just as the same metamorphosis can occur when others get behind the wheel of a car or on to the saddle in the hunting field. He was the Judge Advocate of the Fleet from 1945 to 1973.

Stoner's solicitor, crippled by the poor remuneration available under the Poor Prisoners' Defence Act, had a much less extensive field of talent at his disposal. The English legal system is conducted on what is known as the adversarial system, under which each side puts its best case through the endeavours of its chosen advocate, and the judge, with or without the help of a jury, having secured a balanced picture, provides the decision. Such a system, to be wholly effective, requires that the advocates on either side should be fairly balanced, a situation which is difficult to achieve, if both sides and all parties cannot have recourse to the same pool of talent. Whilst, therefore, Alma could command a King's Counsel and two juniors, the unfortunate Stoner had to be content with a junior, and the task was undertaken by J. D. Casswell.

Joshua David Casswell had been at the Bar for twenty-five years and had not then taken silk, and thus become a King's Counsel. He was by no means without ability and, apart from Ewen Montagu, had better academic qualifications than anyone else appearing in the case, including the judge. He had been educated at King's College School, before going up to Pembroke College, Oxford where he was a Classical Scholar, took Honours in Mods (Classics) in 1907, and an Honours degree in Jurisprudence in 1909. The following year he was called to the Bar. He saw service in the First World War, attaining the rank of major and being mentioned in dispatches. He was tall, with a squarish, rather rugged face; he gave the impression of being a shy man and was certainly a modest one. Unfortunately, as an advocate, it might be said of him, if somewhat uncharitably, as Churchill once said of Attlee, that this was understandable because he had so much to be modest about.

The field of endeavour is littered with men who have failed to fulfil their early promise. Some blossom late, others flower in their early years and progressively fade, whilst a few commence with brilliance and retain it throughout their careers. In the law, however, academic brilliance has never been a guarantee of professional success, although it is a considerable advantage if combined with personality, charisma or a number of other indefinable characteristics. Casswell, although a well-liked man of great integrity, kindness and academic ability, never came within striking distance of the great advocates and barely, if at all, knocked on the door of the middle grade. His innate modesty

1 *Alma as a pianist in Canada*

2 *Alma as a nurse of the Scottish Women's Hospital*

3 Alma signed this publicity photograph 'Lozanne', the name under which she wrote her songs

4 *Francis and Alma Rattenbury in the early days*

5 *A day at the seaside*

6 *George Stoner*   7 *Irene Riggs*

8 *Villa Madeira, Bournemouth*

9 The chair in which Francis Rattenbury was murdered

10 The rear façade of Villa Madeira

11 ABOVE LEFT *J. D. Casswell, Stoner's counsel*

12 ABOVE RIGHT *T. J. O'Connor*, KC, *Alma's counsel*

13 LEFT *R. P. Croom-Johnson*, KC, *prosecution counsel*

14 RIGHT *Mr Justice Humphreys*

15 BELOW *Police forcing the crowd away from the Old Bailey at the end of the trial, 31 May 1935*

16 *A doctor escorting Alma from the Old Bailey*

17 *Three Arches Bend, where Alma committed suicide*

and the nature of his career were, perhaps, exemplified in the autobiography which he wrote, under the title *A Lance for Liberty*, since chapter after chapter bore the headings, 'My First Client to be Hanged', 'My Second Client to be Hanged', and so on, over a considerable number of unwillingly deceased clients.

Following the trial of Alma Rattenbury and Stoner, he became Recorder of Salisbury and then of Southampton, and in 1959 was appointed an Official Referee of the Supreme Court, an appointment which involved trying long and generally highly boring building disputes.

In representing Stoner, he was not assisted by the nature of the instructions of his client, which placed him in an invidious position, as will emerge. But although he had represented Oxford, on three occasions, in the long jump, he conducted the proceedings with a number of very short jumps, and the lance which, on this occasion, he carried for Liberty, appeared to have been rather blunted. It is debatable whether a more assertive and determined advocate would not have coped coped with the dilemma he was to face.

CHAPTER 11

The Trial Opens

The trial at the Central Criminal Court, popularly known as the Old Bailey and situated in the street of that name – was fixed to commence on Monday, 27 May. The accused had been committed for trial only on 1 May so that just short of four weeks had elapsed.

Much is heard about the merits of speedy justice, and Edmund Burke had many years before reminded his listeners that 'justice delayed is justice denied'. There are, however, as in so many matters, two sides to that coin and, with all respect to Edmund Burke, justice hurried can be justice frustrated. The presentation of a case for trial, not least when it carries capital punishment, needs great thought and no less preparation, and the course of the trial of Alma Rattenbury and George Stoner threw up sufficient inadequacies and instances of poor preparation and less thought that even after the passage of fifty years it must give concern to those who respect justice that the trial followed so quickly after committal.

For the prosecution, the Director of Public Prosecutions briefed R.P.Croom-Johnson KC, and Anthony Hawke as his junior.

Reginald Croom-Johnson was born in 1879, and after attending Bristol Cathedral School he took an LL B at London University. He commenced his legal career as a solicitor's clerk, and qualified as a solicitor in 1901. After a few years he decided to change to the Bar and was called by the Inner Temple in 1907. He entered the Chambers of Hemmerde KC and practised on the Western Circuit. In the First World War he joined the King's Own Yorkshire Light Infantry as a lieutenant and went later to Mesopotamia in the Judge Advocate's Department. He developed a busy practice which largely concentrated on tax and finance, and entered and Parliament in 1929 as the Conservative Member for Bridgwater in Somerset. Three years after the trial of Alma Rattenbury and Stoner he was elevated to the High Court bench, but in 1953 resigned on account of ill health, and was granted by the Queen an annuity of £3,500 a year. He died in 1957.

He did not secure an entry in the *Dictionary of National Biography*, but his obituary in *The Times* may have conveyed rather more between the lines than on them. As to his performance in Parliament it read, 'His speeches were competent but not enlivening. With better luck he might have attained the rank of a Law Officer, but during his nine years in the House when the Law Officers were changed, there was just someone else whose claims were considered higher than his own.' It continued, 'In court he was dignified, and a slight pomposity of manner which followed him to the Bench, if it sometimes amused, never affected his relations with the Bar, whom he treated with courtesy and consideration.'

Those who remember him on the bench might question whether his pomposity was slight. He was not a popular figure, and if he did not create the condition known in the legal profession as 'judgitis', he did nothing to eliminate it.

By comparison, his junior Tony Hawke was a much-loved figure with a great width of experience of criminal trials which his leader lacked. Edward Anthony Hawke was a Cornishman, of which he was extremely proud. The son of Mr Justice Hawke, he was forty years of age at the time of the trial, having been called to the Bar in 1920. Educated at Charterhouse, and Magdalen College, Oxford, he was Treasury Counsel at the Old Bailey from 1932 to 1950, passing through all the ranks until appointed Senior Prosecuting Counsel, then he was Common Sergeant and finally Recorder of the City of London. All those who were privileged to know Tony Hawke carry with them only the warmest recollections, and he was a fair, highly skilled but quiet and determined prosecutor, no less admired and effective when he became a judge.

At eleven o'clock at night on 27 May 1935 a queue formed outside the doors to the public gallery at the Old Bailey. At 1 a.m. some unemployed men began offering their places in the queue for sale at a price of £2. The vast majority of those hoping to gain admission were women and they, as a result, predominated amongst those who were successful in gaining admittance.

The Old Bailey had been the site of Newgate Prison, where fever was contained as well as prisoners. When it became a court of justice it was the scene of General Gaol Delivery, and the hearing of cases known as Oyer and Terminer, by specially appointed commissioners, until 1907, when King Edward VII opened the new Central Criminal Court, built at a cost of just under £400,000.

In those days, before the need for maximum security against terrorist attack made it necessary to close the main entrance, there was something majestic about the approach to criminal justice in the building. Parts of the frontage included stone from the old building and the rest was faced with Portland stone. One ascended a fine staircase, impressive and solid, and at the top of the stairs one looked up at colourful paintings on the domed ceiling, depicting Art, Truth, Wisdom and Labour (but not the hard variety), which added an air of theatricality to the setting. The floor and corridors were made of Sicilian marble. But none of these features were uppermost in the minds of Alma and Stoner when they arrived there. Court Number One was to be the scene; a large court, dominated, as were all the courts at the Central Criminal Court, by the vast dock in the centre, which blocked the view of those at the back, and much of that of those located on either side of it.

In the days between the committal for trial and the opening of the case at the Old Bailey, the solicitors for both Alma and Stoner had been preparing the case for each of their clients. They both faced something of a dilemma. Alma Rattenbury adhered to the story she had told the police; Stoner was insistent that nothing should be said or done at the trial to place the blame on Alma. The books which have been written touching this case, *Rattenbury* by Terry Reksten, the Introduction to *Notable British Trials* by F. Tennyson Jesse, herself a somewhat tragic and unbalanced lady who three times attempted suicide, and *Tragedy in Three Voices* by Sir Michael Havers QC, the present Lord Chancellor, Peter Shankland and Anthony Barrett, present and accept a picture of Alma much in love with Stoner, protecting him from his own wickedness, until her concern for her children persuaded her to tell the truth and place the blame on him. Of necessity, that view must carry with it the assertion that Stoner was unquestionably the guilty party. The authors of the last-mentioned book relied heavily on information given to them by Mrs Kingham (Compton Pakenham's sister and Christopher's aunt), who visited her on several occasions while she was awaiting trial. Moreover, Alma's solicitor is on record as being convinced of her innocence, always a happy state for a defending solicitor.

They may, of course, all be correct in their beliefs. Those with longer experience of observing behaviour at closer quarters than any of the above mentioned could be forgiven for at least questioning whether the truth may have been otherwise. According to the account attributed to Mrs Kingham, as a result of a request from the Governor of Holloway Prison, one Dr Morton (though what the Governor was doing interfering in this fashion does not appear) and at the earnest request of Alma's solicitor, she had taken Alma's son Christopher to see Alma in prison a few days before the trial began, and this was the catalyst which wrought the change in Alma and caused her to decide to tell the whole truth. It is a touching version; the lovelorn Alma torn between her great and protective love for Stoner and her undoubted love for her children, finally giving way to her stronger maternal instincts.

There is, however, another scenario, which, in the light of one's experience of human behaviour, might equally be true.

Was Alma so much in love with Stoner that she was prepared to go to the gallows for him, although unwilling to provide him with the means of defending himself, as she was able to do for herself, otherwise than under the Poor Prisoners' Defence Act?

Despite her ability to exude warmth and kindness, Alma was also a highly intelligent and calculating woman who was willing to extract money from her husband by lying stories in order to engage in sexual encounters with her chauffeur/handyman behind her husband's back and in his home. As a highly experienced woman of the world, was her interest in this callow youth, young enough to be her son, one of unselfish love or merely physical and carnal? Could it be that even she, against that background, could not at first face sending Stoner to the gallows for an act that she had committed? And might it not be that, in the final analysis, the reasons for her change of heart, after seeing Christopher in prison, was the realization that she had a higher and more attractive duty not to leave her children orphans, whilst Stoner, if made the scapegoat, had no one to support but himself?

Ultimately, as will emerge, there were other matters which lend additional credence to this possibility. The authors of

Tragedy in Three Voices suggest that Alma's change of heart first emerged when she wrote to Irene immediately after the visit of her eldest son, which they put, following Mrs Kingham, a few days before the trial. This, however, must be inaccurate, since the trial commenced on 27 May and the letter was sent on 18 April.

The story which Stoner required his solicitor to instruct counsel to present was that he struck Francis Rattenbury whilst under the influence of cocaine, a substance which he described in such fashion as rendered it clear that he had never seen the drug, far less taken it. In his autobiography his counsel wrote:

> On the Saturday morning before the trial I had been to see Stoner, together with Mr Bickford, my solicitor's managing clerk, in Brixton gaol. I knew from my written instructions that Stoner was going to insist on a defence which in no way threw the responsibility upon his co-accused; he was not really interested in establishing his innocence, but in ensuring that Mrs Rattenbury was not convicted. The only defence which we were instructed to put before the jury was that he had committed the murder when under the influence of cocaine, but *no one, I think, really believed this.* . . .
>
> Yet the discussion of his drug-taking habits took up very little part of our interview, indeed, Stoner said very little. He sat in the conference room in the gaol silent and completely unco-operative.

Caswell went on to write that he did not press him about his guilt because, had Stoner actually admitted to him that he was guilty, he would have been embarrassed in presenting his case and been unable to challenge the statement attributed to Stoner by the police that he struck Rattenbury.

Does Casswell's account portray a cold, determined, premeditating murderer? Or is it rather what might be expected of a truly lovelorn swain, young, uneducated and inexperienced, believing himself madly in love, riding like the knights of old to the defence of the one person whose life was everything to him? A youth who had sought to claim responsibility not when first seen by the police but after he had received a letter from Alma in prison and gone to Holloway to see her.

Casswell's account raises interesting questions about the duties of lawyers defending in such circumstances. Unquestionably the Bar Council, which governs barristers, and the Law Society, which governs solicitors, would say that each of them might only put before the Court that which they were instructed by their clients to present. Casswell, however, clearly realized that there was no substance at all in the defence of acting under the effects of cocaine. Is it not likely that a stronger man than Casswell, and even the solicitor, had he been present, would not have found by skilful questioning something closer to the truth? Casswell was rightly concerned that 'by the rules of my profession I should not have been allowed to call any evidence to prove that he was innocent' (had he admitted guilt) and should have been restricted merely to trying to show that the evidence against him was insufficient.

When, however, the evidence which he was to call came to be examined it was so weak that it did not amount in value to a string of beans, and he could hardly have been worse off had he subjected his client to the most vigorous catechism.

Moreover, if Stoner's was the hand which struck the blow, why did Stoner sit mute and require nothing to be said adverse to Alma but fight shy of saying to Casswell, 'Yes, it was I who did it,' if, in fact, he did?

Thus, by the time the judge ascended the bench in Court Number One Alma was prepared to place the blame on Stoner, whilst Stoner was unwilling to admit that he had done the act and equally unwilling to contend that Alma had done it. Since, apart from Alma and Stoner, no one else could have done it, the trial gave promise of a great deal of muddle.

The judge was Mr Justice Humphreys, one of the great figures of the world of criminal practice, a man of Victorian outlook, capable of prejudiced views on occasion, which, to his credit, when on the bench he steadfastly and probably successfully overcame.

Richard Somers Travers Christmas Humphreys was born in 1867 in London. His father was a solicitor specializing in criminal cases. Educated at Shrewsbury School and Trinity Hall, Cambridge, Travers Humphreys, as he was always known, was called to the Bar by the Inner Temple in 1889. The *Dictionary of National Biography* records of him: 'The story of Humphreys' life is the story of the criminal law of his time.' He appeared in connection with the trial of Oscar Wilde, the Crippen murder case, the trials of Seddon, Smith and Casement, Bottomley and Bywaters and Thompson. The *Dictionary* also records that it was said of him as a prosecutor, 'He's so damned fair that he leaves nothing for the defence to say.' Like Tony Hawke, he rose through the ranks of Treasury Counsel to become Senior Prosecuting

Counsel at the Central Criminal Court in 1916. He was reputed to be witty, clubbable (he was a member of the Garrick) and popular amongst his colleagues, but viewed from a distance when in court he seemed a fierce and somewhat intimidating figure, especially when he reached the High Court bench in 1928. His appointment was something of a rare break with tradition since it was not the custom then, and is hardly the custom now, to appoint barristers to the High Court whose experience has been limited to the Criminal Bar.

He entered the court carrying the usual posy of flowers, a relic of the earlier days of stench and fever at the Bailey, in one hand and the black cap, it was recorded, in the other. This latter detail, however, seems somewhat premature and is probably untrue.

Every available seat was occupied in the court, the public gallery overflowing with women. The aldermen of the City of London, who always accompany the High Court judge to the bench, decided to stay to hear the opening of the proceedings and took their seats beside the judge. The scene was set. Alma and Stoner were brought into the dock, and a grey-haired wardress with horn-rimmed spectacles seated herself between them. They looked around the court, but avoided looking at each other. Alma, anxious as ever about her appearance, wore a blue suit with blue and white spotted facings, elbow-length blue gloves, and a daisy pinned to her dress. No lady in 1935 ever appeared in public without her gloves. On her head was a wide-brimmed black straw hat, the band of which had a coloured zig-zag pattern, and a heavy fox fur was draped in such fashion that with her wide hat only her lips and the tip of her nose were visible.

The usher came to his feet and intoned, 'If anyone can inform my Lords, the King's Justices, or the King's Attorney-General, ere this Inquest be taken between our Sovereign Lord the King and the prisoners at the bar, of any treasons, murders, felonies, or misdemeanours, done or committed by the prisoners at the bar, let them come forth and they shall be heard; for the prisoners now stand at the bar on their deliverance. And all persons who are bound by recognizance to prosecute or give evidence against the prisoners at the bar, let them come forth, prosecute, and give evidence, or they shall forfeit their recognizance. God save the King.'

The Clerk of the Court came slowly to his feet. 'Alma Victoria Rattenbury and George Percy Stoner, you are charged with the murder of Francis Mawson Rattenbury on 28 March last. Alma

Victoria Rattenbury, are you guilty or not guilty?'

'I plead not guilty,' said Alma softly.

'George Percy Stoner, are you guilty or not guilty?'

'Not guilty.'

The Clerk then called the jurors to the box, from a list which he held, and after the first had been sworn, Casswell rose to his feet to tell the judge that he wished to apply for the defendants to be tried separately.

'It would have been better', said Humphreys, 'if you had made it before any of the jurors were sworn. I will hear your application now. Which accused do you appear for?'

'I appear for the accused Stoner,' replied Casswell. 'It is an application which perhaps had better be made in the absence of the jury.'

'If you think so,' said the judge, and the jury before they had begun were required to retire.

The basis of the application was the letter which Alma had written to Irene and which speculated about Stoner's remorse and responsibility. Any evidence upon which a prosecutor intends to rely, which was not produced at the magistrates' court, must be served before the trial as additional evidence. A notice containing Irene's account of the receipt of the letter, with a copy of it attached, had been served on Stoner's solicitors. Casswell pointed out that a letter thus written by one accused cannot be evidence against the other, but if produced on a joint trial might prejudice the jury against his client.

The application was doomed to failure from the start, despite the fact that O'Connor gave it half-hearted support and did not oppose it. The judge, as must have been foreseen, rejected the application on the time-honoured formula that he would tell the jury not to treat any such document as evidence against Alma's co-accused. No one ever believes that the average juror is capable of expunging from his mind what he has heard or read, but the time-honoured charade is a daily occurrence in joint trials and always has been.

The jurors were brought back into court looking even more mystified than when they first took their places. They were duly sworn, whereupon the Clerk looked at them and said, 'Members of the jury, the prisoners at the bar, Alma Victoria Rattenbury and George Percy Stoner, are charged with the murder of Francis Mawson Rattenbury [which they had heard him say not long before] on 28 March last. To this indictment they have separately pleaded not guilty and it is your charge to say, having heard the evidence, whether they or either of them be guilty or not guilty.'

If all this seemed to those observing to be a great waste of time, they were not wrong. Even these jurors, chosen at random from a list of householders, and not for their great intellect or erudition, at least knew why they had been brought there and that they could not decide until they had heard the evidence.

Croom-Johnson came to his feet to open his case to the jury. He began by relating something of Alma's background and marriage to Francis Rattenbury, going on to the visit to the Royal Palace Hotel, Kensington. 'It is the submission of the prosecution', he said, 'that the relationship between Mrs Rattenbury and Stoner had ceased to be that of the wife of the employer and the man employed and had become an adulterous association.'

He then turned to the nearest he was going to get to the provision of a motive: 'On their going back to the Villa Madeira [from London] where Mr Rattenbury, the somewhat elderly husband, was residing, the situation was likely to be one of some difficulty, and the prosecution submits that Mr Rattenbury stood in the way of their indulgence in this guilty passion.'

Precisely on what Croom-Johnson presumed to base this assertion hardly appears. On their return to Bournemouth there was not the slightest reason to believe that their sexual exploits would have been any more difficult to continue than they were before they left. They evidently moved in and out of one another's bedroom at all hours of the day and night without the slightest interference from Rattenbury or anyone else. Indeed, the better view was that Rattenbury must have known exactly what was occurring and did not in the least object. Certainly, there was no evidence to the contrary. If anything, for all that Croom-Johnson knew, life might have been much more difficult for them with Rattenbury gone than with him providing a love nest for them, with all the security it offered, at his own expense.

Croom-Johnson next proceeded to the dreadful Sunday night, and succeeded in getting the timing wrong: 'A few moments after Irene Riggs returned from her day out, she went to her bedroom, and she saw Stoner leaning over the bannisters looking down into the hall.' As already noted, that was not when she saw Stoner at all.

Turning to Alma's visit to Irene's bedroom after Irene had gone to bed and the conversation in which Alma told of the visit next day to Bridport, Croom-Johnson said, 'I suggest that

Mrs Rattenbury made these statements to Irene Riggs to prepare the notion, which was to develop later, that some unknown person had come into the house and committed an assault on Mr Rattenbury and that she knew nothing about it.'

Could this suggestion, made by prosecuting counsel to the jury, have been accurate by any stretch of the imagination? It was no notion. It was common ground that Alma had arranged the trip to Mr Jenks for the following day well before her husband was attacked. When asked by the police, on their arrival, she had at once said the french windows were locked when she left the room, which was quite inconsistent with a pretence that someone else had entered.

Commenting on the part of his account which told of Alma, having hurried downstairs, calling anxiously for Irene, Croom-Johnson said, 'Stoner, therefore, on this night – and I want you to appreciate the full force of this – from the moment he is seen leaning over the bannisters, is only on the scene for a few minutes comparatively late in the story, Mrs Rattenbury apparently not having called Stoner, the man who, in the circumstances, you might have supposed she would have called if it were nothing more than a case of illness.'

Was this not another instance of 'scraping the barrel'? It was a fair point, and might have had significance that she did not at once call both Irene and Stoner, but very little time elapsed before she did call Stoner, a matter of minutes, which counsel did not see fit to tell the jury. Moreover, it might have been clearer to the jury, who until then had known nothing of the facts or evidence, had he explained what exactly he thought was 'the full force of it'.

He recounted the arrival of Dr O'Donnell and the events which followed, and the arrival in the early hours of the redoubtable Police Constable Bagwell, then he observed of Alma, 'There is no doubt she was under the influence of drink.' What he meant was that witnesses would give evidence that she appeared to them to be under the influence of drink, but no one had subjected her to the slightest test, no one was going to say she smelled of drink and her condition could have been occasioned by causes of a wholly different nature. Far from it being 'certain' that she was under the influence of drink, the evidence in his possession on that score would not have convicted her of riding a bicycle on the highway whilst under the influence of alcohol.

Having previously told the jury that Alma had told a story to Irene to create the notion that some stranger had intruded and assaulted her husband, he described the Inspector's arrival: 'Inspector Mills noticed that the french windows were open and he asked [Alma Rattenbury] if they were open when she came down the stairs for the first time. Her answer was "No, they were shut and locked." If that is right, it would preclude the possibility of a person with murderous intention having come in through the window to administer the blows and afterwards to escape through the window into the garden.'

In fact, there was no evidence of any breaking or means of entry anywhere else. The confusion which this opening speech may have occasioned the jury is evident; it seems that insufficient thought had been given to how the case should be presented to them.

Reaching the point in Alma's statement where she said she struck the blows herself, he observed, 'The reason why they had not killed Mr Rattenbury outright was that her physical strength was not sufficient.'

That must have been a theory of his own making, since he neither possessed nor adduced from any witness at the ensuing trial any expression of medical opinion to that effect. On the contrary, the doctors said the injuries must have required considerable force.

Croom-Johnson concluded by telling the jury, 'The prosecution suggest for your consideration that these two people, Mrs Rattenbury and Stoner, with one common object and one common design set out to get rid of Mr Rattenbury, who, as I suggested earlier, stood in their way.'

That, then, was the way the prosecution was putting its case: contending for an agreement between both of them to kill Rattenbury, entirely unsupported by any evidence of acting in concert, based on an insupportable and misconceived motive. Croom-Johnson should have presented the case that, since no one else was there, either Alma or Stoner must have killed Rattenbury and it was for the jury to determine which, if either. Perhaps he was fearful that the jury might be uncertain which of the two struck the blow and consequently acquit both.

CHAPTER 12

The First Crown Witnesses

The first witness called to the box to give evidence was Keith Miller Johns, a solicitor and Francis Rattenbury's nephew. His evidence, of which none, understandably, was subjected to cross-examination, consisted of a series of answers most of which were hearsay and as such inadmissible in evidence. He recounted his uncle's history in Canada, his marriage in America and the birth of his children, although Johns had no knowledge of any of this other than what he had been told. The only relevant and admissible question related to the identification of his uncle's body.

Johns was followed by a surveyor who produced a plan he had drawn of the Villa Madeira. The surveyor was succeeded by a police officer who had taken photographs. Next came Frederick Clements, a retired police sergeant, who told of having known Stoner for four years and of having seen him driving a car in Ensbury Park at 8.00 p.m., about 100 yards from the home of Stoner's parents. He said that when Stoner stopped he went into his parents' house, which was about three and a half miles from the Villa Madeira.

O'Connor did not cross-examine, but Casswell asked him, 'Did you often see the accused Stoner before he went to Rattenbury's?'

'I used to see him almost daily; at least three or four times a week.'

'He was a decent and respectable boy, was he not?'

'Quite,' was the answer, which evidently meant 'Yes,' and not 'Somewhat.'

'And bore the highest character?'

'Yes.'

Casswell, after a few more questions, elicited from the witness his knowledge of the workshop and the manner of reaching it.

'What I am suggesting', he said to the witness, 'is that if anybody wanted to borrow a mallet, and did not want people to know he was going to do it, his easiest way would be to walk through that gate, and round the back rather than apply to anybody?'

'Yes,' was the answer, 'it is quite easy.'

The simple point that Stoner made no attempt to hide his presence was a good one, but why anyone seeing him would have speculated or assumed he was going to borrow a mallet was not quite clear, and whether he would have taken it without permission was at least arguable.

Mrs Elizabeth Stevens told the Court that Stoner, her grandson, called on her between 8.00 and 8.30 on Sunday, 24 March and said to her, 'Mother, will Dad lend me a mallet?', to which she replied, 'Yes, Dad will.'

'Did he say what he wanted it for?' asked Hawke.

'To drive in some pegs as he was going to erect a tent.' She added that she fetched the mallet for him and he left the house within a few minutes.

After a few unimportant questions from O'Connor in cross-examination, Casswell established from her that Stoner used to stay with her, when his parents were away, from the age of four, and that he was backward in education and growth and did not walk until he was three.

'What sort of a lad was he?' he asked her.

'A good lad, Sir,' she answered looking across to the dock, 'an extraordinary good boy, he was.'

'Never known to be rough, I think?'

'Never. He never wanted to go out in the road to play with other children. He would always stay in and mess about with his old bicycle doing repairs or making up things to try and get electricity.'

'Did he ever go about with girls much?'

'Never. I have never known him to go about with a girl.'

'Did you ever know him to drink at all before he went?' asked Casswell.

'Never. He never drank. In fact, he was very prejudiced against it.' His grandmother went on to remark that after he went to the Rattenburys he began to look very pale, which she 'put down to them giving him too much work driving the car about'.

She was followed into the witness box by her son, Richard Stevens, who produced the mallet which his mother had lent Stoner. It was a fair-sized tool and, in answer to Casswell, he said it was not what you would call a jobbing builder's mallet.

'It is the sort of thing one uses to drive tent pegs with, is it not?'

'Yes.'

Casswell turned to another subject. 'I think you have known Stoner for some time. I suppose you have known him almost as long as your mother has?'

'Oh, yes,' he replied, not surprisingly.

'What sort of a lad was he?'

'A good, honest boy, and the best boy that I have ever seen in my life.'

'Did he go about with girls much?'

'I have never seen him in my life.'

'Did you know of him going about drinking at all?'

'Never.'

Stevens, having left no doubt that he regarded Stoner as an unlikely candidate for murder, left the box and the prosecutor called the name of Irene Riggs. She was undoubtedly the Crown's most important witness, whom Croom-Johnson doubtless believed was no more likely to let him down than she would ever dream of letting down her beloved Alma.

There was the usual rustling and murmur in the court as Irene Riggs, dressed in a vivid green coat with a white hat and scarf, crossed the well of the court, mounted the steps to the witness box and took the oath.

'Is your name Irene Riggs?' asked Croom-Johnson.

'Yes.'

'Are you a spinster?'

'Yes,' was the quiet answer.

From there she was taken to the arrangements in the household and on to Sunday, 24 March and her return, at 10.15 p.m., to the Villa Madeira. When she came to describe seeing Stoner leaning over the bannisters she became confused. At first, aided by the prosecutor, she said that she went to her bedroom, where she remained for five or ten minutes, before leaving and seeing Stoner at the bannisters. But then she was asked, 'A little later on did you leave your room again?'

'Yes.'

'About how long after you had seen Stoner and spoken to him was that?'

'That again I should say was about five or ten minutes.'

'Where did you go on this occasion?'

Irene looked somewhat flustered. 'Well,' she said, 'I am afraid it is a little bit backward; I went downstairs once, but on the first occasion something happened when I went downstairs, and then I went upstairs again and came out of my room, and that is, I think, when I saw Stoner.'

Croom-Johnson, having given a wrong account in his opening address which differed from that in his instructions, had now got still another version, so he decided to try once more. 'Just let us see if we have got it right,' he said. 'You think on the first occasion you went downstairs and then you got back again, and it was when you got back again that you saw Stoner?'

'Yes.'

'And then you went to your room?'

'Yes.'

'Then you went downstairs a second time, is that right?'

'No,' replied the witness, to his consternation. 'I went downstairs the first time and nothing happened. I got back into my room. I left my room again, presumably to go along the landing, and I saw Stoner hanging over the stairs.'

Croom-Johnson tried again. 'Then did you go on downstairs that time?' He waited expectantly.

'No,' was the answer, 'I did not go the second time.'

'When you were downstairs on whichever occasion it was,' said Croom-Johnson in desperation, 'were there any lights on downstairs?'

'No.'

Irene then described how she had heard heavy breathing downstairs, which prompted Croom-Johnson to one last attempt: 'Was it after you had switched on the light in Mr Rattenbury's bedroom, according to your recollection now, and went upstairs, that you saw Stoner leaning over the bannister?'

Irene would not be committed. 'As far as I can remember.'

She had similar difficulties with the timing in relation to Alma's arrival in her bedroom.

'It is very difficult but I know you will do the best you can. About how long was it that you had been in bed before you saw Mrs Rattenbury?'

'I cannot really say, but I should say again five to ten minutes.'

'About the same period of time as before?'

'Yes.'

'Were you in bed?'

'Yes.'

'Did she come into the bedroom?'

'Yes.'

The judge intervened. 'Could you tell us about what the time would be? You have told us so far you came in about a quarter past ten, you went up to your room and then on two occasions you left your room?'

'Yes,' agreed Irene.

'Finally,' continued the judge, 'you got into bed and then Mrs Rattenbury came in. Could you give us within a quarter of an hour or so the time when you think she came?'

Irene paused to think. 'I cannot really say at all. I should say half an hour all the time.'

The judge was perplexed. 'Half an hour after what?'

'Quarter past ten – eleven o'clock perhaps.'

'Somewhere around eleven o'clock,' said Mr Justice Humphreys plaintively.

'Yes, quarter to eleven or eleven,' said Irene, and then after a pause, 'I have no idea at all.'

Witnesses can, of course, have great difficulty in fixing time, and some might believe that Irene's difficulty in her evidence was understandable. She, however, had arrived at the house shortly after ten o'clock, if that part of her evidence was accurate. The attack, it is to be assumed, must have taken place by then. But her confusion could have been occasioned for other reasons, one of which could possibly have been that she had rehearsed an account which would be helpful to Alma, which in the atmosphere of a court she could not accurately remember. Certainly, the prosecution could not be expected to canvass this possibility since it formed no part of their case; O'Connor would desire to strengthen rather than weaken Irene's evidence because she was clearly on his client's side, and the unfortunate Casswell felt precluded from investigating it because of his client's instructions which he considered he must strictly follow.

The questioning continued, whilst Irene very briefly related part of her conversation with Alma, contenting herself, and being left contented, with the comment that the rest of the conversation was nothing of importance. She repeated in answer to Croom-Johnson's questions the account she had given, when interviewed by Inspector Carter, of having been called by Alma, and finding Rattenbury injured in the drawing-room.

'After you had bathed Mr Rattenbury's eye,' asked Croom-Johnson, 'did you call somebody else?'

'Yes, I called for Stoner.'

'Did he come when you called?'

'Yes.'

'How soon after you called?'

'Almost immediately.'

The judge came in again: 'Did you call for Stoner of your own accord, or did somebody suggest you should?'

'I think Mrs Rattenbury had previously called. We both called at the same time practically.'

The prosecutor, conscious that this unexpected evidence disposed of one of his earlier points when he had pointed out to the jury that it was strange that Alma had called for Irene and not Stoner, realized he had to try and retrieve his position. 'You think you both called?'

'Yes.'

'Are you quite sure about that?'

'Yes.'

Then, despite that affirmative answer, he thought it proper to try to ignore the difficulty by observing, 'At all events, *you* did?'

'Yes.'

Croom-Johnson next took Irene to her visit to Wimborne on the Tuesday with Stoner in Mr Rattenbury's car. He did not ask her why they had gone there, nor did either of the two defending advocates when it came to their turn to cross-examine. He elicited the statement that Stoner had pointed out his grandfather's house from which he got the mallet and that on their return about 10.30 p.m. he had been in a 'peculiar state' and had said that Mrs Rattenbury was in jail and he had put her there.

That this statement attributed to Stoner was later not mentioned by O'Connor is hardly surprising since it fitted well with the case he was presenting for Alma; what is perhaps strange is that Casswell, when his turn came, also avoided dealing with it, both in cross-examination of Irene and in his final address. No one at any point, therefore, explained to the jury that the words were at least capable of suggesting that he had a feeling of guilt, not, as it was hoped the jury would believe, at having attacked Francis Rattenbury, but rather for having become involved in a liaison with Alma, which had brought her to a situation where she was held in jail.

Having dealt with Stoner's early departure for London on the Wednesday morning, either Croom-Johnson realized or it was pointed out by one of his juniors that he had failed to elicit part of the statement on which he was basing his questions. 'I want to go back a little bit,' he said, 'because we left out of account some of the events of Monday the 25th. After Mrs Ratten-bury had been arrested in the early morning of Monday, the 25th, or the morning of the 25th, were you and Stoner in the house together?'

'We were in the house together, yes,' replied Irene.

'Did Stoner say anything to you about what happened, do you recollect, on the Monday morning?'

Irene frowned.

'If you cannot remember, just say so.'

Irene was nonplussed. 'No, I do not remember now.'

Croom-Johnson, who was not allowed by the rules to cross-examine his own witness, had to leave it there. This is often a difficulty, if an advocate examining a witness takes the story out of chronological order, and it is especially the case when this occurs with witnesses who have learned a story, since they may forget what they intended to say. It is a technique, often used in cross-examination, to test veracity by asking questions requiring the witness to repeat parts of his account out of sequence. It fell, in due course, to O'Connor, in cross-examina-tion, to make good the deficiency and bring out a statement Irene attributed to Stoner which Croom-Johnson thus failed to elicit.

Having proved, through Irene, her receipt of Alma's letter of 27 March sent to her from Holloway, the prosecutor turned to the question of the garden tent.

'While you have been employed by Mr and Mrs Rattenbury has there ever been a tent in the garden?' he asked.

'A sun shelter,' was the reply.

'I will ask you about that in a moment, but has there ever been anything which had to be kept up with guy ropes and pegs or anything of that sort?'

'No.'

'Is a sun shelter put up with pegs?'

'Yes.'

'What sort of pegs?'

'Just little wooden ones.'

'Ones, as far as you could see, that would be easily driven in?'

'Yes.'

'Had that sun shelter been used the previous summer when you were there?'

'Yes.'

'How late the previous summer had that sun shelter been up

105

in the garden?'

'It was on a very hot day we had it,' said Irene, 'but I cannot remember how late.'

Croom-Johnson left that aspect. His last question, it may be thought, was a curious one. The object of this question was to raise the improbability of the shelter being erected at the end of March, in which case he would be expected to be asking how early, and not how late, it had previously been erected. As a result he established nothing relevant to the case.

He next turned to the production of Alma's second letter to Irene, which contained the references to Stoner's remorse at what he had brought on her head and his frightful responsibility.

Casswell came to his feet to advance his claim, having failed to achieve separate trials for the defendants, that the letter was not admissible in evidence: '. . . it cannot be evidence against either Mrs Rattenbury or against my client Stoner.' Certainly, it was difficult to see what it contained which would be evidence against Alma.

Mr Justice Humphreys was not impressed: 'Surely it is not a reason for excluding evidence because there is nothing whatever in it. . . . Of course, it will not prejudice your client. It is not evidence against him. I would like to hear whether there is any other objection.' And after a pause, 'Apparently not. The letter is *prima facie* admissible in evidence against Mrs Rattenbury if it is a letter in her handwriting. It may help her or be against her – one does not know anything about it at the present. Obviously it is not. No objection is taken.'

The letter was admitted in evidence but it is questionable whether the jury clearly understood what the judge had just said. For his part he was content, as most judges are always content, that the jury would judiciously exclude this matter from their minds as against Stoner whilst carefully retaining it in their minds in relation to Alma. Some lawyers, it would seem, do really believe that.

Croom-Johnson had finished his examination-in-chief. He gathered his robe around himself, and majestically sat down.

O'Connor rose to his feet to cross-examine. A man of excellent appearance and bearing, he knew that every answer which he received from Irene would be helpful rather than the contrary.

He established the close relationship between Alma and Irene and then asked, 'During the whole of these four years that you have belonged to that household, have Mrs Rattenbury's relations with her husband been perfectly friendly?' Such leading questions, which suggest to the witness the answer you require, are fully permissible in cross-examination.

'Yes,' replied Irene.

'With the exception of one trivial quarrel, have you ever known them to have a quarrel?'

'Just little funny affairs, but nothing,' said Irene.

'Just little tuppenny-ha'penny affairs?'

'Yes.'

'You have known for some time, have you not, that the relations between Mrs Rattenbury and Stoner were those of a woman and her lover?'

'Yes.'

'There was no mystery about that either, was there?'

'No.'

'Did Mrs Rattenbury tell you that her life had been threatened by Stoner more than once?'

'Yes.'

Casswell was on his feet. 'My Lord, I object. This is something which was said to this lady by one of the accused.'

'Well?' said Mr Justice Humphreys.

Casswell, looking pained, went on, 'It does not appear to have been said in his presence, and in my submission it cannot be evidence against him.'

It was now the judge's turn to look pained. 'I am not concerned with the object of leading counsel in bringing out something which in my view is clearly admissible for or against his client. I will tell the jury now, if you like, but I have not a shadow of doubt they thoroughly understand it.' The judge who, no doubt, truly believed what he had just uttered, turned himself towards the jury and continued, 'Members of the jury, documents written by "A" in the absence of "B" are never evidence against "B", merely because "B" happens to be sitting in the dock and is being tried with "A". . . . Therefore, when evidence of this sort is being given, whether for the prosecution or the defence, for some person made by one of the persons in the absence of the other, you will understand that evidence in regard to – I do not say for or against; it does not matter – that particular person who made the statement, it is not evidence against his or her co-defender. I hope that is very clear. I have very little doubt you have understood it already.'

If the judge had hoped that a look of massive enlightenment would now transfuse the members of the jury, he must have been very disappointed.

O'Connor rose and resumed his cross-examination, touching on the time when Irene entered Stoner's bedroom to end a quarrel between him and Alma, and saw Stoner with his hand outstretched. 'Of what part', asked counsel, 'did he have hold?'

'I would not definitely say,' said Irene.

Clearly, however irrelevant, if it was to be brought out at all it was important to know whether, if the story were true, Stoner had Alma by the throat or the arm, the former clearly being more violent and menacing than the latter. It is to be further noted that violence towards her by Stoner did not advance one iota Alma's case that she did not assault and kill her husband. At best it sought to establish a predisposition for violence in Stoner towards people other than the actual victim, evidence which the prosecution was not permitted to adduce because it would be so grossly unfair and irrelevant, but which O'Connor was clearly willing and permitted to adduce to make it more difficult for Stoner.

The judge, however, did not feel it necessary again to explain to the jury that evidential proposition; perhaps, as before, he 'had very little doubt they understood'. In any case a different sort of intervention had the unforeseen consequence of allowing the point to escape altogether.

'Can you say whether—' began O'Connor.

He got no further because Casswell, from a sitting position, commented, quite accurately, 'It is rather important if I could hear this.'

Meanwhile, answering Casswell's intervention and without waiting for the question to be put again, Irene volunteered, 'I say I could not definitely say.'

'Just one moment,' said the judge. 'Mr Casswell, may I suggest to you that if you were to change positions with the gentleman who is next but one to you I think you would be able to hear better.' He went on to elaborate on the acoustic difficulties of that particular seat and of the court in general and exhorted the witness to speak up.

The effect was that O'Connor, presumably having by then forgotten how far he had previously progressed, merely asked, 'Was it a firm hold that he had of Mrs Rattenbury?'

Irene replied, 'Yes,' and there the matter was left.

Intent not only on putting in the knife for Stoner but twisting it as well, with evidence denied the prosecution, O'Connor then asked, 'Used Stoner to carry a dagger about with him.'

'Yes,' said Irene.

'What kind of length was it?'

'A blade about four inches.'

'When Stoner went away with some belongings on the 25th was there a box labelled "Air Pistol"?'

'Yes.'

'You saw it yourself?'

'Yes.'

Croom-Johnson must have been very pleased with the help which O'Connor was giving him by presenting irrelevant but supposedly discrediting evidence against Stoner.

O'Connor, however, wisely decided he was not going to become embroiled in the movements, up and downstairs, of Irene on her return home on the night of 24 March.

'You went to your room and came out, and as you have told us – I want to have it quite clear – it was only once that you came downstairs?'

'Yes.'

'But you came out of your room twice, and on one of the occasions, when you came out, you saw Stoner, but you are not quite sure which it was?'

'Yes,' replied Irene.

Irene, when she told her account to Inspector Carter, had evidently left no doubt that she saw Stoner when she came out of her bedroom, the second time, to go to the lavatory; she had repeated this in answer to Croom-Johnson, until he confused her by misunderstanding the sequence she described. Now she was not sure on which of the two occasions when she left her bedroom she saw him.

'Whenever you came down, whether it was before seeing Stoner or afterwards, you looked in Mr Rattenbury's bedroom, did you not?'

'Yes.'

'Did you see that a suit of clothes put out for him in the way that was habitual when he was going away?'

'Yes.'

This was rightly brought out to negate the case for the prosecution, as opened by the Crown, that the trip to Bridport was a 'notion', or part of one, designed to suggest that someone else had assaulted Rattenbury.

'Miss Riggs, had you an uneasy feeling that made you come down that night?'

'I had.'

What brought her down that night, if her original evidence

was to be believed, was a visit to the kitchen; her uneasiness did not arise until she heard, as she said, heavy breathing.

'I suppose you must have been accustomed in the course of the time that Stoner had been there to find him going in and out of Mrs Rattenbury's bedroom?' the advocate continued.

'Yes.'

'There was nothing very remarkable in finding him on the landing. Mrs Rattenbury shortly afterwards came into your room; she was perfectly normal so far as you could see in every way when she came in to talk to you?'

'She was just excited, a little excited,' said Irene before O'Connor skilfully altered the purport of her answer.

'What was she excited about?'

'About the preparations she had made for the Monday.'

'Did she look as though she had just had a great shock or heard something terrible?' asked O'Connor, continuing to leave no doubt about the answers he wanted.

'No.'

'Did she look as though she had any knowledge at that time that her husband was down below struck with a blow upon his head?'

'No.'

O'Connor led Irene through her account of being called downstairs by Alma. 'Were you down in the drawing-room within a few seconds of that cry?'

'Yes.'

'What was her condition then?'

'She was in a terrified state.'

'Was her condition then like the condition that you had seen her in a few moments previously in your bedroom?'

'Nothing at all like it.'

'Was she a changed woman?'

'A changed woman absolutely.'

'Had she obviously had a sudden and terrifying experience?'

'Yes. It was dreadful, and you could not make out what she said, but she said "Oh, poor Rats."'

'Did you hear her say "What have they done to you?"?'

Even Irene was not having that. She replied, '"What has happened?"'

'She was very impatient with you?'

'Yes.'

'What did she think you ought to have done quicker?'

'She was telling me to hurry – "Can't somebody do some-

110

thing?"'

'How did she tolerate the time that elapsed between the telephoning for the doctor and the time he came?'

'Raving about the house.'

'Was she drinking?'

'Yes.'

'Drinking continuously or not?'

'She came out for some whisky. Yes.'

The judge looked up. 'Was she drinking whisky continuously?' he asked.

'Well, she kept going backwards and forwards for some.'

'Was it neat whisky or not?' asked O'Connor.

'No, she had soda in it.'

Having dealt with the arrival of the doctors and reached the
arrival of the police, counsel asked, 'What was Mrs Rattenbury's
condition when the police first arrived? I think they arrived about
two o'clock?'

'Yes. She was still in a terrified state.'

'Was she making up to the police?'

'Yes.'

'Trying to kiss them?'

'Yes.'

O'Connor interrupted his questioning designed to provide
Irene's account of the happenings after the police arrived: 'There
was one question I am afraid I have missed which I have taken
out of its order – I ought to have asked you before – a rather
important one. When you came down to the drawing-room for
the first time that evening and found Mrs Rattenbury with her
husband, did you notice anything about the blood that was on
his head?'

'I saw no blood on his hair.'

'Blood on the chair?'

'On the chair.'

'And the carpet?'

'Yes.'

'In what condition was the blood?'

'Well, not fresh.'

'Thick and congealed, was it?'

'Yes.'

The importance of the condition of the blood never emerged
because no further evidence was offered concerning it. The speed
of coagulation is not easy to assess, because so many factors
affect it. The only importance, which was self-evident, was that

if it was not in a fluid state the injury could not have occurred immediately before discovery, and in this case it was never seriously suggested that such was the fact.

There was a tense and quiet atmosphere in the court as Irene recounted the events on that morning in the Villa Madeira: the police endeavours to arouse Alma from her sleep and to get her from her bed; her arrest and departure from the house; and her whispered conversation about getting Stoner to give her the mallet.

'Did Stoner afterwards on some occasion or other say anything to you about the mallet? Did he say anything about fingerprints?' O'Connor asked Irene.

'I asked Stoner would not there be his fingerprints on the mallet. He said no, he wore gloves.'

'Would you ask her', said the judge, 'what time she is speaking of when she says Stoner made this observation to her. Was it some time afterwards?'

O'Connor replied that he thought it was a day or two later, and turning back to the witness said, 'Was it the next day, the Monday, or the Tuesday?'

'About the gloves, do you mean?' asked Irene.

'Yes.'

'It was on the Tuesday that happened.'

There was some further cross-examination about the time this was said, and Alma's counsel approached the end of his cross-examination. 'There is just one other little matter that I want to ask you as to something that Stoner said to you. Did he say to you on some occasion after the Sunday "I suppose you know who did it"?' By putting the very words into the witness's mouth, as he was entitled to do in cross-examination, O'Connor elicited the assertion which Croom-Johnson had failed to get from Irene in evidence-in-chief.

'Yes,' was Irene's reply.

'Was that on the Monday morning?'

'That was on the Monday morning.'

'What did you say to that?'

'I answered, "Well."'

'Was anything more said?'

'Nothing more was said.'

O'Connor was preparing to resume his place – he had one or two more perfunctory questions; the spectators were getting a little restless – when he had a surprise, as did everyone else connected with the case.

Referring to the remark attributed by her to Stoner, 'I suppose you know who did it,' he asked her, 'Was that before or after Mrs Rattenbury was taken away?'

'It was before.'

'While she was either having a bath or dressing or asleep?'

'Yes.'

O'Connor began to sit down. 'It was some time, you think, during that time?' he asked.

Irene produced her bombshell. 'Yes.' And then she added, 'There was something else on the Tuesday, I remember. I asked Stoner why he had done it.'

O'Connor was back on his feet.

'Wait a minute. Do you want to put any further questions, Mr O'Connor?' said the judge.

'My Lord,' O'Connor replied, not unexpectedly, 'I think I will follow this up if I may.'

It was quite evident that he had been taken completely by surprise and that Irene could not have told anyone of this before, or it would have been disclosed by the prosecution.

Irene was obviously conscious of the confusion she had caused. 'I should have said it when he asked me another question,' she stammered.

'What was it?' asked O'Connor.

'On the Tuesday I asked Stoner why he had done it,' she repeated.

'What did he say?'

'He said because he had seen Mr Rattenbury "living" with Mrs Rattenbury in the afternoon.'

The judge joined in. 'Let me have this. On the Tuesday, was it?'

'Yes.'

'Was he sober when he said that?'

'Quite.'

'Was that on the Tuesday when you had been to Wimborne?' asked counsel.

'Yes.'

'Was it while you were in the car?'

'Yes.'

Here was a vital piece of evidence against Stoner: an unconditional confession, if true; the most important piece of evidence which Irene had given, the importance of which, if true, she must herself always have known. Yet it seems clear that from first to last she had never mentioned it before. It was dynamite for Stoner, especially since it made no mention of his being under the influence of cocaine or anything else, and showed a premeditated and clear intention to cause, at least, serious injury.

Coming as it did at the very end of Irene's cross-examination on behalf of the co-accused there can be few skilled advocates in Casswell's position who would not have decided they had to tackle this statement immediately and with vigour. When had she first remembered it? Why had she never before mentioned it? Why not to the police? Why not in her evidence-in-chief? Had she not realized its importance? If not, why not? And a string of similar questions which would, at least, have made the jury realize the implications.

Casswell, stolid and inflexible, had a prepared series of questions and began as if Irene's last utterance had not been made. 'You had lived in this household for about four years?'

The suppressed excitement in the court aroused by the last evidence subsided like a burst balloon.

'Yes,' was the reply.

'Did you find it a curious atmosphere there indeed?'

'It was just a little unusual.'

'Mrs Rattenbury used to do strange things did she not, sometimes – walk about the garden late at night in her pyjamas?'

'No, I did not think it strange.'

'Did she sometimes stay up all night playing the gramophone?'

'Yes.'

'Did you think that was strange?'

'No, because I used to be with her.'

'All night long?'

'Yes.'

Then came the first of a series of questions which hinted at an unusual relationship between Irene and Alma, but they were delivered in a half-hearted spirit of being willing to wound but unwilling to strike.

'In those days you often went about with her, did you not?'

'Yes.'

'In the car?'

'Yes.'

'When you went away you were more as a sort of friend than companion/help?'

'Yes.'

'Did that stop when Stoner came?'

'Yes.'

Casswell broke his chain of questioning by referring to the visit to Oxford. Irene expressed her belief that no intercourse had taken place between Alma and Stoner then because she had a communicating room with Alma.

'Was not it almost as soon as that trip was over, that Stoner came to live in the house, the Villa Madeira?'

'Yes.'

'Did you approve of that?'

'I did not mind him living in the house,' was the reply.

'You did not mind him being in the house but you knew he was always going into her bedroom, did you not?'

'Yes.'

Then Irene gave a strange answer for someone who was a companion/help, even if treated as a friend.

'Did you approve of that?' asked Casswell, proceeding very competently.

'Well, it was not my duty to approve or disapprove. It just hurt me.'

Was this addition an unguarded response? The judge looked up sharply from his note-taking. He too must have sensed a whiff of scandal. '*How* did it hurt *you*?' he asked.

'Well,' replied Irene, 'just because Mrs Rattenbury, shall we say, hurt my feelings.'

Instead of pushing home the advantage, Casswell began to retreat. 'You were not pleased, were you – perhaps naturally – having been a close friend of Mrs Rattenbury's for four years that suddenly this lad of seventeen should come in?'

'No.'

'You were not pleased about it, were you?'

'Not very.'

Then Casswell put a question which he would never have put unless he had found it in his instructions from Stoner, who in turn could only have learned of the matter by having heard it or having been told about it by Alma: 'I mean before that you used to call her "Jack", didn't you?'

Irene paused. 'Call her what?' she said.

'Jack?' repeated Casswell.

'Never,' said Irene.

Having raised this use by Irene of a man's name for Alma it would have seemed appropriate to have pressed on with it. Once again Casswell retreated. 'What did you call her?'

'Darling,' and there it was left.

Casswell turned instead to the occasion when Alma had got

a black eye and he brought out that Rattenbury, in the course of the same argument, had severely bitten Alma's arm; he touched on the visit of Mrs Price before which Alma had had an attack, although Irene said she could not remember a lot about it. This line of questioning seemed, without it ever becoming particularly clear, to be directed to establishing Alma's peculiar behaviour and her vulnerability from time to time to 'attacks'. However, even when mildly tackled by the judge to indicate what he was getting at and with which object in view, Casswell was far from forthcoming, and indeed did not appear certain himself.

'Let me see', he said, 'if I can suggest to you what these sort of attacks were – that suddenly she became very excited and used to run about a great deal?'

'Yes.'

'And that would last for a bit of time and then she would, perhaps, get drowsy and go to sleep?'

'She would always be in bed. Yes.'

'What I am suggesting is that every now and again she had sudden attacks and got very excited.'

'Yes.'

'And ran about.'

'Yes.'

'Just as if she had taken something?'

'Yes.'

'And then at the end of the attack she would go to bed, would she?'

'Yes.'

'And that used to happen two or three times a month, did it not?'

'Not quite so often as that.'

Casswell seemed to be laying the foundation for a suggestion – not without justification – that it was Alma who was on drugs, but he never made the suggestion explicitly, did not pursue the matter, and left it a mystery why he had raised it at all.

He turned to ask about the chef called Davis who had left Alma's employ, but Irene said it was before her time. He next questioned her about some statement or other, which he enshrouded in mystery, which Irene was said to have given to someone, but he never explained what it was or to whom it was given, either then or at any other time in the trial. He then sought to ascertain what Alma wore under her pyjamas during the day. He established that when Irene first went down the stairs on the fateful night, she had intended going to the kitchen but never got there. In fairness to him, had he pursued his success and made something of it then or later, he might have effectively elicited a number of answers which, from the curious sequence of events in Irene's account of her own conduct on the journeys down and upstairs, would have raised a doubt whether it might have been an invented story. But he never did pursue it.

He established the good relations between Stoner and Francis Rattenbury and, contrary to the impression given by Croom-Johnson, brought out that Stoner was much in evidence in the house when the doctors and the police were there. He then turned to the question of the mallet, and once again, owing no doubt to inadequate preparation, an important chance was missed to make a cogent point in Stoner's defence.

The prosecution had sought to suggest, without achieving it with conviction, that the mallet had been specially fetched for the dark deed, and that no other purpose for it existed in March.

'With regard to the question of the mallet,' said Casswell to Irene, 'do you remember a Mrs Almond being there as a nurse-maid? She was there up to a day or two before Stoner arrived, was she not?'

'Yes.'

'During her time, whatever it was, a canvas sun shelter was put up, was it not?'

'I expect it would be.'

'That was about 24 or 25 September,' he asked, without explaining what help that might be in relation to erecting it on 25 March, 'and was it not a great nuisance keeping the pegs in?'

'They would slip out, yes.'

'At that time there was no mallet on the premises?'

'No.'

'Mrs Rattenbury was the sort of person who would put up a shelter in March, when others would not put it up till June?'

'No, she would only put it up on very hot days when the little boy could sleep out.'

'Was 24 March quite a hot day?'

'I don't know. I cannot remember.'

'You cannot remember that morning, perhaps, but you went out in the afternoon. I suggest it was one of the first hot days this year,' he pressed.

'I do not know,' was the answer, 'I cannot remember.'

There Casswell left it, although the state of the weather might have provided an explanation for the fetching of the mallet. What endeavours, if any, had he made to check it? The *Bournemouth Daily Echo* for 21 March recorded that far from the 24th being one of the first hot days of the year, 'Bournemouth weather continues summerlike. Sunshine enjoyed here yesterday amounted to eight hours. This brilliant spell brought the aggregate for the first 20 days of March to 85 hours. The sun shone continuously again today, the first day of Spring. ... Yesterday saw temperatures in the 60s for the first time this year. Temperature today: minimum shade temperature, 62. ...' The temperature in the shade, moreover, for the 22nd was 61° F and for the 24th the same. Why was this never put to Irene or at any time adduced to the court? And might this sudden Bournemouth warmth have been a reason for getting a mallet, with a view to erecting a shelter facing the sun, and as a wind protection, for Rattenbury in the garden, who, sheltered from the wind, could have enjoyed the sunshine?

The only other reference which Casswell made to the mallet was to ask, 'You have told us, of course, something which is not evidence against Stoner, but which was brought out by my learned friend, Mr O'Connor, for some reason or other he himself knows, and that is, as Mrs Rattenbury went out of the door, when Stoner was not there, she whispered to you something about "Tell Stoner to give me the mallet"?'

'Yes.'

'"He must give me the mallet"?'

'Yes.'

'And you also say that she was not herself at the time?'

'Not quite herself, no.'

'She was going away to the police station, was she not?'

'Yes.'

'How could anyone bring a mallet to the police station?' asked Casswell – a wholly sensible observation.

'I suppose she wanted it before she left,' was the less than sensible answer.

'She wanted it before she left, but it was not until she was being taken away by the police matron and the police officer that she told you to tell him he must give her the mallet?'

'It was when the police were outside the room.'

'When the police matron was outside the room?'

'When she was getting ready; she was not quite ready to go.'

The judge wanted no doubt about it. 'There was no policeman

actually in charge of her at that moment?'

'No, nobody knew she said it to me.'

'Did you tell the police about it?' asked Casswell.

'No.'

'Why not?'

'I did not remember it at the time I was giving my statement.'

Where the sympathies and the loyalty of Irene really lay could be in no doubt, if indeed they ever were. Previously she had volunteered, at the very end of a long cross-examination on behalf of Alma, a statement in which Stoner had, so she said, admitted the crime to her. Now, she disclosed a highly significant statement which, although not admissible against him by the prosecution, could be, and was, introduced by those defending Alma. This statement had not been told to the police, because she had, it seemed, conveniently forgotten it at the time, but it must somehow have been communicated to Alma's lawyers for them to have known of it.

Casswell, admittedly with his hands tied behind his back by his instructions not in any way to implicate Alma, made a very poor showing.

He had demonstrated the absurdity of Alma telling Irene to tell Stoner to give her the mallet as she was on her way to the police station. What, however, might have been fruitfully pursued, then and certainly in the course of preparing his defence, was whether Irene had misheard or misunderstood what in fact Alma said – if she said it at all. She might have said, 'Tell Stoner to tell me where the mallet is,' or words similar to that, since she had told the police she had done the deed with a mallet which was hidden, but clearly had not told them that she did not know where it was. If, for example, she had struck the blows herself, and Stoner, horrified at what his loved one had done, had seized her and the mallet, and in fear for her had hidden it, she would have needed to know where he had put it in order to justify the story she was at that time telling the police.

Casswell moved on: 'Afterwards you said something to Stoner about fingerprints on the mallet?'

'Yes.'

'Did you know at that time he had brought that mallet, had collected it at his grandmother's and brought it back in the car with him?'

'Yes.'

'Did you know also that fingerprints would last for a long time?'

'I heard they would.'

This was a curious answer which Casswell missed. She would have been expected to answer in the affirmative or negative, but the answer 'I heard they would' manifestly needed clarification. Heard from whom? Under what circumstances? And why had she been discussing it? Casswell asked not a word.

He continued, 'So when you asked him about fingerprints he may have thought of that time, may he not?'

'I do not know.'

'Did he always wear gloves as a chauffeur?'

'Yes. I do not know whether he always wore them, but he had them.'

What a singularly ineffective cross-examination this was. He might, as would most experienced policemen, have anticipated more helpful and illuminating answers had he put different questions. For example: 'Miss Riggs, you say that on the journey back from Wimborne Stoner pointed out the house from which he fetched the mallet? When he did so you thought, at once, of fingerprints? And that his might be on it? You had in mind, of course, that his fingerprints might be on the mallet from the time he collected it? And thus might still have been there later? But he told you that he was wearing gloves? You were both then talking of the time he collected the mallet! You did not discuss with him having handled the mallet at any other time?' It hardly called for any brilliance to approach the matter in that way, and thus remove the totality of the sting from the evidence. But it was not done.

Casswell had finished with Irene. Croom-Johnson in re-examination obtained confirmation that when Irene looked into Rattenbury's bedroom on the night of 24 March a suit was hanging in the wardrobe where it was only placed when they were going away; that when Alma went into Irene's bedroom she did not seem excited by drink 'or anything of that sort'; that Irene did not observe Alma having any conversation with Stoner between the time the doctor first arrived and his return to the house. Croom-Johnson sat down to make way for any questions from the judge.

Judges endeavour, as far as their natures will permit, to delay any questions which they wish to put to witnesses until the advocates have finished with theirs. The judge had a few further questions for Irene.

'You have told the jury that Mrs Rattenbury was sometimes excitable, and sometimes drank too much alcohol?'

'Yes.'

'And that she had drinking bouts. How long had that lasted – all the time you were there?'

'Yes.'

'And how often did she have drinking bouts?'

'Sometimes she would go a month or so without having one.'

'And sometimes it was more often than once a month?'

'Yes.'

'You also told the jury that at times she had what you call sudden attacks, when she got very excitable and ran about, and afterwards used to go to bed and sleep. Were those occasions when she had been drinking?'

Irene's answer revealed a slight reservation. 'Yes, more or less,' she said.

'Did it seem to you that her condition at those times was due to drink?'

Had anyone else asked that question there is little doubt the judge would have enquired whether it was believed that Irene was capable of giving such expert opinion in evidence. However, Irene replied, 'Yes, I always thought so.'

The judge clearly and justifiably had other things in mind, since the behaviour which had throughout been attributed to Alma bore fewer of the characteristics of drunkenness than of a condition induced by other causes.

'That is what it seemed like. Did you ever know her to take drugs. Things like cocaine, morphia and heroin?'

Again this produced not a categorical negative but a slightly qualified response: 'No, not to my knowledge.'

This was the first time in the case that anyone had mentioned heroin, which as events might show was not necessarily wholly irrelevant.

The judge continued, 'With regard to Stoner, you have told us that after this tragedy on at least one occasion he was drunk. Had you ever seen him drunk before 24 March, or under the influence of drink at all?'

'No.'

'No sign at all?'

'No.'

After a few more questions from his Lordship and after Casswell was allowed to ask another question which showed that the box marked 'Air Pistol' which Stoner took away with him did not contain one, Irene smiled at the judge and left the witness box with the hope that she might never return there. She was, however, to be disappointed. After a police officer had been called to tell how he had collected a hypodermic syringe, which he had found in a small washstand cupboard at the Villa Madeira, Irene, to her dismay, was recalled to confirm she had seen the syringe there but to her knowledge had never known it used, although she believed that the young boy had once had to have injections for his leg.

This was still a further example of the slipshod manner in which this prosecution had been prepared. The hypodermic syringe when recovered should have been sent for forensic scientific examination. If it showed traces of a drug, as, presumably, the prosecution were anxious to imply, and it thus appeared to have been used for injecting some drug or other, the forensic scientific evidence should have been called. If it showed no such traces, it became useless and irrelevant and should have been forgotten. Merely to put the hypodermic syringe before the jury in such fashion was as unfair as it was incompetent.

Dr William O'Donnell must have been exercising his mind, as he walked across the floor of the court to the witness box, about the questions which were likely to be put to him. The prosecution had throughout been hinting at the presence of drugs, as they might have affected Alma's position, but had miserably failed to produce any cogent evidence about them. O'Donnell, as was customary at that time, may well have had his own dispensary at his surgery, and thus had easy access to drugs, which might conceivably, it could be suggested, have been passed on by him to his friend and patient, Alma. Was someone going to suggest such a thing? He may have pondered this as he mounted the witness-box steps. The doctor, a man in his middle sixties, looked younger. He wore glasses, was smartly dressed, and was agile in his movements as he lifted the Bible to take the oath.

His evidence-in-chief was merely the recounting of what he had found when he arrived on 24 March at the Villa Madeira, and it accorded with what he had told Inspector Carter earlier. When O'Connor cross-examined him on behalf of Alma, the doctor confirmed that Rattenbury had many times, in his hearing, threatened suicide, but he did not agree that these threats distressed Alma. O'Connor was permitted by the judge to put a question which hardly fell within the ambit of O'Donnell's medical expertise. 'As her medical attendant,' he asked, 'and one who has had every opportunity of seeing her temperament at close quarters, do you think it would be possible for Mrs Rattenbury to take part in a crime of this description and then act perfectly peacefully and normally with her maid?'

That was, of course, exactly the question which it was for the jury to decide, and, as such, impermissible, but the doctor manfully took on the task for them and replied, 'I do not consider it possible.'

O'Connor, for the best part of his cross-examination, underlined with O'Donnell that Alma's condition at six, seven and eight o'clock on the morning of 25 March was not such that she would have been capable of making a reliable statement to the police or anyone else.

Casswell's cross-examination on behalf of Stoner produced nothing new, dealing mostly with the number of times the doctor had visited the Villa Madeira and the receipt by Rattenbury of his black eye. Burdened by the task of showing that Stoner acted under the influence of cocaine, he questioned the doctor about the habits of cocaine-takers, but since O'Donnell seemed to know as little about the effects of such drugs as Casswell himself appeared to possess it was not very illuminating. His questions to the doctor about the visit which Stoner had paid to his surgery concerning drugs made the doctor look a trifle silly but achieved little else and nothing which assisted Stoner.

'Here,' said Casswell, 'in February last a man of just eighteen was brought to you?'

'No, he was not,' replied the doctor.

'You were asked to speak to him and the suggestion was that he was already a drug addict?'

The doctor corrected him again: 'That he was taking drugs.'

'Yes, taking drugs, if you please, and, as a result, was becoming violent?'

'Yes.'

'You yourself had very little experience of cocaine or drugs?'

'That is right – the abuse of them.'

'What symptoms did you look for?'

'I did not look for any,' replied the doctor, which was strange since he had said the only purpose for which Stoner had been required to attend on him was to enable him to determine whether Stoner was on drugs or not – if that *was* the true purpose of the visit.

'But you asked him', continued Casswell, 'and he said he had been taking cocaine?'

'Yes.'

'Did you believe him?'

'Well,' replied the doctor, and after a pause to think, 'I suppose I did.'

'Did you ask him whether he had been up to London to try and get it?'

'He told me he had been up to London the day before to get it.'

'Did he say whether he managed to get it or not?'

'No, he said he failed.'

'Did he tell you where the money had come from to get it?'

'He did not.'

'Did you ask him.'

'No.'

'So the steps you took on his behalf were to warn him of the dangers of cocaine?'

'That is so.'

'Do you think it was much good to warn a cocaine-taker of the dangers of cocaine?'

'No, I do not think it is.'

Casswell browsed his way through a variety of other questions, none of which much contributed to the advancement of any defence, and having arrived at the question of Alma's condition at the crucial time asked, 'Do you think, by any chance, she took some sort of drugs without your knowing it?'

'I do not think so,' replied the doctor. 'As a matter of fact she was averse to any treatment which she considered dope.'

'Of course,' continued Casswell, 'the normal way of taking cocaine is by snuffing, is it not?'

'So I understand.'

'That would leave no mark?'

'No,' said the doctor, 'unless you get a mark on the septum of the nose. You do get a perforation of the septum of the nose from cocaine taking.'

'That would be on the inside of the nostril?'

'Yes.'

'You would not notice it unless you were told about it?'

'No, unless you examined for it.'

O'Connor had been at pains to establish throughout that such was Alma's condition at the relevant times that anything which she had said at those times should be rejected as unreliable. Croom-Johnson, for the Crown, in re-examination endeavoured to redress the balance. In answer to his questions the doctor said that the effect of the morphia which he had injected would not have passed off more quickly had Alma been sober rather than drunk when it was administered, and that coffee, walking about and a hot bath might assist in getting rid of the effects of the injection. On further reflection, however, Dr O'Donnell was only prepared to agree that it would keep the patient more wakeful but would not get rid of the effects of the drug. He said such a person would be fuddled and muddled.

'Unable to tell a coherent story?' asked Croom-Johnson.

'Yes,' replied the doctor.

'So that you would not expect anybody under the influence of morphia to be able to tell a coherent story at all?'

'No, I should think not.'

The judge added his assistance. 'Would you like to place any reliance on any statement made by a person under the influence of morphia?' he asked.

'No, my Lord,' was the reply.

Croom-Johnson, in due course, came to the visit Stoner paid to the doctor. 'Did you make any enquiry as to how often he had taken cocaine since he had discovered it gave him a pleasant sensation?'

'No.'

'Or how long it had been going on?' asked the judge.

'No.'

'Does that mean that you did not gather from him whether it was a matter of a week or five years?'

'That is so,' was the reply. 'I did not ask him.'

The judge was as mystified by the course which the doctor's examination of Stoner had taken as must have been everyone else. 'Surely your experience is enough, is it not,' he asked somewhat brusquely, 'to know that it is important to find out whether a person has been taking it for a week or five years?'

'He appeared perfectly normal to me that day. I saw no reason to believe he was taking large doses of cocaine.'

'Or that he had been taking it for some time?' asked the judge.

'I could not say he had taken any from what I saw that day.'

'He said he had?'

'Yes, he told me he had.'

'Did you understand from him whether that was the first time he had been up to London to get it, or not?'

'No, I did not ask him.'

Croom-Johnson took over again from the judge but nothing of moment emerged and the doctor left the witness box.

By now the trial was into its second day. The interest of the public had, if anything, greatly increased. The atmosphere in a court on such occasions is an unusual one. A journalist writing in the *Daily Mirror* during the trial noted, 'After sitting in the Court for several hours you become unconsciously part of the machine. Your heart stops aching for the prisoners. You can look at them now without feeling cruel or inquisitive. You watch the Judge, wondering if he will show by the flicker of an eyelid what he is feeling. You do not bother. You have become lulled into a sort of coma by the droning of the K.C.'s voice.'

The crowds outside the Old Bailey were still anxious to get in. One man told the *Daily Mirror*, 'I've been here since before midnight. I'm hoping to get married and if I sell my place in the queue I may get enough money to set myself up in a little business. I am unemployed, and a man I met yesterday told me he had sold his place for £2, and while I don't like doing this – my girl knows nothing about it – I am quite prepared to wait. I've been out of work, apart from odd jobs, for several months and I would probably be sleeping out during the night in any case. I intend to come each night while the trial lasts.'

At least he was not lonely in the street. Women still predominated in the crowd, and some of them carried picnic baskets with vacuum flasks and sandwiches, and picnicked in the court as the trial proceeded.

There is something unhealthy about the way in which the public even today will rush to court to gloat over and presumably enjoy the suffering and humiliation of those in the dock. The prisoners, for their part, sat there impassive as ever. Alma's dark hair was uncut, braided over her ears; her face was florid and lightly powdered. All the while that each succeeding witness was in the box, her eyes never left him or her. When the statements attributed to her were read out she showed not the slightest trace of emotion. Stoner, his fair, gold-streaked hair brushed back from his forehead, wearing his grey striped suit, the relic of the Harrods shopping expedition, sat through the evidence with his elbows resting on the edge of the dock, his face on his hand, only sitting up and taking more notice when evidence given from the witness box more directly concerned him.

On the bench, beside the judge, sat a woman spectator. Her identity was not revealed, but it was assumed she was the judge's wife.

Little that was new came from the evidence of the surgeon, Alfred Basil Rooke. He described the three wounds which he found on Rattenbury's head. One above the ear on the left-hand side had irregular jagged edges and was about three to three and a half inches long; the bone was exposed in the deep parts of the wound and there was an obvious depressed fracture of the skull. He said he could feel where the bone had been driven into the brain. The second was approximately in the midline at the back of the head; it was a lacerated wound which reached down to the bone, but he could not feel a fracture. The third was similar to the second, and was a little further round to the right. There was no fracture there either. The real interest in his evidence, had anyone been following the forensic medical aspects with greater interest than the participants in the trial appear to have done, was his evidence on the striking of the blows.

'Did you form any opinion', asked Croom-Johnson for the Crown, 'as to whether the blows had been struck from the front or from behind?'

'From behind,' was the reply.

Rooke was shown the mallet and agreed that the blows could have been inflicted with such an instrument. The nature of the injuries was further taken up when O'Connor cross-examined him on behalf of Alma.

'The most serious injury was the one to the left on the skull?'

'That was the most serious,' was the reply.

'So far as one could apportion the cause of death, that probably was the wound which caused it?'

'The injuries associated with that wound were, in my opinion, the cause of death.'

'It was a very formidable wound, was it not?'

'A very formidable wound,' he agreed.

'And it must have been caused by a blow delivered with such force that it caused contracoup on the other side of the brain?'

'Yes.'

A contracoup injury, as the name – 'against blow' – conveys, occurs because the brain is sited in fluid, so that a severe blow on one side propels the brain, in the fluid, against the opposite side of the skull, thus setting up a double injury.

O'Connor, having established the existence of the contracoup, continued, 'Which presupposes great violence on the left?'

The surgeon was, quite rightly, not having this. 'Not very great violence,' he observed.

'A considerable degree of violence?'

'Yes.'

It was certainly not in the interest of his client to pursue this aspect further, and there O'Connor wisely left it. He endeavoured to establish, for good measure, that the surgeon had never seen any sign of drug addiction in Alma's behaviour, but got no more than the answer: 'It never occurred to me. I had never looked for signs of it.' Rooke did, however, helpfully agree that her reaction to the situation on the night of the attack was compatible with the ordinary reactions of a very highly strung person.

'To the horrible situation in which she found herself?' added O'Connor.

'Exactly,' he replied.

'In association with alcohol?' added the judge.

'Yes.'

'She was a perfect nuisance when you arrived?' asked O'Connor.

'She made an examination impossible.'

'Making utterly incoherent remarks, but nevertheless solicitous for her husband's welfare?'

'So solicitous,' replied Rooke, 'that when I was making futile efforts to conduct my examination I said, "If you want to kill him, you are going the right way to do it. Do let me get near him and attend to him."'

'*Embarras de richesses?*' said O'Connor, knowing that some members, at least, on the jury would recall their French lessons at Hoxton Boys School.

'Exactly,' said the surgeon.

'You have no doubt it was done with the sincere wish to help?'

'I cannot speak for the sincerity,' the witness wisely responded. 'There was the apparent wish to help.'

When Casswell's turn came, he reverted to the nature of the blows. Dealing with the fracture, he asked, 'Was the blow very near to the top of the left ear?'

'It would be from one inch to one and a half inches above it.'

'Why do you say it was a blow from behind?' asked Casswell.

'I feel justified in swearing to it being a blow from behind because of the direction of that blow absolutely shown by the contracoup.'

'Why cannot I hit a man from the front behind his ear with that mallet and cause a contracoup in that way?'

'Because your position makes it mechanically impossible.'

'Assume that the patient is sitting in a chair,' commented Casswell, physically demonstrating a way he thought the blow might be achieved from the front, but without explaining what a doctor might be doing sitting his 'patient' in a chair and then taking a good swipe at him with a mallet. The surgeon was, in any case, unimpressed.

'Have you ever swung a hammer?' asked Casswell.

'I have,' said Rooke.

'One swings it almost towards one, does one not, as if driving in something?'

'Yes, but I think the swing of a hammer is rather a different thing from this; the action is different.'

'One further point about the direction of the blow. I think it important whether the blow was struck from in front or behind—'

The judge came to the witness's aid: 'All that the doctor has said is that the direction of the blow was from behind.'

'I understood him to say', said Casswell, 'that the person who delivered it was standing behind.'

In fact Rooke had not said that at all.

'With great respect to him,' said the judge, 'he is not in a position to say.'

'That is the whole point of my enquiry,' persisted Casswell.

'It is not a medical question at all,' said the judge. 'It is a surgical question what was the direction of the instrument which caused the injury, and that, he said most distinctly, came from the back towards the front. Whether it is possible for a man who is standing in front of another, who is sitting, to hit that man a blow which comes from the back to the front, the jury know as well as any surgeon does.'

Casswell was not satisfied. 'I understand the witness to say it was, in his view, struck by a person standing behind.'

'I do not think I said that,' said the surgeon. 'I said the direction of the blow, by which I mean the direction of the force.'

'I was trying to make you understand that might be the direction of a blow from someone standing in front, and I understand you do not agree with me?'

'No.'

'Then it comes to this, that you say it was struck by someone standing behind?'

The witness stood firm. 'The direction of the force was from behind.'

Casswell was slightly losing his cool. 'Still you will not answer me?'

'I cannot say more than that the direction of the force was from behind.'

'Do you say that it was possible to have caused the blow standing in front?'

The judge added, 'Or at the side?'

'From the side, yes, but from the front, I cannot stretch my imagination sufficiently.'

Casswell was becoming quite exasperated. 'What you are in fact saying is that you, a medical man, who has seen the marks on the skull and the cracks in the skull, and have seen the contracoup, cannot stretch your imagination to that blow having been struck by somebody standing in front of the victim?'

'I cannot,' and there the surgeon's evidence was left.

From that point there was neither evidence nor further canvassing of the question where the assailant was likely to have been standing when the blows were struck. It might not have been unimportant, since coming up behind a man sitting and perhaps dozing, or half drunk, in a chair with a moderately high back has an element of predetermination about it, whilst striking him three blows in the front is more consistent with an argument, loss of temper, or even the conduct of someone in a state of frenzy or hysteria, perhaps brought about by drugs. In a case which was badly prepared and badly presented, save by O'Connor for Alma, this aspect was perhaps the most disturbing and surprising of all. It is true that Stoner was represented under the Poor Prisoners' Defence Act with little money available and that his counsel never reached the front rank of his profession. The Crown, however, had a Silk who became a High Court judge, and the presiding judge was one of the great figures of the criminal law. What is more, although several books have been written about this case, some vital but simple matters appear never to have been considered. No one, in the course of the trial, appears ever to have discovered, in evidence or otherwise, Francis Rattenbury's height, or the height of the chair back from the cushion on which he was sitting when struck. This was clearly relevant to whether the blows were struck by someone at the back or the front. Secondly, no evidence was ever adduced on whether the accused were left-handed or right-handed, nor, it seems, was the question asked. The only other medical witness was a local police doctor who acted as police surgeon. No trained and experienced forensic pathologist was called as a witness, or even, it would seem, consulted. It was also somewhat unfortunate that when the judge did intervene during these discussions, with a man and a woman in the dock, he chose to deal with the matter before the jury only on the basis of whether '*a man*' might have been in front or behind the chair, rather than 'a man or woman'.

If a blow or blows had been struck from behind the chair by a right-handed person, he or she could not have inflicted such an injury as caused death on the left-hand side of Rattenbury's head. Only a left-handed person could have done that, but a right-handed person standing in front could and probably would have hit the left-hand side of the head.

The back of the chair might have made the second, midline injury difficult to inflict from the back unless Rattenbury's head had fallen forward after the first blow, as it probably did. This would equally have been a possibility if the assailant had been in the front. Why were these matters never made the subjects of enquiry? Certainly, despite the curious comment of Travers Humphreys on the bench, forensic pathologists would have regarded these matters as having a forensic medical interpretation on which they could have expressed strong views. It was not, as the Judge wrongly said, a matter only for the jury.

CHAPTER 13

The Prosecution Case Concluded

The remainder of the second day of the trial was taken up by
a procession through the witness box of six police officers, who
gave their account of the part they had played in the investigation. At the head came PC Bagwell, whom Alma, it was said,
had been so anxious to kiss.

No one said anything about the other person present at the
Villa Madeira on the night of 24 March, Alma's small son John.
He was clearly in bed asleep when the fateful blows were struck
and he was reputed to be a heavy sleeper, but such were the
activities going on in the house that night it is surprising he
was not disturbed, even when Alma was taken up to her bedroom, in which he was sleeping, and given an injection by the
doctor.

PC Bagwell, looking every bit the stalwart and honest town
policeman, was in due course questioned by O'Connor. The
object of O'Connor's first questions was to show that it was
unlikely to have been Alma who had hidden the mallet.

'Look at Photograph 2,' he said to Bagwell. 'In order to get
to the place where the mallet was found you have to bend down
and get under an overhanging tree?'

'Yes.'

'And the ground there looks pretty rough?'

'Yes.'

'Do you have to squeeze through a narrow passage?'

'Well, it is a bit narrow there, yes.'

'It is not the sort of expedition that anybody would be likely
to undertake in their bare feet, in their pyjamas?'

Bagwell had little experience, if any, of walking about gardens
with bare feet and in pyjamas, although Alma could have told

him a lot about it, judging by Irene's account of her activities. 'The ground is quite even,' Bagwell contented himself by replying.

'Do you think it is?' asked O'Connor, trying to ignore the rebuff.

'Yes.'

'Whoever went would have to crush in between the trellis work and the wall?'

'They would have just to bend down,' came the bland reply.

O'Connor had very little of significance to put to Bagwell, and Casswell put virtually no questions to him at all for Stoner.

When Inspector Mills had given his account of events at the house O'Connor asked him whether, when he got to the nursing home, he had said, as Dr O'Donnell had told the court, that Alma was drunk. He denied this and said that all he had said was that she had been drinking.

Mills had described in his evidence how, when he arrived at the house from the nursing home, at around 3.30 a.m., Alma, having been told of her husband's critical condition and having been cautioned by him, then said, 'I did it; he gave me the book. He has lived too long. He said, "Dear, dear." I will tell you in the morning where the mallet is.'

O'Connor, understandably, wished to challenge this, on behalf of Alma, and asked Mills, 'She said, "I will tell you in the morning where the mallet is." Did you ask her where it was?'

'No, I did not question her.'

'Why not?'

'I did not question her at all.'

'Did you not question her because you did not think she was in a fit condition to give intelligent answers?'

'No, not at all,' said Inspector Mills.

'Why did you not?'

'I had taken that statement.'

'Was this the first you had heard of a mallet?'

'That is right.'

'You knew this man had been injured with some heavy weapon, and here is this woman telling you, "I will tell you in the morning where the mallet is." I am suggesting the only reason you did not follow that up was because you thought you could not place any reliance on the statement?'

'Not at all. I started searching for the mallet,' said Mills.

'Why did you not ask her where it was?' rightfully persisted

O'Connor.

'I did not ask her.'

'That would have helped, if she knew?'

'Yes,' conceded Mills.

Clearly this was a competent and proper cross-examination, but the judge decided to come in. 'Do you really suggest, Mr O'Connor, if after a woman has said – believe it or not – that she was a party to a crime like this, this police officer would be justified in cross-examining her at all?'

Alma's counsel was duly rebuffed. 'I accept your Lordship's suggestion at once, and apologize for the question,' he said, and turning back to the witness, he observed, 'I'm not blaming you for not having pursued the point.'

It is difficult to decide which is the more surprising: that Travers Humphreys, a master of the criminal law, should have said what he did, or that a King's Counsel of O'Connor's standing – he was shortly to become Solicitor-General – should have allowed himself to be thus sidetracked.

In 1912 and in 1918 the judges of the King's Bench Division formulated a set of rules, called the Judges' Rules, to regulate the questioning of suspected criminals. These were certainly operating in 1935 when the trial occurred. Rule III, it is true, required that, save in very special circumstances, questions should not be put to a suspect after he has been actually and formally charged with an offence. Rule II, however, reads:

As soon as a police officer has evidence which would afford reasonable grounds for suspecting that a person has committed an offence, he shall caution that person or cause him to be cautioned, before putting to him any questions, or further questions, relating to that offence.

According to Mills' evidence, he had cautioned Alma and it followed, as the Judges' Rules provided, that there would have been nothing improper in asking Alma, as Mills should have done, where the mallet was. What the judge was thinking about is difficult to imagine. Certainly his comment was wrong and inappropriate, and with no less certainty O'Connor should have drawn his attention to the Judges' Rules and got on with his cross-examination.

When it came to Casswell's turn to cross-examine Inspector Mills, on behalf of Stoner, he had little to ask. He reverted again to the mallet, but only re-established that, when Mills had asked Stoner whether he had seen a mallet about the place, he had replied in the negative. Mills then departed to make way for Detective-Inspector Carter.

Carter's evidence retraced the events which had occurred while he was at the Villa Madeira, and he declared that, with his long experience as a police officer, he had no doubt that Alma clearly understood what she was saying when she spoke to him.

This was the first line of attack by O'Connor when he began his cross-examination.

'Had you ever seen this woman before in your life?' he asked.

'Never.'

'You took a statement from her at 8.15?'

'Yes.'

'And you have told us that she was then normal?'

'I did.'

'Did you say at the police court that she was quite normal?'

'I said she was normal, I know.'

'Did you say she was quite normal?'

'Possibly I did.'

'Was she quite normal?'

'Yes.'

Then came the familiar punch-line.

'How can you judge whether a person you have never seen in your life before was quite normal?'

'I saw Mrs Rattenbury when she woke up at 6 a.m. and she was then not in a normal condition, but it was at 8.15 that I decided she was in a normal condition, before I attempted to take a statement from her.'

After a few similar questions, O'Connor asked, 'Do you agree with Dr O'Donnell that no reliance could be placed on any statement taken from her at that time, 8.15?'

'No, I do not.'

The Inspector was not interested, he said, in how much morphia she had been given or how much drink she may have taken, despite the fact that he was taking a statement from her. O'Connor, continuing his attack on Carter's evidence, turned to the time when Alma awoke on the Monday morning.

'Did you intend from what you had heard to arrest her?'

'I had definitely made up my mind to arrest Mrs Rattenbury.'

'And the quicker the better,' suggested counsel.

'No,' replied the Inspector, 'otherwise I would have done that at six o'clock when she first woke up.'

'What?' ejaculated O'Connor.

'I said "No." If I had been of the mind – the quicker the better – directly she woke up at six o'clock, I should have arrested her then – had I been of that mind, but I was not. Her condition at that time was not such as she should be charged, therefore I did not charge her at that time. I took the precaution of sending for coffee, sending her to have a bath, and waiting for her to be definitely normal before I charged her, and I asked her no question, I charged her immediately.'

He agreed, however, that Alma had vomited at that time and that her hand may have been shaking so that she could hardly hold the cup of coffee, but disputed that she was unable to walk, adding that if Dr O'Donnell had said that was so, it was untrue.

'Supposing', asked O'Connor, 'you had seen that woman, and had never seen her before, would you have said, "This woman is neither drunk nor incapacitated in any way from anything I can see"?'

'I should say so, yes.'

A number of further questions dealt with the movements of the police about the house, before O'Connor returned to the question of Alma's condition. 'Not only was this lady in your judgment fully in possession of her senses, knowing what she was saying, but she was able to read it out with a clear voice?'

'With deliberation,' replied the Inspector.

'With a clear, deliberate voice?'

'Yes, with deliberation.'

'None of that incoherence that you would expect from a person who had been drunk and drugged within a couple of hours? No slurring over or anything?'

'No.'

The Inspector revealed that he had verified with Mr Jenks that Alma had made arrangements, between six and seven o'clock on the Sunday, to visit him with Rattenbury the following day. He also indicated that the texture of the wood of which the mallet was made – it was rough wood – would be such that it was unlikely that fingerprints would have been detectable on it, irrespective of the presence or absence of gloves on the hand of whoever held it.

Casswell had few questions to put to Inspector Carter. He did, however, ask whether there were two swords hanging over the mantelpiece, above the very chair where Rattenbury was killed, and was told there were.

'And also a pistol with a heavy butt?'

'Yes, there was,' replied the Inspector.

'And the pistol with the heavy butt could easily have been used to give this man a very bad hit on the head?'

'Yes.'

'And yet', Casswell effectively continued, 'for some reason or other apparently this mallet was used?'

'Yes, that is so.'

'I suppose there were other things about the premises which could have been used?'

'I suppose there were several.'

This was clearly an important point, rendering it still more unlikely that the purpose in fetching the mallet had been to kill Francis Rattenbury. It seemed quite irrational, when there were so many other weapons which could have been used, that Alma and Stoner would have been so stupid as to have brought a mallet from his grandmother's house with her knowledge.

Detective-Constable Sidney Bright, the next of the Hampshire constabulary to enter the witness box, was as adamant as Carter that, at 8.15, Alma's condition was 'normal' and that she spoke with deliberation. He saw in her none of the signs you would expect in a person who had been drunk or drugged.

'Would you have let her drive a motor car?' asked O'Connor in cross-examination.

For a young provincial police officer hitting people with mallets and making incriminatory statements was one thing, but driving a motor car was a horse of a very different colour. He hesitated. 'Well . . .' he said.

O'Connor urged him on. 'Why not, if she was quite normal?'

'But I didn't know whether she could drive,' which from the officer's point of view was logic carried to the maximum degree. Realizing, perhaps, that that was not quite the purpose of the question, he added, '. . . whether she is a fit person to drive a car,' which was no more germane to the question.

Pressed further he asserted that she was not in such a state that he thought she was under the influence of drink.

Detective-Constable Gates told the Court of the statement Stoner had made to him while they were waiting for the hearing at the magistrates' court, in which he 'confessed' to the crime, and he told Casswell that he was also the officer who had been called to see Stoner on the Wednesday night when he had been drunk.

'Was anything said by him or by any of the officers in your presence', asked Casswell, 'about taking "snuff" on that occasion?'

'I do not remember.'

'You know what I mean, do not you, by "taking snuff"?'

'Well, I have seen "snuff".'

'I mean by "snuff", cocaine.'

The second day of the trial was drawing to its close. The judge told the jury a great deal had been made of the statement which Alma had made at 8.15 on the morning of 25 March. Sometimes, he told them, you can get some assistance from a person's signature in judging whether they are capable of knowing what they are doing and what they are writing and whether they are in a fit state to write or not. He left copies of her statement with them overnight, together with, for comparison, copies of her signature on a number of cheques which had been put in evidence and which it was not disputed she had signed.

The newspapers continued to report virtually the whole of each day's evidence, giving front-page prominence to the trial, and only passing mention to what must have been a singularly unusual occurrence, namely that an Official Receiver in Bankruptcy had himself, that day, been made bankrupt.

When the Court reassembled on the Wednesday the foreman of the jury, having noticed that the mallet appeared to have been split in two from side to side, asked the judge whether it could be ascertained if it was in that condition when found by the police. The judge merely replied 'Yes.' O'Connor then told the judge that he had hoped in due course to call a Dr Morton from the prison, but he was ill and the prosecution had agreed that in the circumstances they would have no objection to the doctor's statement being read in his absence.

Bagwell was then recalled, in deference to the jury, to say he had not noticed the state of the mallet although he had handled it carefully. To overcome this indecision, Croom-Johnson said he thought his next witness might clear up the matter.

This was Dr Roche Lynch, a senior Home Office analyst. Roche Lynch had at that time built for himself a very considerable reputation – mostly for being inaccurate and unreliable.

A good example is documented in J. D. Casswell's own autobiography. He defended in 1936 a Mrs Bryan, also charged with murder, but on this occasion by arsenical poisoning. Roche Lynch gave evidence for the Crown to the effect that some ashes found under a boiler contained 149 parts to the million of arsenic. This, he said, was so abnormally large a proportion that it proved that something containing arsenic must have been burned in the boiler. A professor of science at the Imperial College, having nothing to do with the case, was so outraged when he read in the press what Roche Lynch had said that he got in touch with Casswell. He told him that as long ago as 1900 it had been established that the normal arsenical content of house coal was not less than 140 to the million, which was under the proportion found in the boiler ashes, and that usually it was about a thousand to the million. Thus, far from the arsenical content of the boiler ashes being excessive, it was remarkably below what could be expected. Moreover, on the hearing of Mrs Bryan's appeal against conviction (she was described in the autobiography as Casswell's second client to be hanged) the Solicitor-General, who may well have been Terence O'Connor, told Trapnell KC who had been brought in to lead Casswell for the appeal, 'Lynch had certainly made a dreadful blunder. He knew nothing about the contents of coal himself but got his information over the telephone. He must have misheard what was said. It's quite obvious he was wrong and you were right.' So much for the reliability of Roche Lynch.

Lynch was first asked about the mallet. He said that he had noticed there was a split but he did not bang it and there was no evidence that the two pieces were readily coming apart. He described his findings in relation to the mallet and had no doubt that it was human hair and part of the scalp that had adhered to it. Finally, he was asked in examination-in-chief whether he had made a study of the properties of cocaine and replied in the affirmative, but did not say whether this study had been conducted over the telephone, as had been his study of the proportion of arsenic and boiler ashes.

In cross-examination, by Casswell, he made an unpropitious start.

'Have you had any experience of cocaine addicts?' he was asked.

'No,' came the reply.

'In what capacity or in what position have you examined cocaine addicts?'

'I have not really examined cocaine addicts. My knowledge is based upon what I might call the toxicology of cocaine.'

He was asked if he was familiar with certain books on the subject. He had heard of one of them. Casswell having thus effectively established that, whilst Lynch claimed expertise in the chemical and toxic properties of cocaine, he knew absolutely nothing about and had no clinical experience of the symptoms of the drug-takers or its effect on their behaviour, proceeded to ask a series of questions on those very aspects of which Lynch claimed only ignorance. Arguably, such evidence was inadmissible and should have been forbidden by the judge. Only an expert is allowed by the rules of evidence to express opinions, in contrast to stating facts, and Lynch had disqualified himself, by being inexpert in these aspects. The judge, however, allowed the evidence to proceed.

Casswell was trying to establish that those who were addicted to cocaine suffered a condition called the 'cocaine bug' in which the addict felt as if bugs were moving around under his skin, although there was in fact nothing there. He also wanted to establish that addicts had periods of unreasonable jealousy and delusions of persecution, and that they might carry weapons, but even Lynch would not agree that cocaine was perhaps the most dangerous drug in producing violent criminals. He thought it would take months or years for a cocaine addict to become emaciated. Since his opinion on matters about which he had conceded he neither knew anything nor had any experience was quite valueless, it was to be expected that that would be the first matter which Croom-Johnson for the Crown would have clarified in re-examination. He ignored it. The rest of the re-examination, although no one involved in the case appears fully to have realized, could have been of very great significance.

'Cocaine', said the prosecutor, 'is, of course, sometimes given medicinally?'

'Yes.'

'Can you tell me what is the usual dose according to the British Pharmacopoeia?'

'Yes, one-eighth to one-quarter of a grain.'

'What is the colour?'

'It is a colourless, crystalline substance, or, when seen in chemist's shops, a colourless white powder.'

'Is it sometimes mixed with other substances such as boric acid?'

'Yes, it is, more especially when it is used by addicts for snuffing up the nose.' When mixed with other substances, he said, they were always of the same colour.

'Have you ever known cocaine that was brownish in colour?'

'No.'

'Or brownish with dark particles in it?'

'No.'

'If anybody had said that they had a heaped-up eggspoonful of cocaine could you tell us approximately how many grains of cocaine that would contain?'

'A heaped-up eggspoonful of cocaine – which is about half
a teaspoonful – contains about thirty-six grains of cocaine.'

'Would that be a fatal dose?'

'More than a fatal dose.'

'And if a spoon of the same size as you have in mind were
filled up level to the sides of the spoon about how many grains
would that contain?'

'About half, eighteen grains.'

'What would a fatal dose be to someone who was not an
addict?'

'It is difficult to fix accurately a fatal dose of cocaine, because
it affects people differently. The lowest recorded dose is two-
thirds of a grain and there has been recovery after a very large
dose. I should be inclined to say in my opinion ten to fifteen
grains would be the average fatal dose.'

'But the lowest recorded is two-thirds of a grain?'

'Yes.'

'Now, take a person who has taken eighteen grains. That
might, or might not, as I gather from your evidence, be a fatal
dose?'

'Yes, I think the chances are it would be a fatal dose.'

'Would a person who had taken such a dose exhibit any symptoms of poisoning?'

'Become desperately ill, yes.'

'Within what space of time?'

'Within a short space of time – within half an hour or less.'

'And how long would that condition last?'

'If death takes place, it takes place within an hour of the taking
of the poison. If they are going to recover, of course, they will
be some days before they are completely well again.'

'Would they be able to go about?'

'Not for twenty-four hours, anyway.'

'To drive a motor car within twenty-four hours?'

'No.'

Re-examination is limited to clarifying matters or correcting
errors which occur in cross-examination. Most of this evidence
elicited by Croom-Johnson had not arisen before, but Casswell
neither sought, nor was he afforded, any opportunity of putting
further questions.

Croom-Johnson concluded by asking a number of questions
directed to clarifying matters upon which the witness clearly
had no expertise. Then a juror asked whether a person using

a mallet in the way described would get blood on him. It was a sensible question in regard to an area which no one had attempted to canvass, but it was quite outside the expertise of Roche Lynch. Lynch said, 'I think if one single blow were struck it is quite likely no blood would be on the clothing of the assailant but if more than one blow were struck it would be quite likely to get on to the clothing. On the other hand I have seen cases where blows of this sort have been struck where no blood got on the clothing.'

Travers Humphreys, far from questioning what Lynch could possibly be expected to know about such matters, asked him whether it depended on whether the blood spurts out or not. When, however, the juror went on to ask about fingerprints, he did point out that it was not this witness's department.

Then another of those incidents occurred which, having regard to the quality of the judge and some of the performers, seems quite astounding, as did so many matters in this trial. Croom-Johnson, no doubt alerted by the juror's question to the fact that the prosecution had boobed once again, said to the judge, 'I have spoken to my learned friend and what I am saying I am saying with his approval, and I expect with the approval of my learned friend, Mr Casswell. Of course, both the accused persons in this case helped Mr Rattenbury to his bedroom where there was any amount of blood about, and it has not occurred to the prosecution accordingly that any deduction can possibly be drawn adversely to any of the accused on the question of blood being on their clothes.'

'I entirely agree,' said the surprisingly pliant O'Connor.

'That is very fair,' said the judge, and, turning to the jury, 'I daresay it answers your question. The probability is that you would find blood on both of them and the prosecution say finding it would lead to no deduction against them at all because in all probability that would come from the handling of the man that was bleeding.'

O'Connor must have had second thoughts. He rose to his feet. 'If I might add something to that. There is evidence that there was no blood on the lady's pyjamas. One would expect to find some but in fact there was none.'

That statement was inaccurate; there was no evidence that there was no blood on them or otherwise. No such evidence had been adduced although it was obviously not unimportant. This strange interlude demonstrated how badly the case had been presented. In the first place, the police-work was poor.

Possession should have been taken of the clothes the accused were wearing at the time and they should have been sent to the laboratory for forensic examination. Secondly, whilst it may have seemed just and gracious to acknowledge that no guilt was to be deduced from the presence of blood on their clothes, it might have been vital to the interests of the accused to show that there was, in fact, no blood on them at all. Moreover it is not, as Mr Justice Humphreys seemed to think, a mere question of whether blood spurted out or not; the nature, position and direction of blood stains may reveal a great deal. No one came out of this part of the trial with any credit.

In view of the cross-examination of Roche Lynch on the habits and behaviour of addicts, and perhaps realizing that he should have had properly admissible evidence available, Croom-Johnson sought permission to call Dr A. Grierson, the Senior Medical Officer at Brixton Prison.

Grierson testified that under his care Stoner had been normal in behaviour, rational in conversation, had taken his food and slept normally; he had also gained eight pounds in weight whilst in prison. In answer to Casswell, he said he had only had experience of one cocaine patient and if Dr Weatherly of Bournemouth, a brain specialist who was to give evidence later, were to say (as Casswell told him he might) that when he saw Stoner in prison his eyes were dilated and this was a sign of cocaine, he would not have thought that this was so. 'Many people', he commented, 'have normally dilated pupils.' He agreed that Stoner's pupils were not dilated now but he did not notice anything unusual on any other occasion.

Referring the doctor to Stoner's arrival at Brixton Prison, Casswell ascertained that he arrived there on 14 May. 'And the day', he continued, 'upon which he could have had the last dose of cocaine would have been 28 March?'

'Yes, that was the day of his arrest.'

'Do you really say you would expect to see distinct symptoms then?'

'If he was a drug addict I should certainly expect to find some signs and some desire for the drug.'

'I suggest to you that the desire for cocaine becomes more violent a few days after the effect of the previous dose has worn off?'

'That may be so. I do not know.'

'Have you any experience of it?'

'No. I do know addicts, if they are addicts, certainly crave for the drug.'

'If that craving had ceased by the time he came to you there would be no reason why he should not put on weight under the healthy diet and prison life?'

If Casswell thought that Brixton Prison provided a healthy diet he must have been singularly easy to please.

'I quite agree,' said the doctor, who it would also appear was no gourmet.

'Did he tell you he had been taking cocaine between slices of bread and butter?'

'Slices of bread,' replied the doctor. 'Not bread and butter.'

'And did he tell you he took a double dose at about 4.30 on the 24 March?'

'He said he took two eggspoonsful.'

'It has been suggested to Dr Lynch that two eggspoonsful would be more than a fatal dose. You would agree with that I suppose?'

'Certainly.'

'But it would depend', persisted Casswell, 'to what extent that cocaine was mixed with some other substance?'

'It certainly would.'

Casswell elicited the statement that cocaine sold by chemists was usually diluted. Re-examined by Croom-Johnson, the doctor said that Stoner had told him the large dose he had taken on 24 March had made him excited, and that cocaine usually made him curse and swear.

Then came still another important example of the general ineptitude of the trial. Croom-Johnson asked Dr Grierson, 'Did he tell you anything about the colour of the cocaine he took?'

'Yes,' the doctor replied, 'he said it was a brownish powder with black specks in it.'

'Is that the right colour of cocaine?'

'I have never heard or seen cocaine like that – of that colour.'

'Never?'

'Cocaine itself is what may be called whitish – colourless.'

Nothing more was made of this most important answer by anyone involved in the trial. It is also noteworthy that Dr Grierson was only summoned as a witness at the last moment, on an entirely different aspect. Here was Stoner giving a wholly unacceptable description of cocaine. It was highly improbable, if he had never seen cocaine, that he would have given such a description. If he did not know the colour of cocaine he might have ventured red, black, green, blue or brown, but it is inconceivable that he would have said 'brownish with black specks in it'. No one appears to have noticed, however, that Stoner's description, although nothing like cocaine, was an exact description of heroin. This strongly suggests that Stoner must have seen someone taking heroin and it raises the question whether this may not have been Alma. She was suspected of drug-taking and perhaps addiction in Canada, and her behaviour was more like that of someone on a drug of this nature than like that of someone who drank cocktails to excess. But no one caught on for a moment to the fact that Stoner had been describing not cocaine but heroin.

Trying again to make up the deficiencies in the preparation of his case, Croom-Johnson next called the Medical Officer from Dorchester Prison, of whose evidence he had likewise failed to give previous notice. Indeed, this brought a protest from Casswell, who sought, and was granted, further time to cross-examine later. This doctor also confirmed that Stoner's condition and behaviour in prison was quite normal.

The remaining Crown witnesses were merely formal, called to prove the purchases which had been made on the trip to Harrods.

'That', said Croom-Johnson, 'is the case for the prosecution.'

He sat down. It was now Alma's turn to present her case to the jury.

CHAPTER 14

Alma's Defence

The court room was exceedingly quiet and the atmosphere tense as Alma Rattenbury, dressed in blue with a chinchilla cape, made her way across the court towards the witness box. She made a striking figure; her feet seemed to tap their way quite steadily over the court floor. It was 12.15 p.m. as she took the oath in a quiet and virtually inaudible voice.

O'Connor asked her to try and help by speaking up and speaking slowly so that all might hear, and in answer to his questions she told the Court she had married Francis seven or eight years before; that she had been twice married and that her first husband had been killed in the war. Then he asked, 'You had no children by that marriage?'

'No,' she replied.

'You divorced your second husband?'

'Yes.'

'And by him you had a boy, Christopher?'

'Yes.'

'How old is he now?'

'Thirteen.'

'He is away at school, I think?'

'Yes.'

'Just to clear one matter up right away, did he suffer from glands some years ago?'

'Yes.'

'Was certain treatment prescribed for those glands?'

'Yes, arsenic injections.'

'Used you to administer those injections?'

'Yes, I went to the school to administer them.'

'With what instrument?'

146

'With a hypodermic syringe needle.'

O'Connor held up the syringe. 'Is that the hypodermic syringe produced here?'

'Yes.'

'Have you ever used that syringe upon yourself?'

'Never.'

She described some drawings which she attributed to her son John, aged six, which showed a person using a hypodermic needle and which the police had found in the house; and she explained that since the birth of John she and Francis had not lived together as man and wife, but occupied separate rooms. Then O'Connor asked, 'On what terms were you with your husband?'

'Quite friendly,' said Alma.

'No marital intimacy, but were you cordial?'

'Absolutely.'

'Was your married life happy?'

Alma half threw her hands up in front of her, and replied, 'Like that,' conveying, as a journalist in the *Daily Express* described it, 'timeless indifference'.

The same writer observed that as he had watched her enter the witness box he had the same kind of exhilaration as when at Lords, in a Test match, some great player goes in to bat. The stakes at a Test match were not, however, as high as in this trial, although both could equally result in the disposal of ashes.

Asked about quarrels and whether they were severe or trivial she said it all depended whether Mr Rattenbury got into a temper or not. She described the incident when she got a black eye, and was then asked, 'Used you to have to say things of which you are ashamed in order to get money from him?'

'All my married life, yes.'

'Tell him lies?'

'Yes, it saved rows.'

Stoner, she claimed, was engaged mostly as a chauffeur.

'Did you become Stoner's mistress?' counsel asked.

'In November,' she replied.

'Was that before or after he had come to live in?'

'Before.'

'Just taking it quite generally, from that time until your husband's death did relations take place between you and Stoner regularly?'

'Yes.'

'In his room or in yours or both?'

'Yes.'

'One or the other. What attitude did your husband take towards this, if he knew?'

'None whatsoever.'

'Did he know of it?'

'He must have known of it because he told me to lead my own life quite a few years ago.'

'As I understand it, there was no occasion on which you told him about Stoner, but your husband knew about it?'

'No, I told him I had taken him at his word and was living my own life.'

'Oh, you told him that, did you? Can you tell me when that was?'

'No,' she said, and then added, 'I would say it was around Christmas.'

'We have heard evidence of quarrels between you and Stoner, partly in your room and partly in Stoner's. Where would your husband be at that time?'

'In the drawing-room. He always sat there.'

'That is immediately below your room?'

'Yes.'

'Emotion', said James Agate, writing in the *Daily Express*, 'was plain for all to see in the hollow eyes of a woman, no longer young, and in the full red, moist lips, continually pouting and twitching. . . . Over and over again she knocked two questions into one . . . as when asked to say whether her banking account was overdrawn she replied "Always".'

'Was there an occasion', asked counsel, 'in the early part of the year when there was a quarrel between you?'

'Stoner and myself?' she queried, calling her lover by his surname as evidently she always did, and thus never losing the status of mistress in the better sense of that word.

'Yes,' indicated O'Connor.

'Yes.'

'An occasion when Riggs came into the room?'

'I cannot quite remember that but I daresay that is so.'

'What can you remember of the quarrel?'

'Well, I wanted to sever the connections on account of the difference in age, if you understand, and Stoner said' – she hesitated – 'well, he did not want to and that was all the quarrels were about.'

'What did he do on that occasion?'

'Nothing very much. He lost his temper, but it was not

very . . .'

'Was not very serious?'

'No.'

She asserted that Stoner had threatened her life but she did not take it very seriously. She said that she had contacted Dr O'Donnell because Stoner had told her there was something the matter with his head and that he had to take medicine twice or three times a year and that was making his head much more normal again. 'I could not quite understand it,' she commented.

This was a significant departure from the account given by the doctor, which the judge noticed. 'Do I understand that the only time Stoner spoke to you about taking medicine was on this occasion when he said that two or three times a year he had to take medicine for his head?'

Did Alma, perhaps, quickly realize she had blundered and hastily correct her account? 'No, he afterwards changed it,' she answered, 'and said he was taking drugs, and it was then that I got Dr O'Donnell.'

'Have you ever taken drugs in your life?' enquired her counsel.

'Never,' replied Alma, encompassing within that answer the period of her life spent in France and in Canada.

'At any time or description?'

'No.'

O'Connor carefully led her through the relevant events. The lie to her husband, the journey to London with Stoner, the return to the Villa Madeira and on to Sunday, 24 March. She told how in the morning her husband was rather depressed about his building project so she took him for a little drive and to the kennels to see her little dog's puppies. They lunched together, she said, but he was still depressed.

'After lunch what did you do?' she was asked.

'After lunch Mr Rattenbury went to sleep, and I played with John – you know the usual Sunday afternoon.'

'And did you have tea with your husband?'

'Yes – upstairs in my bedroom.'

'Who brought tea to you?'

'Stoner.'

'That was the usual practice, I think, was it not?'

'Yes.'

'Riggs was out, we know?'

'Yes.'

'Now, can you tell me this: after Stoner had brought you your tea what happened to the door?'

'The door was always open with a basket in between, but sometimes the basket would be moved, John might move it going backward and forward, and it closed.'

'On this particular afternoon was the door closed?'

'For a little while.'

O'Connor led Alma to the episode about the book, observing, presumably because the book contained matter with sexual connotations, 'We have maintained a discreet silence about the name of the book, so we will not mention the name.' Alma said that Francis had brought a book to the bedroom when he came up for tea and read her a page from it. She said that Francis was depressed and that after he had read the page from the book, he had said he admired a person who could ... At this point the judge interrupted her. 'You said he admired a person who could do what? What had the person done?'

'The person in the book', she replied, 'said he had lived too long and before he became doddering, as far as I could understand, he finished himself.'

'Committed suicide?'

'Committed suicide, yes.'

Alma went on to describe the arrangements she made to go to Bridport in the hope of cheering Francis up, and how Stoner came into the room carrying a revolver, which she had the previous day learned was a toy pistol. He was, she said, very angry, and as Francis would have overheard their conversation they continued it in the dining-room.

'What did he say to you,' asked O'Connor, 'about your relations with your husband?'

'He accused me of "living" with Mr Rattenbury that afternoon with the bedroom door closed.'

'What did you say to him about that?'

'I assured him that I had not, and he must put that revolver away and not make an ass of himself.'

'What did he say as regards the future? What did he say as regards how you were to behave in the future?'

The use of leading questions, by means of which O'Connor was suggesting the answers he required, became too much even for the judge. 'It is much better', he said, 'she should tell her story. You see you are putting it into her mouth; it is really much better she should tell it.'

Alma said Stoner warned her she must never have that bedroom door closed again and he would not drive to Bridport, because he thought she would have to share a bedroom with

Francis. She assured him they would have separate bedrooms; he believed her and it seemed everything would be all right. She described how she had put out Francis's suit for travelling and how, having played cards with her husband, she had let out the dog, Dinah, and closed the french windows after her. She then kissed her husband good-night and went to bed at exactly 9.30. She continued her description of the events of the night by saying she went to the bathroom and lavatory, but did not bathe, and when she returned to her bedroom – about five minutes later – the little dog had reached there ahead of her. She prepared for bed by removing all her clothes and replacing her pyjamas, made some preparations for going away next day, and climbed into bed. She got out again whenever she thought of something else to put into her suitcase and was reading a magazine when she heard Riggs come in. She went along to her bedroom to talk to her, which she did for ten minutes before returning to her own bed, after which Stoner came in.

'About how long after you had got back to bed?' asked counsel.

'That I am not certain about because I did not look at the clock.'

'I mean was it long? Minutes or what?'

'Well, I did think it was shortly afterwards, but after hearing the evidence here I have become rather confused in time; it seems later than I thought it was.'

'Had you seen Stoner till he came in?'

'Not all the evening.'

'Since the time you had seen him in the dining-room?'

'No, not all evening. Not that I remember.'

It is to be noted that neither O'Connor nor anyone else asked her whether she knew where he had been all that evening, bearing in mind the size of the house, the fact that he usually joined her when she played cards with Rattenbury, and the myriad possibilities his presence in the house might have presented. She said that when he entered her bedroom she thought he looked a little queer. He was dressed in pyjamas and got into her bed.

'He seemed agitated and right away I said, "What is the matter, darling?" He said he was in trouble and could not tell me what it was, so I said, "Oh, you must tell me," and we went back and forth like that for two or three minutes, and he said, "No, I could not bear it." I thought he was in some trouble outside, you know – his mother or like that – and then I said I was strong enough to bear anything and he told me he had hurt—'

151

'What did he say?' interposed her counsel. 'Put it in direct language, if you can. What did he say to you?'

'He told me I was not going to Bridport next day as he had hurt Rats. It did not penetrate what he did say to me at all until I heard Rats groan and then my brain became alive and I jumped out of bed.'

'Yes.'

Rats, it might be observed, had chosen a highly convenient moment to groan. Evidently he had not done so before or after, but had done so at the most propitious moment to give a measure of confirmation of what she said Stoner had just told her.

'And went downstairs?' O'Connor continued.

'Did Stoner say anything about how he had done it?' asked O'Connor by means of another splendid and improper leading question.

'He said he had hit him over the head with a mallet,' replied Alma, not in the least to O'Connor's surprise.

'Anything more about the mallet?' asked O'Connor helpfully.

'That he had hidden it outside.'

From there Alma was led, in every sense of the word, to describe how she had discovered her husband.

'Did you call for any help?' she was asked.

'Not right away. I tried to speak to him, and then I saw this blood and I went round the table and I trod on his false teeth, and that made me hysterical and I yelled – I cannot remember, only vaguely. I took a drink of whisky to stop myself being sick.'

'You yelled for whom?' asked her counsel, with another leading question, since she had only said she had yelled and not that she had done so for anyone.

'Irene,' she replied.

'Did she come down?'

'No.'

She went on to say she remembered being sick and pouring out another whisky but did not remember the police officers coming. In fact, she could remember nothing after putting a white towel round Rattenbury's head, the vomiting and treading on those . . .

Travers Humphreys interrupted her. 'Do you say you were sick after drinking the whisky?'

'Yes.'

Apart from that she could remember nothing.

'Mrs Rattenbury, did you yourself murder your husband?' asked O'Connor.

'Oh, no.'

According to an account given by Margaret Lane, the famous novelist, in the *Daily Express*, when this question was asked of Mrs Rattenbury 'the air in the hot Old Bailey court . . . was very still; only the silk gowns of Counsel ruffled stiffly as they leaned forward, waiting for the woman's answer. The woman in the dock [she must have meant the witness box] thrust her hands convulsively out from under her fur cape. For a moment the words would not come, and she moistened her lips wretchedly. "Oh, no", she said "Oh, no . . . no".'

It is proper to point out that the official shorthand typescript which, with great skill, records every word, merely attributes to her the answer 'Oh, no.'

'Did you take any part whatsoever in planning it?' asked O'Connor.

'No.'

'Did you know a thing about it till Stoner spoke to you in your bed?'

'I would have prevented it if I had known half – a quarter of a minute before, naturally.'

That was the end of her evidence-in-chief. Her defence was clear. She knew nothing of the murder; she had played no part in it, and it was pointless to ask her what occurred after she discovered her husband badly injured because she was suffering from total amnesia. It may seem to some that it is clever to elicit a witness's story by a series of leading questions, but, as the judge implied, it is really self-defeating, because if the words are put into her mouth by her advocate, it is he who is giving evidence and not the witness and, moreover, he is giving it from the contents of a written statement in front of him. Such evidence is, as a result, that much less credible.

To satisfy the enquiring juror, a police witness was next interposed to testify that no fingerprints could possibly be traced on the mallet. Casswell then rose to cross-examine Alma on behalf of Stoner.

Any hope of ever ascertaining the truth disappeared when he began by saying, 'Mrs Rattenbury, I want you to understand from the start that I am not suggesting that you had anything whatever to do with what happened on 24 March or that you ever incited Stoner, or knew that he was going to do it.'

The unfortunate Stoner, through his counsel, was evidently freely and openly admitting that he alone had executed the homicide. Understandably, what is usually called a murmur went round the court.

Casswell, in his first questions, which can be so vital, merely wanted to know whether she had had a manservant before. When she replied 'Yes, several,' he perforce asked whether she had had a chauffeur before, and she said no. He suggested she first had connection with Stoner at Oxford, which she denied, but she reiterated that it was on 22 November. She denied she had first suggested it and asserted it was mutual.

'Mutual?' queried Casswell. 'Because, you see, he was in the position of a servant, was he not?'

'Yes.'

'And quite a young man?'

'Yes.'

Here, at least, was the opening for an effective challenge of the veracity and reliability of the witness. The court waited anxiously for the next rapier thrust. It was, unfortunately, another blunted lance.

'Did you think it might have a very deleterious effect on him?'

It was a question the uselessness of which defies description.

'No,' replied Alma, 'I never would have started if I had.'

She said she did not tell him she was not living with her husband as man and wife because it was obvious, and she had not been looking to Stoner for sympathy. Nor was it an infatuation. She said she thought it was more than that. She absolutely fell in love with him, she told his counsel as he struggled manfully under the Poor Prisoners' Defence Act to earn his miserable fee.

'Now tell me,' said Casswell, 'when did you first come to the conclusion that he was taking drugs?'

'She has not said he was,' commented the prosecutor.

'He told me about his head, I think, some time around the beginning of November, but not as if he were taking drugs,' said the accused.

Casswell corrected this to 'taking medicine'.

'What you thought then was that there was a danger of his becoming addicted to it?'

'Yes.'

'Whatever it was?'

'Yes, but he assured me he was taking it less, and it was only two or three times a year, and that at the end of a few years he would not have to take it at all. I could not have him around with the children if he had been like that.'

'I understood you to say in evidence he said he was taking

drugs?'

'Yes,' she replied, 'later than that,' thus disclosing her real reason for concern to have been his presence with the children when he had something, as he said, wrong with his head.

She said that she took no further notice of it in November because he seemed quite normal.

'How did you expect to find him abnormal?' asked Stoner's counsel. 'In what way?'

'Well, it's difficult to explain,' she said. 'His temperament – he seemed to be so absurdly jealous at times, and that made me worried.' She said he did not get worse whilst he was with her and that she gave him various things – such as lighters – about the house because that was her disposition.

Casswell then asked a series of questions which at least raise the inference that his instructions differed substantially from the account she gave him in reply.

'Now, you told us you never took drugs yourself at all?'

'No,' she said, 'absolutely not.'

If that was the answer he expected, it is reasonable to assume he would have left it there, but he pressed her. 'You are quite sure of that?'

'Positive.'

'From time to time we have heard that you used to get very excited at times and then get drowsy afterwards?'

'Well, all my life with Mr Rattenbury was so – what we call – monotonous that at times I used to take too many cocktails to liven up one's spirits – take them to excess say, or wine.'

'And you say that was the result of cocktails?'

'Not spirits, not like that night, hard liquor.'

'Did Stoner take them also?'

'No, he was very much upset. He did not like me taking them; in fact, I stopped taking them after he came.'

Casswell asked Alma whether she had gone to see Dr O'Donnell in February because Stoner had been taking drugs and had been violent.

'I would not say violent,' replied Alma, 'more agitated.' She said that she could not stop Stoner going to London.

'Now,' continued Casswell, 'have you any doubt that that boy at that time had such a craving that he went to London and nothing you said would stop him?'

'To be perfectly candid,' she replied, 'I was not certain then, and I am not certain now. I cannot answer that and say yes or no. I do not know.'

Casswell later asked her, since she had learned from the doctor that Stoner had said he was taking cocaine, 'Did you do anything more about it?'

'No,' she told him, 'because Stoner was better from then onwards, and he said he could not get the drug, and I did not want to agitate him, in case he was longing for it and he went on just smoothly, and I never brought the subject up again. He said he had stopped it from then onwards, and, well, everything was all right. I thought he had.'

'I do not quite understand. You mean to say from that time onwards there were no more threats from him?'

'Not with the drugs.'

'What with then?'

'No, I am afraid that is a misunderstanding. I do not think I used the word "threat".'

'I thought Miss Riggs said – I may have been wrong – that you complained to her on several occasions that Stoner had been threatening you?'

'No, I am afraid that is rather an exaggeration to say threatening.'

'Not on several occasions?'

'No, he was never like that.'

'Did you know his age when he came to you?' asked the judge.

'I thought he was older,' Alma replied.

'Did you ask?' the judge rejoined.

'I thought he was twenty-two when he first came and afterwards he said he was nineteen.'

'How did you come to think he was twenty-two?'

'Because that is what he said.'

'He said so?' persisted the judge.

'Yes.'

'When did you learn that his real age was eighteen?'

'I think – I am not quite certain – on his birthday.'

Casswell took up the reins again. 'You advertised, did you not, for a boy between the ages of fourteen and eighteen?'

'Yes.'

It certainly seemed odd, since she had specified age limits in the advertisement, that Stoner had given a much greater age. Even he might have realized that such a lie would probably disqualify him for the vacancy rather than increase his chances of obtaining it. The rest of Casswell's cross-examination related, in the main, to the visit to London. It did not significantly advance matters, but before he sat down he asked Alma, 'Had you suggested somebody should get a mallet?'

'Oh, no.'

He pressed her further on this. 'Had you not?'

'No, absolutely no.'

The fact that Casswell put that question and then put it again clearly shows two things. First, that it was based on what Stoner had told him was the fact, namely that Alma had suggested somebody should get the mallet, and secondly that he did not believe her and did not, therefore, accept her denial. Indeed, all the probabilities must have been that getting the mallet was her idea and not Stoner's.

Margaret Lane, describing the trial, as it proceeded, in the *Daily Express*, commented, 'I doubt if anyone – even prosecuting Counsel – leading her through a maze of questions – can look without misgiving into the face of a woman on trial for her life. This woman, Mrs. Rattenbury, so discreetly well dressed in her Navy blue, with the little accustomed touches of feminine vanity in the daily brooch at her neck and the strong clips holding in place the level waves of her dark, heavy hair, has a haunted look in her face that gleams through the desperate effort of her self-control. . . . Prosecuting Counsel, Mr. Croom-Johnson K.C., got slowly to his feet, fixed her with the expressionless gaze of his grey, pouched eyes . . .' and put, in the silent court pregnant with expectation, his first two questions.

'Mrs Rattenbury, you appreciate, do you, that there is only one person alive who can check your story of what went on in this house from the time that Irene Riggs went out until Irene Riggs came back on that Sunday evening?'

'Yes,' she replied.

'That person is Stoner?'

'Yes.'

The fairness, relevance to Alma and, indeed, the propriety of that form of question must be doubtful. It was anticipating, as Croom-Johnson had learned or guessed, that Stoner was unlikely to give evidence in his own defence. It could be regarded as a backdoor method of criticizing, for the benefit of the jury, Stoner's expected failure to go into the witness box. The Criminal Evidence Act of 1898, which first gave an accused person the right to give evidence on oath in his own defence, expressly precluded the right of the prosecution to comment on his failure to do so.

He continued, 'Tell me this: you have already been asked what the point was in the journey to London with this boy whose mistress you were. What was the point if in fact you and he had been living together practically as man and wife since 22 November 1934?'

'I tried to explain that just now; it was all for Mr Rattenbury's benefit.'

'Mr Rattenbury's benefit?' Croom-Johnson echoed, incredulously, misunderstanding her use of language.

'Because I said I was going to London to have an operation, and I had to leave home.'

The objective which Croom-Johnson had formulated, assuming he had conceived one, was difficult to fathom from the course of the questioning. What was he seeking to establish in his questions about why she went to London? How did it advance his case to take further time by regurgitating her own evidence of her habit of telling lies to her husband to get money? How did it help him that she spent money on various things, when it came from her husband's resources with his consent and agreement? What did it matter, in the final analysis, that she bought Stoner expensive clothes in London? It all seemed fairly pointless. Obviously she had gone to London to have a good time and please her lover. So what? The fact that she was able with such ease to get money from her husband and spend it made her desire to murder him less likely, not more. The fact that she bought Stoner expensive clothes was doubtless to keep him happy and as a token of her appreciation of the sexual relief she received which she had previously been denied. All this was already well established in evidence before the jury.

It is difficult to select from Croom-Johnson's cross-examination any passages which could have been of great significance in the trial. For the most part he took her through the evidence she had already given.

Of course, in putting her story to her again he can be said to have been testing her veracity.

'Tell me this, Mrs Rattenbury,' he said, 'until Stoner told you during that time and in that bed about the mallet and about the hiding of the mallet, can you recollect any other occasion that evening when he had that opportunity?'

'You mean was that the only time in—' she began to ask.

'I am asking you this,' interposed the prosecutor. 'I am asking you this: you say that on that occasion he told you he had hit Mr Rattenbury with the mallet and had hidden it?'

'Yes.'

'Can you recollect any other occasion—'

'No.'

'—that evening—'

'No.'

'—when he would have had an opportunity—'

Alma was not waiting for the question but interrupting with her answers. 'No.'

'—of making that communication to you?'

'No.'

'Tell me one other thing—'

Now it was the judge's turn to interrupt his questions. 'I am not sure I follow that. Do you mean that after you found your husband injured, during the whole of that night you were never alone with Stoner?'

Alma seemed to be in some difficulty, although it was a plain question. 'Do you mean . . .' she began.

In view of her hesitation the judge commented, 'I thought it was quite plain, but I will put the question again. Were you alone with Stoner—'

'No.'

The judge ignored her interruption. '—at any time after you found your husband injured?'

She seemed to be flustered. 'Oh, after. No. I cannot remember that – after Mr Rattenbury was injured.'

'That was my question,' said the judge.

'No, my Lord,' she replied.

There are two things which are singular about this evidence, which counsel for the Crown might have been expected to pursue with some vigour. First, it seemed inexplicable that they should both have been in the house, not a vast mansion, after Rattenbury had been injured but were neither together nor in a situation where she knew of Stoner's whereabouts. Secondly, as her story was one of total amnesia only from the time she had the morphia in the early morning, why then could she not remember whether she saw or had any conversation with Stoner before the conversation which took place in her bed, which she clearly could and did remember?

She again described finding Rattenbury injured and said she poured out as much neat whisky as she could get down and was then sick.

'How long was that before the doctor came?' asked Croom-Johnson.

'I cannot remember the doctor. I cannot remember that. I am—'

'Cannot you remember the doctor coming at all?'

'I have pieced together from hearing here . . .'

Croom-Johnson half turned to look towards the jury. 'Are you telling the members of the jury that from the time practically you were sick and poured yourself out a glass of whisky that your memory does not serve you at all?'

'I can, yes, a few things. I remember like in an awful nightmare.'

'You remember, as I gather, placing a wet or white towel – I am not sure which it was – round Mr Rattenbury's head?'

'Yes, and I remember rubbing his hands and they were cold.'

'And according to you that is the last thing you remember?'

'I remember one or two things more.'

'Tell me the things you recollect on that night.'

'Nothing that night. It was a shock to me to hear—'

'Nothing that night?'

'No.'

'Do you recollect Dr O'Donnell coming?'

'I cannot.'

'What?' Croom-Johnson was again incredulous.

'No. I have tried so hard even with piecing from what I have heard to remember and I cannot.'

'Do you recollect the second doctor arriving?'

'No.'

So it proceeded; Alma repeating that she remembered nothing more than she had already told.

'Tell me,' said Croom-Johnson, 'had you a sunshade put up in the garden the previous year?'

'Yes.'

'Had you a mallet for that?'

'No! No mallet for that. We used to take – I think he used to put it up with the axe.'

'Was there any intention that day, Sunday the 24th, of putting up a sunshade in the garden?'

'Not to my knowledge.'

'Not to your knowledge. That day you had tea with your husband?'

'Yes.'

'Did you see the mallet?'

'No.'

After Croom-Johnson had once again canvassed her statements that she could not remember most of the later events, he asked, 'I am suggesting to you, you know, that Stoner never undressed that night?'

'Oh, he was undressed,' Alma replied.

'And had never been to bed?'

'Oh, yes; he got into bed.'

Croom-Johnson tried a new tack. 'Are you suggesting to members of the jury that you wanted to go to Bridport?'

'That I wanted?' she repeated, evidently not hearing.

'That you wanted to go to Bridport?'

'No, not I. I wanted to cheer Mr Rattenbury up to make a change for him and he did not want to go to London, so I suggested Bridport.'

'Did it occur to you that if you went to Bridport Mr Rattenbury might want to treat you as his wife?'

'No, if I thought it was going to happen like that I never would have suggested going.'

'You know what I mean by treating you as his wife?'

'Yes, exactly.'

'Were you fond of your husband?'

'I did not love him, no; I was more of a companion than anything.'

'If he had wanted his rights as a husband would you have been ready to grant them to him?'

'If he had wanted what? Oh no, I do not think so – decidedly not.'

'Were you fond of this boy?'

'I loved him.'

There was then a discussion about the bedrooms in which they had intercourse, and the fact that on the Saturday night they had had intercourse with the child John asleep in her bedroom. She explained that when her elder son was home she would go to bed in Stoner's room.

Croom-Johnson put to her the events of the later part of the night as described in evidence. She remained adamant that she could remember none of it and that her mind was a complete blank. When Croom-Johnson resumed his place the judge confirmed from her that she had a clear recollection of what Stoner said to her when he got into her bed, including the trivial detail that he mentioned hiding the mallet.

'Are you sure', he asked, 'that is when you learned that he had hidden the mallet?'

'Absolutely. I never spoke to Stoner again.'

'Well now, we have evidence that next morning you said to Irene Riggs, "Tell Stoner that he must give me the mallet." Did you say that?'

'I presume I did.'

'Do you mean you do not remember?'

'Absolutely not.'

'You must have remembered at that time all about it or you could not have said that?'

It was a difficult proposition to refute. Alma said, 'I wish I—' but the judge interrupted.

'Do you really mean', he said, 'that you have no recollection of any conversation you had with anybody?'

'No.'

'The whole of the time?'

'No, I felt as if I was the one who had been hit over the head.'

'But you remember quite well what was said to you, and every word that was said to you by Stoner, just before?'

'Oh, yes.'

'In bed?'

'Naturally.'

'You say naturally?'

'Well, I had not had that dreadful shock then. We were quite happy: I was quite happy then – life was different.'

She was insistent that she had not heard Irene and Stoner talking on the landing, although she later heard her husband groaning downstairs. She explained this on the basis that it was easier to hear what happened downstairs.

'When Stoner told you he had done this thing,' continued Mr Justice Humphreys, 'did you believe him?'

'No.'

'When you found your husband, did you believe him?'

'Well, I had to believe him then.'

'You did?'

'I hardly knew what to think.'

'Had you any doubt at all when Stoner told you he had hit your husband on the head with the mallet, and you went downstairs and found your husband had been hit on the head, that what Stoner had said was true?'

'Well, one would naturally think so, would you not?'

'I do not know,' said the judge. 'You are here to answer my questions. I would like to have a plain answer from you. Had you any doubt that what Stoner said to you was true?'

'I did think it was.' She said she did not, however, tell anybody of this at the time and the first person she mentioned it to was her solicitor.

When O'Connor rose to re-examine and to make good as far

as he could any damage which might have been done to her
evidence in cross-examination, he asked her, 'What was the
thought uppermost in your mind when you heard the news
from Stoner?'

'Upstairs?' she queried.

'Yes.'

'After he had actually told me,' she began, and after a pause
added, 'he was about five minutes—'

O'Connor interrupted her. 'After he had told you in your bed?'
he said.

'To try to protect him,' she at last replied.

This worried Mr Justice Humphreys. 'To protect?' he asked
in a rising voice.

'To protect him – that is Stoner?' asked O'Connor.

'Yes. Do you mean after I had seen Mr Rattenbury?'

'I mean when Stoner told you this story, what did you desire
to do as regards Stoner?'

'I thought he was frightened at what he had done because
he had hurt Mr Rattenbury. He wanted me to . . .' She stopped,
clearly uncertain where she was being led. 'He just sort of, what
I thought, hurt him bad enough to stop him going to Bridport,
and when I said I will go and see him then he said, "No, you
must not." He said, "The sight will upset you," and I thought
all I had to do was to fix Rats up and that would make him
all right.'

O'Connor referred to the evidence that she had told Inspector
Carter, 'He dared me to kill him as he wanted to die.'

'Has he ever dared you to kill him?' he asked.

The leading question misfired.

'Suicide has come in several times with Mr Rattenbury. In
the afternoon it—'

O'Connor had to stop the rot, 'Did he ever dare you to kill
him?' he asked firmly, and the penny dropped.

'No,' said Alma, 'not to my knowledge, except that he has
talked of suicide and said the gas oven and things like that;
that would be a dare. That is why I had the quarrel that night.
I was getting rather fed up with—'

O'Connor had to jump in. He saw that his latest leading question had indeed misfired and she might be getting into deep
water. 'Very well,' he firmly interposed. Then he turned to a
new statement, namely 'I picked up the mallet.' 'Do you have
mallets lying about the drawing-room?' The irony also misfired.

'I could not have picked it up; it would be an impossibility

163

to pick up a mallet that was not there.'

Wearily O'Connor said, 'What I was asking was: are mallets part of your drawing-room furniture?' But fearing a further lack of understanding he added, 'Have you ever seen that mallet before?'

'Never before in my life,' said Alma. She added that she first saw it in the Bournemouth police court.

'Did you hear the Police Sergeant say there was no sign of any struggle on the part of Mr Rattenbury? Did you hear that in court?'

'Yes.'

'Did you hear it said that the blow was probably struck from behind?'

'Yes.'

'"I hit him with the mallet,"' O'Connor read from the notes of evidence. '"I hid the mallet outside the house." Except from what Stoner told you, had you any idea where the mallet was for the rest of the evening?'

'No, I did not know where it was, because he said outside and I did not know where.'

The judge observed that, if you took Alma's statement and substituted 'Stoner' for 'I', it was all practically 'true'. It would then have been: Stoner picked up the mallet; Stoner hit him on the head with it; Stoner hid the mallet outside.

'My Lord,' protested O'Connor, 'with respect, no. You can hardly apply that to the story of going to fetch the mallet and bringing it back to the house and doing it in that way.'

This was rather difficult to fathom. Alma's statement had said nothing about going to get the mallet and bringing it back to the house. The judge was correct, but did not say where his observation was meant to lead. It would have been more to the point to explain why someone under the alleged influence of drink and suffering from total amnesia, should have given an accurate account of what occurred, blaming herself, but now said the same things occurred, but blamed Stoner.

As to Alma's alleged reference, in her statement to the police, that Rattenbury's son had done the act, she confirmed he was in Canada and had been there on the 24th; she also said she did not know what a coroner was, although she was said to have mentioned one.

O'Connor's last task in re-examination was to deal with 'a passage from something I am going to read a little later on.' He said, 'I want to ask you whether it corresponds or not with your recollection after the day of 24 March. This is what Dr Morton, the Governor of Holloway Prison, has written about you. "She was received into my custody on the evening of 25 March and I saw her early next morning for the first time. She was very depressed and seemed confused and kept repeating the same sentence over and over again. On 28 March she was somewhat better and appeared to have forgotten what she had said and how she behaved the previous days since her reception." Does that correspond', asked O'Connor, 'with what you recollect about your own mental condition during that time?'

'Absolutely.'

No one, however, mentioned, and it was not for O'Connor to do so, that she had been arrested that day, under distressing circumstances, that she had been taken from her home and her family and that she had appeared to be demonstrating classic symptoms of shock.

Alma's ordeal in the witness box was at an end, as was the presentation of her case. She returned to the dock beside Stoner and shortly afterwards the Court adjourned.

CHAPTER 15

Stoner's Defence

In opening the case for Stoner Casswell, addressing the jury, indicated that he would be calling evidence. He could not tell them, though, how unenviable was his task. He was advancing what could hardly be dignified by the name of a defence: that Stoner had acted under the influence of cocaine. He did not have the slightest grounds for believing it probable and indeed had no evidence available to show that it was even possible. If there was any reason for suggesting that Stoner had been insane, which there was not, he would have succeeded in shutting his client in a mental asylum, which some might see as a worse fate than the death penalty.

He told the jury, when he came to face the task before him, that they might think the case as presented by the prosecution to be a little perplexing. 'They have put both the accused in the dock and said, "We cannot show you one did it more than the other."' In fact, if the jury remembered, the prosecution had said no such thing. Croom-Johnson had opened the case on the basis that the prosecution suggested 'these two people ... with one common object and one common design set out to get rid of Mr Rattenbury, who stood in their way.'

Casswell recalled for the jury the case of Thompson and Bywaters at the Old Bailey some years before. In that case Bywaters, who was aged twenty, was charged with his mistress Edith Thompson, aged twenty-eight, with the murder of her husband by stabbing him to death in the street. Humphreys, as a junior to the solicitor-general, had prosecuted in that case. Both the accused were convicted and hanged, and there had been considerable public disquiet, including suggestions that the case for the Crown had not always been fairly presented. It is most unlikely that the jury had that case in mind, despite some of the similarities to the matter they were trying, but Casswell may have thought it wise, if he was capable of that degree of subtlety, to mention it to the jury, not for their benefit, but to remind the judge that his earlier case had brought some criticism and that he should be careful not to bring about a similar result in the case currently before him. Indeed, the judge may well have had that need in mind from the outset.

At all events Casswell said to the jury, 'If you remember that case, and have confused it with this in any way, think again, because in that case there was evidence beyond dispute that the two people before the jury were both there when the fatal blow was struck. You might have read about the case, since many doubts have been expressed as to whether one of those two people was rightly convicted. That is the sort of thing you will be particularly careful to see does not happen here. There must be no mistake. Can you imagine any crime which bears less evidence of having been the result of two people working it out before?'

He was on very strong ground here, and was putting the point well and forcefully. He continued in equally compelling terms: 'My submission to you is that the only explanation of this case is that it was the act of one, and the impulsive act of one, and I might add the mad act of one. What was the position of the solicitor who was asked to defend Stoner?'

He went on to explain how the solicitor had at once sought the advice of a psychiatrist, one Dr Weatherly, who, said Casswell, 'came to the conclusion without the slightest hesitation that the boy had been taking cocaine, had been taking it frequently and was in the position of what you would call an addict.'

Events might show that this was the problem with Dr Weatherly, namely that he had indeed come to such conclusions 'without any hesitation'. This is often the trouble with far too many so-called experts.

'This is the position,' continued Casswell. 'The Crown accusing two people, each one trying to take the blame on him or herself – a cocaine addict whose statements could not be relied on.'

That may have been true, it is to be noted, at one stage, but Alma had now made it clear that she was no longer taking the blame herself, but was putting it squarely on Stoner's shoulders.

'You can imagine', said Casswell, with a great deal of truth, 'that the defence of Stoner has been an anxious task. You can imagine that few stones had been left unturned and that every endeavour has been made to find out what is the truth.'

That statement was not quite so reliable. A fair analysis reveals stones, littering the place, which had remained unturned. One of them, if not a stone, was certainly a Stoner, named George – his own client, who carefully questioned and strongly advised might have revealed the truth of what had occurred.

'If this had not been a joint trial,' continued Casswell, 'if I could have been in the happy position of representing Stoner and Stoner alone [despite the presence of the co-accused, he was representing only Stoner and his duty was to him alone] I could have said boldly that the prosecution had not proved their case; the evidence against this boy is practically nothing. How can I do that when there is somebody else in the dock?'

This was a more difficult argument to follow. If there was, as he said, no evidence against Stoner on his own, there could still be no evidence against him however many people had been in the dock. Casswell alone knew what he meant by this. He said he intended to call Dr Weatherly, whom he described as 'one of the oldest and most experienced brain and nerve specialists in England' and also a Dr Gillespie. Certainly, he could not be faulted in describing Dr Weatherly as one of the oldest experts in England. He had been in general practice since 1873 and assuming he had qualified at the age of twenty-four this made him eighty-six years of age. He must also have been, poor fellow, one of the deafest experts on his subject since he had great difficulty in hearing what was said to him and had to leave the witness box for the well of the court in order to hear and comprehend the questions. The length of his experience was beyond question; the depth of his expertise, as events would show, was capable of more than one opinion.

Casswell told the jury that the two doctors had 'both examined the boy and would say they had come to the conclusion that the story he had told the prison doctor was correct, that at 4.30 on that Sunday evening he took what he called – nobody knew exactly what it was – a double dose of cocaine.' There are many things which experts can do but there are a number of things they cannot, and should not be allowed to, do and one of them is to usurp the functions of the jury. It was for the jury to decide whether they believed the prison doctor on the question of what he said Stoner told him. Even if they believed him, that proved that he said it and not that what Stoner told him had really happened. Unless Stoner went into the witness box and told that story, it remained unproved and it was certainly not permissible for doctors, however experienced and however old, to try to make up the deficiency by giving inadmissible opinions.

Casswell, who had made it plain he would not call Stoner in his own defence, then proceeded, mostly improperly, to give evidence himself to the jury, telling them of Stoner, 'He had for months been taking cocaine, perhaps as much as one dose every six days.' Apart from this statement from counsel, which in law was of no significance, there was not a shred of evidence to this effect. He then described the act as 'an insane fit of jealousy on the part of the boy; an insane and unreasoning jealousy which leads to a state of mind without forming a sufficient intent to make it a crime of murder'.

'What was the state of that boy's mind', he asked the jury, 'when he did, as he said he did, knock that man on the head with a mallet? What was his intent? It was a mad and unreasoning thing to do. It looks like the impulsive act of a child. What an absurd thing to use.'

This was hardly advocacy at its highest level. It might be queried of Casswell, 'What was the state of his mind in so presenting his case?' It is sensible to pitch arguments to ordinary members of the public in terms which cause them at once to relate to their own daily lives. It seems unlikely that anyone on this jury had children who so frequently coshed their grandfathers on the head with mallets that they could regard it as no more than a childish impulse, and they may have thought that, if you had it in mind to crack someone's skull with anything, far from being 'absurd' a mallet was as useful a sort of weapon to have in hand as any.

Casswell finished his address by suggesting to the jury that 'guilty but insane' was a possible verdict or they might come to the conclusion that 'the confusion in Stoner's mind was such and the toxic effect of the cocaine was such that he was not capable of forming the necessary intent to make the crime of murder'. Casswell had completed his address to the jury in opening Stoner's case and he sat down.

The fourth day of the trial opened with a request by O'Connor to have Rooke, the surgeon, recalled for further cross-examination on behalf of Alma. It transpired that Rooke had communicated with the DPP and Alma's solicitor, and had told them of his experience of patients under the effects of morphia. He said that, in his considerable experience of operating under spinal anaesthesia, he had given pre-operational injections of one-quarter grain of morphia, and patients lost their memory for events which occurred for up to two days after the injection. Answering the prosecutor he said he had never known retrospective amnesia involving loss of memory of events prior to the injection. Neither Croom-Johnson nor the judge asked him whether it was unusual to have selective or partial amnesia, or even a memory loss of a spasmodic nature. However, the judge himself had pointed out earlier by his questions that, if the police evidence was to be believed, Alma had remembered what (according to her) she had been told by Stoner about hiding the mallet, despite having morphia well within Rooke's forty-eight-hour period of amnesia.

At this point Casswell apologized to the judge. There was something, he said, which he had intended to tell the jury the previous day, but which he had forgotten to do. He sought leave to do so now. Leave was given and he proceeded to tell the jury about a recent decision of the House of Lords. This was the case of *Woolmington v Director of Public Prosecutions*, which had become one of the leading cases in the criminal law. He told the jury what the Crown must prove to establish the necessary intent in murder, saying, 'It was pointed out in the recent decision of the House of Lords ... if the accused's defence i⠆ "I did the act, but I had not sufficient intent owing to a disease of the mind" – which is the way in which we lawyers speak of insanity or drunkenness or of taking drugs – "which rendered me in such a state that I was incapable of forming that design", that is a defence.' (In fact, this was a reference to quite a different decision of the House of Lords.)

Casswell added that that was for the accused to prove and went on to say, to the surprise of many in court, including the judge, and many outside it, 'You have now heard the evidence of Mrs Rattenbury and on his [Stoner's] behalf I accept and endorse the whole of her explanation of the facts and matters which happened leading up to that day of 24 March, and what happened after that day. It necessarily follows that she, in my submission, did not commit this act, and had nothing to do with it, and the accused does not deny, in fact admits, that it was his hand that struck the blow. ... The onus therefore remains upon the defence to show you that when he struck the blow he, by reason, as I shall submit to you, of his addiction to cocaine, was incapable of forming the necessary intent, that is the intent to kill or the intent to cause grievous bodily harm.'

It is not without its irony that the case of Woolmington was one in which Casswell had appeared for the defendant who, in keeping with a number of his clients, had been found guilty of murder. When he appealed to the House of Lords it was decided that the case should no longer be left to Casswell to argue, that it needed a more senior person, and O'Connor had been brought in to lead him. The decision of the Lords had been given immediately before he decided to tell the jury about it. Few lawyers, moreover, would have accepted then or now his explanation of the meaning in law of disease of the mind.

Presenting his evidence on behalf of his client, he called, 'George Stoner.' The prisoner stood up, the warder opened the dock door, and he stepped down into the well of the court, followed by the warder, making his way to the witness box. No one had anticipated, in face of all that Casswell had been saying, that he had any intention of calling his client, although many may have thought he should have done so. Someone at the solicitor's table, presumably his solicitor or his clerk, uttered a loud, 'No, no, no,' and the warder, understanding what was going on, cried, 'Wait.' Someone whispered something to him and he took hold of the prisoner's arm and guided him back, retracing the steps he had taken into the well of the court and into the dock. It was George Stoner the father who was required.

Stoner's father now made his way into the court. A poignant figure, spare, with greying hair, he looked indeed like a useful bricklayer. He fingered his tortoiseshell glasses nervously as he entered the well of the court, glanced up at his son and smiled at him. His son, upset no doubt at the thought of what he had inflicted on his father, looked straight ahead. The father said that the accused had always been backward, had had little schooling, perhaps four years at most, but had an excellent character, never gave trouble, was always protective of his smaller friends, but after he had gone to Rattenbury's he had begun to look pale, with sunken eyes, which was particularly noticeable when he fell asleep in the chair, as evidently he was wont to do when he went home. Anyone who had any inkling of Alma's sexual appetite would not have been amazed. Presumably, however, the jury were being invited to assume it was all attributable to the drugs about which Casswell had 'given evidence' in the absence of any evidence being available.

At the end of Mr Stoner's description of his son's character, Casswell asked him, 'It has been suggested by some witness that your son said he found cocaine in your house, and that that first started him. Have you ever had cocaine yourself?'

Stoner had never said this, but, if Dr O'Donnell was accurate, he said he found cocaine 'at home', which might have meant Villa Madeira.

'No, never,' the father replied.

'As far as you know has there ever been any in your house?'

'There has been no cocaine, or morphia, or any drug of any description in my house,' he firmly replied, leaving no doubt that that was a wholly truthful response.

The prosecutor put a few perfunctory questions in cross-examination and the sad witness left the box, to be followed by Stoner's mother, an equally poignant figure. Why she was subjected to the ordeal was not apparent, since all she said was that her son called on her on the Sunday afternoon, at three o'clock or soon after and left at about 4.30.

The only witnesses remaining were the expert witnesses which Casswell had promised the jury he would call. Expert witnesses if they are to be called in a court of law need to be chosen with great care. Throughout the years there have always been a few who were truly expert in their field and were men of undoubted wisdom and experience. Equally, there have always been a considerable number whose only expertise is in being expert witnesses. The latter, if pressed hard enough, will generally say almost whatever is required of them.

Lawyers in general, and judges in particular, are often sceptical about the evidence of 'specialists'; to be convincing they must always show they have taken an objective view and are able to speak clearly, concisely and with undoubted authority.

Dr Lionel Weatherly gave his qualifications as a Bachelor of Medicine of Aberdeen, a Member of the Royal College of Surgeons, and President of the Society of Mental Nervous Diseases. Casswell was putting to him that he had also been Vice-President of the Annual Meeting of the British Medical Association, when the judge intervened. 'Dr Weatherly,' he said, 'would you mind answering, because the shorthand writer has to take your answer down, and he cannot take down a nod.'

'I am very deaf, my Lord,' replied the unfortunate doctor.

'Did you hear the question?' asked the judge.

'He asked me if I was President of a certain section last year.'

In fact, he had asked no such thing and the doctor had not been the Vice-President of the Annual Meeting of the British Medical Association. The judge addressed him again: 'If you hear the question, will you be good enough to answer the question, yes or no. Do not just nod. You understand the reason

– the shorthand writer has to take down your answer.'

'Yes.'

This was not the happiest of starts, since experts are always anxious, and wisely so, to make their presence and authority manifest from the outset. Moreover, the Court, as a result, was never to learn what he had vice-presided over since Casswell moved on to establish that he had for some years been the proprietor and residential licensee of Valebrook House, a private mental hospital at Bath.

The doctor said he had had three cases of cocainism under his care and several cases of other drugs, and that he had lived amongst mental cases all his medical life.

'You have specialized in that particular branch of medicine?' asked Mr Justice Humphreys.

'Absolutely. I have done no general practice since 1888.'

He said that he had seen Stoner at the prison on 8 April, and that he had read the statement Stoner had made to the police and the depositions.

'When you interviewed Stoner, did you notice any physical symptoms?'

'Yes.'

'What were they?'

'The physical symptoms,' repeated Dr Weatherly, 'I hardly expected to find it so long after the last dose of cocaine, that physical symptom was a very definite dilation of both of his pupils.'

'Did you test that with the light?'

'I tested it with the ordinary normal light and with electric light.'

'With what result?'

'With the result that the pupils did not react at all either to normal light or to electric light.'

'Is that consistent or not with the taking of cocaine?' led Casswell.

'Undoubtedly, it is one, and very important, and it is due to a definite cause.'

At this early stage the doctor was demonstrating that he would not be many lawyers' first choice as an expert witness. His academic qualifications were commonplace, adequate for the practice of medicine, but hardly in the front rank of expertise. His experience of cocaine subjects was very limited indeed; he had seen the subject under enquiry only once and evidently not for long; he was describing one symptom and attributing it to cocaine addiction when it could have had many other causes;

173

and he had not sufficiently established to the satisfaction of a true expert that the patient had really been on cocaine.

He said he did not find Stoner mentally deficient, but he was backward because his education had been interrupted.

'Physically, what was his condition?' asked Casswell.

'The boy was anaemic, a poor circulation.'

Casswell lunged in with another leading question, leaving the witness in no possible doubt about the answer he required and thus devaluing the weight of any answer he was given. 'Did you come to any definite conclusion as to whether he was an addict or not?'

'A very definite conclusion that he was a cocaine addict.'

For a doctor, and an expert, to express such a view on one meeting and on one symptom was about as valuable as if he had said he had come to the conclusion that he was a smoked haddock, rather than a cocaine addict.

'Did you form any conclusion as to how long he had been an addict?'

'I could only form that conclusion from what he told me himself.' He said he had found no other physical symptoms but added that Stoner had described to him 'fairly, feasibly and accurately the effects of cocaine which last some hours'.

'Did the description tally with your own experience?'

'Absolutely.'

Any lawyer listening to this evidence, in anticipation of cross-examining this witness, would be mentally noting the imperative need to ascertain how the doctor's interview with Stoner had been conducted, since what he had been told by this poorly educated young man might be crucial. It would be necessary to ascertain skilfully and with some care whether the doctor himself had suggested the symptoms to Stoner and thus induced affirmative answers. All this was never to be known, however, because no one ever asked.

The doctor said that Stoner had experienced the hallucination of touch, which was 'described in a way that I had never heard before, but it was very pathognomonic', namely he had a rash under his skin which 'seems to move about'.

'Is that a typical hallucination of cocaine?' led Casswell again.

'Oh, definitely,' came the expected answer.

This evidence, from an expert, was somewhat singular. First, he did not tell the Court the words Stoner used which described his symptoms in a way Weatherly had never heard before. Secondly, if he had never heard them before it was difficult, in making his diagnosis, to match them with his own earlier experience, if any. And thirdly, what he did attribute to Stoner, far from being unusual as he suggested, was precisely what Stoner's counsel, Casswell, had previously put to other witnesses as being contained in the published textbooks as a symptom of drug addiction. Asked how long a person would have to be an addict before such an hallucination appeared, he said it would depend on the constitution of the patient and the size and frequency of the doses he took.

'Supposing a man', said Casswell, 'were to take it in fairly large doses about once a week, how long do you think it would take then?'

'I should think two or three months at the outside.'

It is not known what was the reaction of those sitting in court to this examination. Most of the questions appeared to be founded on the purest fantasy. There was no evidence at all that Stoner had taken large doses once a week; no evidence that, had he wanted it, he could have had the money to buy it; and no evidence that he had any source from which to get it. Yet there *was* evidence that he did not even know what cocaine looked like. Casswell turned to ask Dr Weatherly to describe the effects of cocaine addiction with particular reference to hallucinations.

'The hallucinations of hearing and sight,' said the doctor. 'I had a case under my care of a doctor who took cocaine. He had the most horrid hallucination of sight. He saw insects crawling over his clothes, over his bedclothes, and it kept him in a terrible state of agitation.'

This sounded marginally worse than the horrors sometimes produced by expert witnesses. Even Casswell could see the danger he was now facing. 'I daresay we all know that that is one of the results of delirium tremens, is it not?'

'Yes,' was the reply.

Casswell had rightly anticipated that almost every symptom already described might equally be attributable to the effects of other drugs including alcohol, and to many other causes as well. Indeed, that, in effect, would not be an unfair summary of the whole of this witness's evidence insofar as he was describing clinical symptoms. Told that Stoner once carried a dagger he said that that was a common symptom of cocainism attributable to a sense of persecution.

'Are the descriptions of what Stoner did – the sudden threat with a revolver and his sudden turn of violence and threat when

175

she was telephoning – consistent with his having taken a dose of cocaine or not?'

'No,' replied the expert.

Casswell was flabbergasted. Here he was, feeding this expert doctor one splendid leading question after another and now he was refusing to take the bait. 'What?' he asked incredulously.

'No,' came the answer again.

'What are they consistent with in your view?'

'They are quite consistent with the story I heard as told by Mrs Rattenbury in the witness box yesterday.'

'You did not catch my question,' said Casswell, trying to hide the fact that he was a little beside himself. 'I was asking you whether the story she told was consistent with Stoner having taken a dose of cocaine that afternoon?'

At last he was home and dry.

'Yes,' said the doctor.

The judge was less happy. 'Are they also consistent with his not having taken a dose of cocaine, but being very angry and jealous of his mistress?'

'I doubt it, my Lord.'

'You doubt it? Very well.'

Casswell went manfully on. 'You have heard that the blow struck in this case was struck by that big mallet, and you have heard the other evidence as to where the mallet was put. Is that consistent or not with the after-effects of cocaine?'

'What on earth', interjected the judge, 'does that question mean? I don't know.'

The willing doctor did, however. 'I think', he said rather recklessly, 'any assault would be consistent with the after-effects of cocaine if those effects had created an abnormal, unreasonable and insane jealousy.'

Casswell ineptly elicited from him confirmation that had Stoner taken a dose of cocaine as large as the one he had told Dr Grierson he had taken, it would have killed him, but the doctor explained that cocaine was often sold adulterated.

After a small number of other questions which produced only highly inconsequential answers, Casswell asked, 'Is there any more you wish to say to my Lord and the jury about this case?'

'That', commented the judge dryly, 'is a rather wide question,' whereupon the trial lapsed into considerable confusion.

'I think I have told all I can tell, my Lord,' said the unfortunate Dr Weatherly.

'Apparently the answer is no,' volunteered Croom-Johnson.

Casswell decided to try bowling another ball. 'Dr Weatherly, are there any other conditions which, according to you, lead you to believe that Stoner had taken cocaine that day as he says.'

'I cannot quite catch that question,' said the doctor.

'Are there any other medical matters you desire to mention?' tried the judge.

'Any other medical matters?' echoed the doctor.

'Yes,' said the judge, 'that's what you are here for, you know – as a medical expert.'

'I do not think any more than I have already said,' replied the doctor.

O'Connor having indicated that he had no questions to put, Croom-Johnson began his cross-examination for the Crown.

'Dr Weatherly, have you known people get very, very jealous who are not drug addicts and not suffering from acute alcoholism?'

'I did not hear your question,' said the doctor.

The prosecutor repeated it.

'I have only had my experience that I have told you of definite cocaine addictism. I told you of one case of hallucination of sight. May I, my Lord, tell you of another case that I have had?' he asked, turning towards the judge.

Humphreys seemed as uninterested in hearing the doctor's anecdotal accounts as he was in his evidence generally. 'No,' he answered, 'try and answer the question. I am sure you can answer it. Do you know after sixty-two years as a medical man that some people get very jealous without cocaine or drink having anything to do with it?'

'Oh! of course,' was the reply.

'So far as pupils reacting or failing to react to light are concerned, is that quite a common symptom of many things besides what you call cocainism?' asked Croom-Johnson.

'I do not think so,' was the surprising reply.

'Have you given evidence in cases which have to do with neurasthenia?'

'I am not hearing.'

The question was repeated.

'I have given evidence in all sorts of cases on all sorts of diseases.' The witness was non-committal.

'Let me put the question in a perfectly plain form. Is not one of the symptoms of great nerve shock that the pupils fail to react to light?'

'Not in my experience.'

Croom-Johnson did his best to get from the doctor acceptance of the clearly reasonable and accurate proposition that the symptoms which he had indicated as existing in his examination of Stoner for part of one day were equally consistent with other causes. The doctor was clearly unwilling to make the concession, although good expert witnesses will always bow to the inevitable. Moreover, the witness, who may at his advanced age have been tiring, had increasing difficulty in hearing the questions.

'Do you hear?' asked the judge.

'No, I cannot, my Lord,' the poor old fellow replied.

'Perhaps it is my fault,' said Croom-Johnson generously. 'Is dilation of the eyes met with in many things besides cocaine?'

'I cannot hear. I cannot follow the question so I cannot answer.'

'Did you hear it? Did you hear the question?' said Croom-Johnson, beginning to wonder whether the doctor may have been exaggerating his inability to hear in order to avoid a straight answer.

'No,' said Dr Weatherly, 'I could not hear it at all and I could not answer.'

'Would you like to come a little nearer ... down here? Do you think you would hear better here?' asked the judge, indicating the well of the court.

The witness accepted the invitation, left the witness box and made his way to the floor of the court between the judge and the counsel, and further from the jury. Even from that position, however, his evidence contributed little that was significant to the sum of knowledge as it affected the case, and his evidence was no more illuminating when Casswell, shortly afterwards, re-examined him.

The next witness called on behalf of Stoner was Mrs Louise Maud Price, the owner of the Villa Madeira, who revealed that she also kept a tobacconist's shop. Her evidence was short and even more undramatic than that of the previous witness. She said that Stoner used to make purchases in her shop and on an occasion in February when he called she thought he looked exceptionally pale. Not surprisingly neither Croom-Johnson nor O'Connor thought this evidence worthy of challenge or, it is to be suspected, of much else.

The qualifications of the next witness called by Casswell looked far more promising. Robert Dick Gillespie, was, he told the Court, a Doctor of Medicine of Glasgow University and a Fellow of the Royal College of Physicians, and he held the Diploma of Psychological Medicine. He was a physician for psycho-medicine at Guy's Hospital, London and held other appointments. His principal activity, he said, was the study of functional, nervous and mental diseases. In the course of his practice he had treated cocaine addicts but there were few in England and still fewer consulted doctors. His evidence was sound on the symptoms which were to be found in addicts but threw little light on whether they had any application to Stoner, whom he too had seen only once in Brixton Prison. He said that the symptoms he looked for in a cocaine addict were inexplicable oscillations of mood, elation and, on other occasions, depression without ascertainable reasons, lethargy and tiredness and, later, more profound physical and mental effects. Sleep and appetite were interfered with, so that addicts lose weight. They become pale and emaciated; ultimately they hallucinate, develop morbid jealousy and do impulsive acts.

'You had the opportunity', Casswell said to the witness, 'of interviewing the accused Stoner in Brixton Prison last Saturday?'

'Yes, I did.'

'Can you tell us anything you noticed about him?' asked Casswell, giving him a very wide brief.

'I understand I am precluded from saying anything about his previous disposition.'

'You are entitled, I think,' explained Casswell, 'to give us any symptoms which he described.'

'At the time he was very tense and anxious, but I do not think it was relevant.'

That was all the doctor said in his evidence which related to Stoner, and it was hardly supportive of any suggestion that he found him to be, or ever to have been, a cocaine addict. He went on to elaborate on the effects of addiction, which were clearly highly competent observations but added little to the description he had given at the outset of his evidence.

'What is the effect of cocaine on the sexual male?' asked Casswell.

'In the male it produces very definite morbid jealousy, rather akin to the morbid jealousy of alcoholism, which, for example, is described by another authority in this country, Dr Sullivan.'

'Supposing a person to be under that morbid jealousy, is he likely to misinterpret what goes on around him?'

'Extremely likely.'

'Is that not true of all jealousy?' asked the judge.

'Yes,' said the expert, 'but I should have thought it was more likely to happen with a diseased jealousy.'

179

'Have you ever read the play of *Othello*?' the judge enquired.

'I have, a long time ago.'

Dr Gillespie agreed with Casswell that when addicts committed violence their conscience was often clear but they were unlikely to make a balanced judgment, weighing the pros and cons of a situation.

'Unfortunately, a great number of people in this world', observed Croom-Johnson, when he rose to cross-examine, 'do not think beforehand of the consequences of their acts. Do you agree?'

'I agree.'

'Perfectly healthy people?'

'Yes.'

'And perfectly normal people?'

'It depends on how you use the word "normal" but I suppose in ordinary language it would be so.' He agreed that one of the effects of cocaine was to reduce sexual power, before Croom-Johnson moved him into a field which hardly seemed to be covered by his expertise.

'Is regular sexual intercourse with a member of the opposite sex, by a boy of eighteen onwards, likely to do him good or harm?'

Without so much as a smile on his face, the witness answered, 'I should think it is a very difficult question to answer. I should not say that it did him good, if you are thinking of it from the moral point of view.'

'No,' said Croom-Johnson, 'I am not talking of it from a moral point of view. I am talking to you as a doctor. Is it likely to make him look pale?'

'I should not think that necessarily it would.'

'Would you think it likely?'

'It depends on the frequency with which it occurred.'

'Frequently, is my question,' said Croom-Johnson.

'It depends on what you mean by "frequently".'

'Do you think one would look sleepy or have the appearance—' Croom-Johnson was saying when the judge stopped him.

'I think you might take it in this way,' he said to the witness. 'To speak quite plainly, the learned counsel means as frequently as the nature of the woman would permit.'

This was hardly putting it plainly; indeed, without knowing both the woman and her nature it made it more obscure. An answer would first require an evaluation of the stamina, energy and sexual appetite of both the eighteen-year-old and the woman.

'In that case,' said the doctor, 'unless he was very worried about it, I should think it might not have any physical effect but it would obviously depend upon the constitution.'

'Is it likely to induce fatigue?' asked Croom-Johnson, presumably in all seriousness.

'Again the answer is similar to that I have just made.'

The doctor rightly persisted in refusing to commit himself on the bases of purely hypothetical questions. At least the jury may have realized, whilst this rather futile discussion was proceeding, that the one thing which most eighteen-year-olds do require is a good eight hours' sleep and if they are deprived of it night after night and engaged instead in frequent sexual activity they would certainly be likely to look tired, pale and probably ill.

When Dr Gillespie was being cross-examined on the effects of suddenly cutting off the supply of cocaine from an addict, the judge asked him, 'In those cases did you give something else?'

'I did.'

'What?'

'One of the other drugs that we fall back on to quieten the nervous system.'

'Bromide?'

'Yes, bromide, aspirin, etc.'

The evidence was nearing its end. Casswell asked only one question in re-examination before the judge said to the witness, 'Do you know in your experience any such case as this: a cocaine addict suddenly cut off from any supply, given no drug of any sort or kind to take the place of cocaine, and from the day the supply is cut off, for a period of two months, has been a person who can properly be described in this way: thoroughly rational, sleeping well, taking his food well, and been perfectly healthy?'

'I should be surprised, except on this one condition, that the doses had a considerable space between them. Then I should not be quite so surprised,' the witness replied.

'For how long after a dose of cocaine would this distension of the pupils continue?' asked an obviously intelligent juror.

'Quantities of cocaine have been found in the pupils for as long as twenty-four hours after the drug has been taken, but how long, still after that, it might in certain cases be observable, I do not know.'

The doctor left the witness box. The taking of evidence was concluded; it was time for the closing speeches by counsel, the summing-up and the jury's decision, which would determine life or death for Alma and Stoner, sitting anxiously in the dock.

CHAPTER 16

The End of the Trial

Commencing his final address to the jury Casswell reiterated that he had made it clear that Stoner did not deny that it was his hand which struck the blow, but he contended that such was the state of his mind that he was not responsible. He told the jury they had to decide whether the accused had the requisite intent or 'did he have some sort of intent merely to do something very different?' One has to assume that Casswell – an experienced junior counsel – had given thought at some stage to how he would put his case. His first endeavour had to be to persuade the jury, in simple terms, that they had open to them an acceptable way of acquitting his client. Even if one ignores the lack of any credible evidence that Stoner was under the influence of cocaine addiction, it remains difficult to know what Casswell was suggesting. The requisite intent which had to be proved by the Crown was to murder or, at least, to cause serious injury. Casswell was not arguing that his client did not know what he was doing but that he lacked the necessary intent. What then was he suggesting was such intent? It was certainly not an intention to hit his employer with three stout mallet blows to the head, so as to kill a fly that was on it. Presumably, Casswell meant an intent to injure Rattenbury, so that he could not make the journey to Bridport. But if Stoner intended to cause him serious injury for that purpose it was still a sufficient intent, if Rattenbury died, to amount to murder.

'How', he asked, 'are we to find out what was the state of Stoner's mind on that day ... and were the motives which actuated him when he did this act?' There would be little purpose, he suggested, in putting Stoner in the box, because that would not have helped the jury. He did not point out that had he really hoped to establish cocaine addiction, in the absence of any other evidence, it might have helped Stoner to have demonstrated, in evidence, his state of confusion. He said Stoner was under the influence of a drug at the time and 'what he would know would be of little assistance to you'.

He invited the jury to consider all the evidence they had heard. 'When you have looked at that,' he continued, 'I shall ask you to say that this crime is, in my submission, almost inexplicable in a young Englishman – you might, perhaps, expect it in a sadist, a man who killed for the joy of killing, a man killer – you might expect it in a man of hot blood and of a Latin race, urged on, perhaps, by jealousy or some kindred emotion, but is it the sort of thing that one expects in a lad of seventeen or eighteen and an English lad?'

It is to the credit of the English jury – as Casswell would no doubt have described it – that not one of them laughed or even sniggered. The idea that only a hot-blooded Latin and never an English lad of eighteen could clout his employer three times with a mallet was an odd proposition in the extreme. Moreover such evidence as he had called had been directed to the proposition that the blows had been struck in an irrational drug-induced fit of jealousy.

Having proceeded in this strain for a while, he then addressed himself to one of the more valid arguments available to him. 'The motive suggested by the prosecution', he reminded the jury, 'is this – it was put very forcibly by my learned friend and very fairly as he always does – "They wanted to get him out of the way." Whose way was he in? Here was a lad who probably had to look at every sixpence before this first job of his; there was nothing to keep him from what has been termed an adulterous intercourse; everything was ready for him, everything was there. There was no Mr Rattenbury standing in the way. As far as we know, Mr Rattenbury knew about it and did not care, or else he was in entire ignorance, and there is no evidence before you that here was a man in the way whom somebody wanted to get out of the way. Why should they need to get him out of the way? In order to live together?'

He pointed out, with some force, that had anyone wanted to get someone out of the way, they would have done it in a fashion which would not at once fix the guilt on one or other of them. There was an absence of motive, other than one which involved stopping the journey to Bridport. If there was a motive, the method employed was the clumsiest possible, including the obtaining of the mallet when there were already equally effective weapons in the house. There was no chance of an alibi and no possibility of escape. It could never have been presented as suicide and it would be inconceivable that it could have been an accident. It was an act of impulse, and one which was uncontrollable at that; but he was forced to explain that uncontrollable impulse was no defence, which made it the more curious that he should have told the jury that such was the cause.

He reminded the jury of Stoner's excellent and inoffensive nature and his history as it had been recounted. He described the household and Irene Riggs, who 'became and was jealous of this new helper in the house'.

So he continued until he came to the stage when Stoner heard Alma telephone to Bridport. 'What must I do?' he suggested must have been Stoner's reaction, making a valiant endeavour to provide the evidence which was missing due to Stoner's absence from the witness box. 'What must I do? Something to stop that visit to Bridport.'

'In my submission,' he urged the jury, 'that was the only intent in that poor lad's mind at nine o'clock at the Villa Madeira.'

It is unlikely to have been lost on the jury that, in contending that his client had a definite intent to cause the injury for such a specific purpose, it fitted ill with his earlier suggestion that his mind was so befuddled by cocaine that he could not form any intent.

After Casswell had reminded them of the statements which Stoner had made to the police, he invited the jury to find that his client was not in his right mind when he did this act and did not understand what he was doing. He concluded, 'I say to you as reasonable men and women that the verdict which you ought to find is one of these two: either he was guilty but insane or he was guilty of manslaughter only and not of murder.'

He resumed his seat.

It was a singularly muddled speech which was far more likely to have left the jury confused than responsive to any argument which could have assisted 'the young English lad'.

Next to his feet was the prosecutor Croom-Johnson. His approach was that the visit of the two accused to London less than a week before the fatal Sunday suggested that the opportunities available to them at the Villa Madeira were not sufficient for their purpose. He had hinted at this in his original opening but nothing had emerged in evidence which gave such a motive the slightest support. Doubtless, realizing this, he tried to cover the situation by explaining that a motive is not required in law to support a conviction for murder.

The question which arises, however, is whether, had the case been properly prepared, he might have been able to suggest a suitable motive. Alma clearly liked spending money and generally contrived to spend considerably more than she possessed. She liked the bright lights, the glamour of the metropolis, and her life with Rattenbury was, as she said in evidence, one of 'monotony', with sex limited to such as she could herself arrange with her acquaintances, of whom one, for sure, was Stoner. In their book *Tragedy in Three Voices*, the three authors, Havers, Shankland and Barrett, assert that Rattenbury had left his money equally to Alma's two children, Christopher Pakenham and his own son, John Rattenbury. This suggested that Alma had more to lose than to gain from her husband's death. It is, however, incorrect. His will, which was dated 18 December 1929, left to Alma all his jewellery and personal trinkets for her use absolutely, together with his 'automobile' and an annuity of $4,200 a year. The children only inherited, by the will, on Alma's death. The value of his estate here and in Canada was not shown in the aggregate, but manifestly it would have enabled Alma to live, at least, in the style to which she had become accustomed, with or without Stoner. Allowing for the change in the value of money over the last fifty years she could rightly have regarded what Rattenbury left as a very considerable sum. Why was this will never produced at the trial and why did Croom-Johnson not use it to support the motive that it was convenient to remove Rattenbury, because, without him, she would not have had to lie to get money, his wealth would have been under her control for life, and with or without Stoner she could have been relieved of the 'monotony' of her life?

Croom-Johnson asked the jury whether they had any doubt in their minds that throughout this unhappy story Stoner was dominated by Alma. He told them that in assessing Alma's story they must remember she was a self-confessed liar in the way she misled her husband or as he put it 'has been engaged in a constant life of the grossest deceit of her husband'. He reminded them of her pleas that she suffered amnesia, but rightly stressed that there was no evidence that those who took morphia ever had retrospective amnesia. She was given the drug at half-past three in the morning, why then could she remember nothing between finding her husband and that hour? He did not say so, but it was a convenient period through which to suffer a loss of memory since it covered the whole of the time when a story might have been cobbled together between Alma, Stoner and, perhaps, Irene. This may, of course, never have occurred and there was no evidence to support it, but it was, at least, a subject suitable for close enquiry. That period of amnesia also enabled her to have forgotten, and be unable to comment on, the evidence of PC Bagwell that she told him she had done the act with a mallet, that she immediately retracted it and then said that her 'lover had done it'. Croom-Johnson referred to each of her statements and conceded that Dr O'Donnell had declared he would not have accepted anything she said even at 8.15 on the morning after the assault; but the prosecutor invited the jury to accept that the statement which she made at 8.15 was both reliable and correct. He concluded that part of his address, which related to the position of Alma, with these words: 'Does it suggest to your minds that Stoner and she had a common object that night, that Stoner was the person who had gone away to fetch the mallet, and that she, thinking she was strong enough, had aimed the blow or blows at her husband's head, but [quoting her statement] "made a muddle of it"? For the purpose of examining as to whether the facts do not lead to that conclusion, I suggest for your consideration that you should consider whether it is right or not to come to the view, on the facts in this case, that Stoner was a person who was likely, to say the least of it, to be acting under her domination.'

With regard to Stoner he was on more fruitful ground and he made a number of forceful points. The first related to Alma's suggestion that, when he got into her bed, he had told her he had hurt Rats, which was wholly inconsistent with the way he behaved immediately afterwards. For some reason, Croom-Johnson stressed, Stoner remained quiet and watched her go to jail, 'and it is not until some little time afterwards when he makes first of all his statement to Irene Riggs and later on, when he makes his statement to the police, that you get any statement incriminating him'.

As to the verdict suggested by Casswell of 'guilty but insane' he drew attention to the fact that Stoner's statement, as Alma left under arrest, 'You have got yourself into this mess by talking too much' indicated a person in possession of all his faculties who quite understood the position. He also fairly commented that the things which, by common agreement, Stoner had got up to were hardly what the jury might expect from 'an ordinary

English lad of eighteen'. 'It is no good', he observed, 'inviting people to come to a conclusion of "guilty but insane" because they may not expect things of this sort to happen. His Lordship', he said, 'will direct you as to the effect of a statement by Stoner's own counsel that he accepted the position that Stoner is guilty.'

The judge thought it a proper moment for him to clarify the position. 'I think I ought to say at once', he said, 'that I shall tell the jury to put out of their minds entirely that statement, not only against Mrs Rattenbury but also as against Stoner. They have to decide the case upon the evidence and not upon any quasi-admissions which counsel may think it desirable to make from his point of view. Stoner is the only man who can say "I am guilty." His counsel cannot say that.'

'I anticipated that would be the direction your Lordship would give,' said Croom-Johnson, before telling the jury that for an insanity verdict there had to be something akin to disease of the mind; he reminded them that Stoner, after having taken two heaped-up spoonfuls of cocaine at about four o'clock (he omitted to point out that there was not a shred of evidence before them that that had occurred), had got into his master's car, driven three to four miles, borrowed a mallet, had a conversation, returned the three or four miles, arrived back, presumably about half-past eight, waited two hours 'before he struck the blows, which eventually ended fatally, somewhere about half-past ten, just before he got into bed with Mrs Rattenbury'.

He had been doing quite well but, muddle being par for the course at this trial, he had once again got the last part wrong. Casswell was on his feet.

'What story is that?' he asked angrily, reacting against Croom-Johnson's version of the evidence.

'He is talking of the story told by Mrs Rattenbury,' said the judge.

'That's not the story told by Mrs Rattenbury,' interposed O'Connor.

'There is no evidence of Mrs Rattenbury', persisted Casswell, not quite correctly, 'that the blow was struck later than nine o'clock and the evidence of the prosecution is that when Miss Riggs went down there the blood was clotted as if it had been there some time. I hope my friend [he had lost his 'learned' appellation], if he is going to suggest to the jury that this took place at half-past ten—'

'I am not,' interrupted Croom-Johnson.

'—will at least', continued Casswell, 'put his finger on the evidence upon which he bases his statement.'

'Go on, please, Mr Croom-Johnson,' was the judge's response.

Croom-Johnson tried to redeem his error. He pointed out that Alma had said she went to bed at 9.30, so the attack must have been after that, and that very soon afterwards, certainly not half-past ten, this man was in her bed, telling her he had done the injuries. Thus, without the slightest apology for his error, he had retracted and corrected it.

As he drew towards his peroration, he said, 'The object of my observation, when I was interrupted by my two learned friends, was to point out to you that if you accept the suggestions which are made on behalf of Stoner, they do appear to involve premeditation by him, carried out with premeditation over a fairly long time, some hours at the very least.'

There can be no doubt that, in contrast to those who had preceded him, when it came to O'Connor's turn to address the jury, he did so in terms which had been carefully thought through and which were delivered with very great skill and per-suasion. Having reminded the jury of the nature of their duty and heavy responsibilities, he urged them to separate in their minds the natural revulsion which they might feel against beha-viour which nobody would seek to condone or commend, to dissociate in their minds evidence of evil character and beha-viour, of ill or damage done to other people – to divide all these prejudicial elements and features of the case from the crime of which that person is arraigned.

He then turned to the arguments which had been advanced on behalf of the Crown, leaving aside the statements made by his client, Mrs Rattenbury. The first was motive. 'Is it suggested', he asked rhetorically 'that this designing, self-indulgent woman, as the Crown wish to make her out to be, would desire to exchange her comfortable middle-class surroundings with her car and villa and reasonably ample means for life with Stoner on a pound a week? I venture to suggest that the case of motive is so impalpable and flimsy that you will discard it out of hand.'

On the evidence O'Connor had every justification for saying that, but it would have been different had the prosecution in general, and Croom-Johnson in particular, done their homework and ascertained the terms of Rattenbury's will and the fact that Alma, without the burden of her husband, were he dead, would certainly have been no worse off financially – indeed, having control of the whole of his income for life, would have been substantially better off.

O'Connor next urged upon the jury the likelihood of Alma's story, that she rushed down to find her husband sitting in the chair badly injured, being true. 'The medical evidence', he said, 'shows that the blows were inflicted from behind.'

In fact, it will be recalled that Casswell had got himself into hot water with the judge and into argument with Rooke when he asserted the same thing and attributed it to the doctor. He had only said that the force came from behind the head towards the front, perhaps from the side, and not from a blow struck from behind Rattenbury, as appeared to be asserted. The second prosecution lapse was that they had not bothered to ascertain whether the accused were left- or right-handed.

O'Connor went on: 'If the case for the Crown is to be accepted, while she was talking to Riggs about the morrow's arrangements in this way, she knew that Rattenbury was bleeding to death in the room below. You have seen Mrs Rattenbury in the witness box. Can you credit her with such diabolical finesse, with such exact and careful preparation of her defence? . . . The suggestion of the Crown, of course, is that this was part of a premeditated scheme. Can you believe that possible?'

Clearly, it was indeed highly improbable. He did not, however, adopt the obvious argument, which Casswell had advanced that, if this was premeditated, it was the most incompetent plan for murder ever devised, with one or both of the two accused indubitably being caught and convicted for it. All indications were that what had occurred had happened in a sudden burst of frenzy or anger. But would it have been so inconceivable, if Alma struck the blows, that the two co-accused had urgently accepted that Stoner, if necessary, would take the blame? Since none of this had been canvassed by the prosecution, it was certainly no part of O'Connor's duty to do it for them. However, it is difficult to imagine that Alma had not known of the terms of her husband's will throughout or, at the least, before the commencement of the trial. It is odd, and indeed probably a measure of the negligence of the Crown, that they neither made any enquiries nor asked a single question of Alma when she gave evidence. It is also difficult to believe that O'Connor had not asked about the will and been told, albeit incorrectly, of its contents since it was an obvious subject for routine enquiry.

O'Connor turned, as he had promised, to consider the statements attributed to his client. Understandably he relied heavily on her first statement made at 2.00 a.m. on the fateful night, that she had rushed down to discover her injured husband, as she had told PC Bagwell. He no less relied on her repetition of this, in similar vein, shortly afterwards to Inspector Mills. He wholly repudiated as unreliable all her subsequent statements at the Villa Madeira in which she implicated herself. 'On no occasion', he told the jury, 'does she tell the police where the mallet is hidden. Can you imagine any reason for the omission other than the fact that she did not know?'

It was a fair proposition for him to advance, but had the prosecution really done its work this argument could and should have been foreseen and countered. First, one reason why she did not deal with the whereabouts of the mallet was because she was never asked. When O'Connor was questioning the police about this, during the trial, he was improperly stopped by the judge and he wrongly abandoned the enquiry. Moreover, if she had used the mallet, was it so unlikely that her lover had taken it and hidden it to protect her, in which case her absence of knowledge of where it was hidden was easily explained? O'Connor argued that by the time she left the house under arrest her befuddled brain was beginning to clear and that she hissed in Riggs' ear, 'You must find out where the mallet is.' In fact, he stated, what she said to Riggs was, 'Tell Stoner to give me the mallet.' He suggested that this clearly showed she was inventing a confession which she knew would be incomplete unless she could indicate where the weapon was hidden. That was not necessarily the case.

O'Connor was preparing to read some of the statements to the jury when his junior drew his attention to a notebook of one of the police officers in which the statement was contained. They had a whispered consultation together. This went on for some minutes whilst the judge and all in court patiently waited. Mr Justice Humphreys at last decided something had better be done and said, 'Mr O'Connor. . . . There is something which I noticed in the Inspector's notebook which may or may not have been noticed by counsel. It was entirely new to me and caused me some surprise. I thought counsel on both sides ought to see it before I handed it down. I was looking at something quite different. Of course that would not be admissible in evidence as a statement, but if you want to enquire into it, by all means finish your speech tonight and come back to it in the morning.' The judge had discovered a note in Inspector Carter's notebook which related to the statement made to him by Alma at 6.00 a.m. on 25 March when she first awakened and to which

Carter had omitted to refer in his evidence.

Meanwhile, O'Connor continued his address. He considered a number of arguments to show that this could not have been a premeditated crime, before putting in the knife for Stoner. 'Perhaps the most horrible part of my task', he said 'is, in the performance of my duty to Mrs Rattenbury, to have to call your attention to facts which clearly indicate that Stoner conceived and executed the crime.'

These facts, O'Connor said, were that Stoner was a lad of simple upbringing, few friends, no girl friends, and 'was flung at the age of eighteen into the vortex of illicit love'. He was, said O'Connor, unbalanced, melodramatic and given to violent outbursts; he had assaulted Mrs Rattenbury and gone about with a toy dagger and toy pistol. He was taken to a West End hotel and dressed sumptuously. The jury may have been impressed, but if all those factors were true (and some of them were not consistent with the evidence which had been called) they hardly added up to evidence of murder beyond reasonable doubt, particularly since O'Connor ignored a number of matters, such as statements by Stoner, upon which the prosecution more heavily relied.

Having again asked the jury not to judge Alma on her morality, he concluded: 'I beg you, as I began, to discount your horror at her moral failure and to remember that the worst misery which you could inflict on this wretched youth would be to convict her of something for which he knows she is not responsible.'

It did not fall to him to say, as a more objective bystander might have said, that equally the worst and most insupportable misery they might inflict on Alma would be to assist the wretched youth to shoulder the blame for deeds that were really Alma's – if, of course, they were.

O'Connor continued, 'Mercifully you may say to yourselves, "She has been punished enough. Wherever she walks she will be a figure of shame." That is not your responsibility; that is hers. Weigh carefully all the evidence, bearing in mind the considerations I have put before you, remembering that the Crown must prove its case unerringly to your satisfaction, and remembering that if you allow prejudice or moral turpitude to cloud your judgment and to blur the true issue, you will not be faithful to your oaths but you will be debauching the law and degrading our conception of justice.'

Our conception of justice, however, presupposes that every care will be taken and adequate skill employed to ensure that justice is achieved. Justice, he could have observed, is one of the most sensitive blooms in the garden of civilized society and, as with all blooms, requires infinite care. Was that care sufficiently evident at this trial?

The judge, it seems, had second thoughts about his proposal that O'Connor might consider how best to deal with the newly discovered contents of Inspector Carter's notebook, and brought O'Connor back to his feet. 'Mr O'Connor,' he said, 'I think on reflection it would be better, perhaps, that I myself should enquire as to the explanation of that copy in the book. If either of you desire to put any questions to the witness afterwards you can do so. Will you let me have the book, please?' The notebook was handed to him via the usher, and he asked, 'Who was the witness who produced this book? Let him come into the witness box.'

It was Inspector Carter, and he was recalled.

'Inspector Carter,' said the judge, 'you have told the jury that arriving at half-past four in the morning at the house you found Mrs Rattenbury asleep?'

'Yes.'

'At six o'clock she woke up?'

'Yes.'

'After about ten minutes you called for Miss Riggs to get her some coffee?'

'I did, my Lord.'

'Then at seven o'clock Matron arrived, and while Matron was with Mrs Rattenbury you went downstairs and did other work?'

'Quite correct.'

'You took a statement from the male prisoner. I want you to look at page 89 of your notebook.'

'Yes, my Lord.'

'Did Mrs Rattenbury make any statement to you about this alleged crime before 8.15?'

'No statement to me, my Lord. Mrs Rattenbury said the words that I have written in that book whilst she was lying on the bed, directly she woke up. I did not put them down in statement form. I did not refer to it in my evidence for this reason: when Mrs Rattenbury woke up, I said in my evidence that she was not then in a normal condition, and I did not caution her, and for that reason I made no reference at all in my evidence about those remarks that I put down in my book that she said. I was not entitled, in my opinion, to give anything in evidence if I had not previously administered a caution and in my opinion she was not in a condition normally to make—'

The judge interrupted. 'Then in your opinion she was not in a condition to make a statement at 6.15?'

'At 6.10. No, my Lord.'

'Then what she said at that time was something said by a woman who was not in a condition to make a statement which could be acted on?'

'Not in my opinion, my Lord.'

O'Connor was invited to put further questions. 'It is only the same thing as she said at 8.15?' he enquired.

'Very similar.'

'Word for word, is it?'

'No.'

'What are the differences?'

'Read it,' said the judge.

The Inspector read from the notebook, '"I picked up the mallet, and he dared me to hit him. He said, 'You have not got guts enough to do it.' I hit him. Hid the mallet. He is not dead, is he? Are you the coroner?"'

'With the exception of the statement as regards the coroner, the words are very nearly word for word the words which appear in the 8.15 statement?'

'With the exception of the words "He is not dead, is he?" and the question of playing cards.'

'This was at a time when she, according to Riggs, could not recognize Riggs?'

'I am not in a position to say what Riggs said.'

'This was before she had coffee and a bath?'

'Yes.'

Little more emerged from the few further questions which were put by Croom-Johnson. The judge told the jury that they would have to remain together for one more night, as it was too late both for him to sum up and for them to reach their verdict, and he adjourned the case to the following day.

The moment when the accused in the dock would learn their fate was fast approaching. Alma, who according to a report in the *Daily Mail* had sat motionless for some four and a half hours, appeared to sway and hesitate as she got up to return to the cells. 'She took a few uncertain steps', wrote Margaret Lane, 'towards the door of the dock through which she had come in many times during the last four days, but the wardresses beside her grasped her elbows and urged her towards the flight of stairs leading down from the inside of the dock itself to the cells below.

Thinking that she had become faint, spectators in the gallery craned forward, but her hesitation was due evidently to her confusion as to which exit from the dock she was meant to use. She walked steadily down the stairs without assistance. Stoner, his face still wearing the mask of bored indifference that has concealed whatever emotions he may have had from the very beginning of the trial, slouched down the stairs after her without so much as giving a glance.'

Thus the fourth day of this most unusual trial ended in a further exhibition of muddle brought about by inadequate policing and poor preparation. Certainly, Carter should have brought to someone's attention the statement which Alma had made when lying on her bed at 6.10 in the morning, as the judge was later to observe in summing up. That, from a sense of justice, he did not disclose it was commendable, but still wrong. Secondly, if the totality of the evidence was to be believed, Alma, that night and the ensuing morning, had been cautioned by Bagwell and Mills at different times. The law only requires that a caution should be administered before any statement or statements is admissible in evidence from a suspect. It does not require it to be constantly repeated by one officer after another. The judge has a discretion which enables him to exclude statements on the grounds of unfairness and it was, perhaps, fair that the statement which she made at 6.10 should be excluded as evidence for the Crown. In the way in which the case was presented for Alma by O'Connor, however, he might have wanted it admitted for her benefit. As it was, the point was neither taken nor argued; the existence of the statement was, in any event, adduced in evidence as has been described. It emerged only after counsel had concluded their addresses to the jury, and they were not afforded, nor did they seek, any opportunity to add to what they had said. The judge in his summing-up did not allude to its possible significance, if any.

What, however, was its possible significance? O'Connor relied heavily on the fact that Dr O'Donnell gave it as his opinion that none of Alma's statements, after having morphia, were to be treated as reliable. When he cross-examined Carter on his recall to the witness box, he sought to show that both Alma's utterances, at 6.10 and 8.15, were virtually identical. From this he was seeking to imply that if what she had said was unreliable, to Inspector Carter's mind, because of her condition at 6.10, precisely the same statement made about two hours later was unlikely to be any the more reliable. That, however, might not

necessarily be correct. It is, of course, for question whether a
police officer is the best person to decide whether a person's
condition is such that their statements should be relied upon,
but it was his judgment which was being accepted. If Alma's
statement at 8.15 was to be taken as reliable on behalf of the
Crown, then the converse of what O'Connor was implying
obtained and, when she said precisely the same thing at 6.10,
it could be no less reliable. Moreover, what was the significance
of her assertion on both occasions that it was she who had struck
the blows? It is anyone's guess what weight ought to be given
to such an admission, but the fact that the idea had been formulated in her mind on both occasions, whether she was then
affected by morphia and alcohol or not, must have some evidential force.

The judge commenced his summing-up to the jury when the
Court reassembled for the fifth and last day of the trial. He told
them in customary style that he alone could determine and direct
them on the law, but that they alone were the judges of the
fact; he explained that if two people agreed to murder or to
cause serious injury to another they were, if death resulted, both
guilty of murder. He described the fashion in which the Crown
had originally presented the case to the jury and said, 'You will
remember facts were elicited from witnesses on behalf of Mrs
Rattenbury as against Stoner and vice versa, and it appeared,
and apparently was so, that the prosecution was quite unaware
of that evidence. We know that Miss Riggs had made a statement
to Mrs Rattenbury's solicitor, who is instructing Mr O'Connor,
and apparently told that solicitor things which she had not
thought it necessary or proper to tell the police, and you may
think that as the result of that evidence as a whole, the case
that is made against these persons now, is rather a case in which
the evidence points, whether it proves it is quite another matter,
to Stoner as being the person whose hand caused the injuries
to Mr Rattenbury and that Mrs Rattenbury was a party to, but
not an actual assailant of Mr Rattenbury – party to a crime but
not an actual assailant.'

It was not, however, correct that the jury knew that Irene
Riggs had made a statement to Alma's solicitor; at one stage
of the trial she had been asked if she had made another statement, but to whom or what it contained had never emerged.
Moreover, the judge might have observed that she had clearly
given some evidence of facts which, if true, she had never previously disclosed to anybody at all.

He went on to explain that, if Stoner had struck the blows in Alma's absence and she had advised or procured the blows, she was equally guilty of murder, and the same result obtained if he did it in her presence and she had aided and abetted him. He gave the usual direction of the need for the Crown to prove the case beyond reasonable doubt, expressing the personal view that the words 'beyond reasonable doubt' were customary but unnecessary, because in English 'to prove' meant to establish beyond reasonable doubt; if there was a reasonable doubt it was, by definition, not proved. He explained that, although they were tried together, the case against each had to be considered separately. He outlined the essential facts and referred to Alma Rattenbury. 'It was not disputed', he said, 'that you should form an opinion in your minds of that woman's character, the sort of woman she is from two points of view. She has given evidence. Of the three people concerned in this tragedy, one is dead and can give no evidence, one has preferred to remain in the shelter of the dock and, although an admissible witness, has preferred not to give evidence, and so it is that in respect of many of the matters in this case, all that week beginning 18 March and ending on the 24th, the only person who has given evidence first hand about the events of that week is Mrs Rattenbury. . . . It is the case for the prosecution, as I understand, that this woman is a woman so lost to all sense of decency, so entirely without morals, that she would stop at nothing to gain her ends, particularly her sexual gratification, and if that be true, so say the prosecution, do you think that woman would stop at the killing of her husband, particularly if she did not have to do it herself, if she were once satisfied that that would enable her to live the sort of life she was living more comfortably or with less interference or prospect of interference?'

As far as it went it all sounded jolly good stuff, but it bore little relation to what the prosecution had begun to prove. They could have proved Rattenbury's will, which might have supported the judge's statement, but they had miserably failed to do so. Nor was there evidence to show that Alma could have lived as comfortably as hitherto, and O'Connor had made this very point to the jury. Similarly, there was neither evidence nor reason to believe that the continued presence of Rattenbury had or would have made the slightest difference to her ability, sexually, to satisfy herself with Stoner.

Mr Justice Humphreys pointed out the improbability of Stoner having said he was much older than eighteen when the advertise-

ment was for a lad between that age and fourteen; he referred
to the lies she told her husband to obtain money, which she
spent decking out her young lover. He warned the jury that
if they could have no feeling for her but one of disgust they
must not allow that to prejudice them against her when deciding
whether she was guilty or not.

As to Stoner, he said that one could not but feel pity for his
presence in the dock. He reviewed his excellent character and
difficult upbringing. 'It is a pitiable thing that he should be in
that position.'

He left the jury in no doubt that Irene Riggs had become jealous
of Stoner. 'He rather took the place which she had had,' he
said, adding hastily, 'I am not, of course, talking about sexual
matters, but that he took the place in the affection of Mrs Rattenbury which she had got.'

The Crown had to prove that the injuries which were inflicted
were the cause of the death. 'Look at this in the ordinary way,'
he said, 'and assuming it was not a performance by somebody
who wanted to give a performance' [whatever that meant] 'but
something which was a blow by a man probably behind Mr Rattenbury, or possibly at the side. I do not think it matters in
the least.'

It remains surprising that someone with the extensive experience of criminal trials which Travers Humphreys had should
clearly not have seen that this was quite incorrect and that a
right-handed person standing behind Rattenbury's chair could
never have inflicted the killing blow on the left-hand side of
his head. It is just as strange that no one ever ascertained whether
the accused were left- or right-handed. At least his comments
were unimpeachable when he said that it seemed a waste of
time, to him, to discuss the question of whether anybody could
ever deliver three blows of that nature to the head of a sitting
man without intending to do grievous bodily harm, but he would
have been on far safer ground had he added, 'unless it was
done in a frenzy induced by drugs or in a drug-assisted temper'.
He did, however, go on to say, 'I am not speaking now of the
question of whether the man was mad, or anything of that sort.'

That was, it may be thought, another unfortunate lapse when
addressing a jury which was, of necessity, one of inexperienced
laymen. There were in the dock both a man and a woman, and
to speak, however loosely, in a way which indicated only that
the assailant was a man, thus excluding the woman, might well
be taken by the jury as the wink which is as good as a nod

to a blind horse.

His comments were also far from impressive when he turned to the money which Alma had spent on Stoner during their stay in the London hotel. 'Do you think', he asked, referring to Rattenbury, 'that he was a man who would willingly find large sums of money for her to spend on her lover? Do you believe that while they were in London the future was not discussed? What were they going to do when they got back? Could life go on in the same way? Would not something have to be done about Mr Rattenbury? ... Do you think that those two persons in London imagined that life could go on just the same after their return, after an absence of four days, as before? We have not heard a word about it from Mrs Rattenbury and, most remarkable of all, I want to remind you now of what she said happened when she got back on 22 March.'

He then recounted Alma's story of how on her return she found her husband 'jolly', by which she meant drunk, and that he was quite uninterested in where she had been, what she had done, and even the nature and result of her operation. 'Do you believe that?' he asked, '... and if you do not believe it, if it seems to you to be utterly incredible, then, has Mrs Rattenbury told you in the witness box the truth, the whole truth and nothing but the truth, or has she not?'

This passage in the summing-up is indicative of a number of defects which too often prevail in the British courts. The judge told the jury that they alone were the judges of fact, but here, as invariably occurs, the judge is leaving the jury in no doubt that it is his belief that the defendant was not telling the truth. Why did he not leave them to form their own judgment within their own province? Secondly, it demonstrates how the judge is too often constricted by his own subjective judgment based entirely on his own experiences in what is, invariably, a wholly different way of life. What significance in real terms would an absence from the Villa Madeira of only four days have made to the two of them? Once again, there was not the slightest reason, within the evidence adduced or outside it, for believing that their activities would be in any way curtailed or limited in the future. The life they were living could certainly have gone on in the same way, and the reasons why he and the jury heard nothing of what was discussed between Alma and Stoner in London was simply because Croom-Johnson on behalf of the Crown did not ask her in cross-examination, as he should have done. Finally, in the atmosphere and the conditions under which

Alma and her husband were living, when he had reached the
level of a bottle of whisky a night, it was not merely plausible,
but virtually inevitable, that he would not have shown the slightest interest in her trip, nor perhaps cared or even fully realized
that she had been gone for four days.

The judge then took the jury through the facts as they related
to the relevant days. They must by now have heard it so often
that they could recite it in their sleep. When dealing with the
evidence of Irene Riggs, he observed, 'Then she said that on
one occasion in October 1933, Mrs Rattenbury had a sudden
attack. "She used to have attacks [he read from his notes]. She
was very excitable and ran about and then became drowsy, and
then she went to bed." The object of these questions, it turned
out, was, it was being suggested on behalf of Stoner, that Mrs
Rattenbury was addicted to drugs. . . . It is only fair to this woman
to say there is not a rag of evidence that she was ever addicted
to drugs, and whether Stoner was or whether he was not, if
he was, there is certainly no evidence that he got the habit from
her. . . . There is really no evidence that this woman was addicted
to drugs at any time.'

There can be no doubt that everything which Travers Humphreys had said concerning this aspect of the trial was wholly correct. No evidence had been adduced that Alma was so addicted.
It is interesting to note, however, that the judge had himself
noticed that Casswell, on his client's instructions, had been seeking to establish – albeit weakly and ineffectually – that Alma
took drugs. Unless Stoner knew this to be the truth, why would
he have allowed his counsel to put such a suggestion when he
was otherwise moving heaven and earth to protect her? Why
did that peculiarity in the situation occur neither to the judge
nor, it seems, to anyone else?

Between 24 March when the assault occurred and 27 May when
the trial began, only two months had elapsed. How could any
case of any size be properly investigated and prepared in that
space of time? It was prepared by provincial police officers who,
in those days, may have had limited experience, and does not
appear to have received the sort of skill and attention which
should be accorded to such a case by the Director of Public Prosecutions or the prosecuting counsel. Until it was cursorily raised
at the trial no one had ever really considered whether Alma
did take drugs. Why were no enquiries made at the chemists,
in the doctors' records, in Canada? And why did not someone
realize that when Stoner had wrongly described the appearance

of cocaine he was giving a textbook description of heroin? With his background and more recent habits, where was he likely to have seen heroin? Where, that is, other than the Villa Madeira?

The judge continued with his review of the case, suggesting, when he came to the fact that Stoner was seen asleep outside the nursing home whilst Dr O'Donnell was inside, that it was what five out of six chauffeurs would be found to be doing if they had been up for some hours at a quarter to three in the morning. That was perhaps correct, but the judge might have asked whether such sleep would have come so easily if they had earlier given an elderly man three devastating blows to the head with a mallet, and the victim was fighting for his life inside the nursing home?

He reminded the jury that when Stoner was later asked if he had seen a mallet about the house, he replied that he had not, which, the judge said, was untrue. But neither then nor at any other point of the trial did the judge or anyone else canvass the possibility that this young 'English lad' was simply covering up for his more mature lover, with whom he was infatuated to the point of self-destruction.

Methodically, the judge took the jury through all the statements and comments which, according to the evidence, Stoner had made, finally explaining that whilst statements made by others in the absence of the accused were not evidence against him, the evidence which Alma gave in the witness box which was adverse to him was admissible.

He was at some pains to mitigate the unusual behaviour of Casswell in his conduct of the trial. 'Members of the jury,' he said, 'as I intimated to you yesterday, a little mistake was made by those who thought that Mr Casswell, in his address to you, intended to say that his client admitted striking the blow. It would be quite improper for counsel, who was not going to call any evidence, to say anything of the sort, and it is not what Mr Casswell meant at all. All he meant was that, it being the case for the prosecution that they had proved in one way or another that it was Stoner who struck the blow, he was not in a position to, or at all events did not intend to call evidence, to contradict it, and therefore that he did not intend to address you on that part of the case, and he had to leave it there. Counsel is not in a position in a criminal case when his client has pleaded not guilty to make admissions on his behalf, and assuredly not in such a terribly important matter as that his client has done the thing for which he is being tried, and therefore you must pay no attention to that. .... As I rather expected would be the case, I noticed, as I left the court last night, that those newspapers which seem to regard this sort of terrible tragedy as a godsend to them, had found one thing, and one thing only, in the course of the day to put upon their posters and that was "Stoner's counsel says he commited the crime." That is just the danger of that sort of thing – the one thing that appeared on the posters.'

As the judge said, that was unquestionably the law at that time. Today, since the Criminal Justice Act of 1967, such admissions may be freely made in a criminal trial, but it is a fair reflection on the manner in which this trial had been conducted that such an improper admission should have been made. It was very clear that the construction which the judge put upon Casswell's address and the question of motivation bore no relation to what Casswell had in fact said and intended.

When he dealt with the so-called defence advanced on behalf of Stoner, he said, 'In this case it is not said Stoner was drunk, but it is suggested by learned counsel – I cannot say this was given in evidence by anybody – that you ought to find as a fact that, at the time, he was in such a state, owing to something which may have taken place in this case ... that you ought to say he was incapable of forming that intent. ... Here I have to point out to you something which you may think is the most important matter, and perhaps is conclusive, and that is that there is one human being who knows whether Stoner was in the habit of taking cocaine or whether he was not, and whether, if he took it, he took it frequently or once or twice, or all the rest of it, and whether he took it that afternoon, and that person is Stoner himself. Nobody suggests that he is insane; nobody suggests that he is suffering from the effects of any drug at all. He is an admissible and available witness, and if he wishes, or those who defend him wish, to prove that he is, or was, addicted to drugs – had ever taken cocaine – was then under the influence of cocaine – is there any witness on earth who can do it as well as Stoner?'

He stressed that Stoner had told Dr O'Donnell that he had acquired the cocaine habit from having seen cocaine in his father's house and said that that was untrue. The judge was assuming that 'home' did not refer to Villa Madeira. He went through the evidence of Dr Weatherly and rightly indicated that it did not begin to amount to evidence of insanity or much else; and as to 'the distinguished gentleman' from Guy's Hospital, 'he was not asked the question whether he found any symptoms about him of cocaine poisoning' when he saw Stoner in Brixton. Turning to the evidence that Stoner looked ill and worried, he asked, 'Is it not to his credit that he looked worried?'

The judge rightly described as an incredible story the statement which Stoner had made to Dr Grierson that he had two egg-spoonsful of a stuff he called cocaine of which Stoner had given 'a remarkably bad description'. And he concluded on this aspect by directing the jury, 'I have come to the conclusion, and it is my duty to deal with the matter, that there is no evidence, and I so direct you as a matter of law – no evidence upon which you can come to the conclusion in this case that the accused Stoner, if he was guilty of this crime, was insane at the time so as not to be responsible in law for his actions.'

No one could gainsay a word which the judge had said in this regard, and that he would come to such a conclusion ought to have been more than evident from the outset to the most inexperienced legal practitioner.

The judge then took the jury through the statements attributed to Alma in the course of the evidence, and repeated that Dr O'Donnell and Irene Riggs did not consider she was fit to make statements at any time between taking the morphia and leaving the house and that both Carter and his colleague did not feel she was fit to do so, prior to 8.15 on the morning of the 25th. He read from his notes of Alma's own evidence, but before doing so he gave his opinion in relation to the evidence of Dr O'Donnell: 'That is his evidence and I am quite sure that I am voicing the view you yourselves would form, that it seems to me that, after that evidence, it would be very unfair to form any conclusion against the woman on the ground of a statement made in those circumstances. It is quite a different statement [it was of course the one in which she admitted to striking the blows] from the statement which she made when she had merely taken some whisky.'

That was the most helpful statement which a judge could make for Alma Rattenbury, as every discerning person in court must have realized. In retrospect, however, one might consider whether the Crown, had it been properly engaged about its business, ought not to have had available some truly reliable forensic medical evidence which may have thrown an entirely different light on the mental abilities of Alma at the relevant time and the cause of her condition throughout that night.

By now the time had arrived for lunch, and, in adjourning, the judge asked the jury not to discuss the case over their lunch but to wait until he had concluded the whole of his summing-up.

On their return he concluded his reading of his notes of Alma's evidence and, having explained to them again the nature of the duty which they were required to perform, at 2.48 he sent them to the jury room to consider their verdict.

Then began what is always the most trying time for everyone concerned in any way with such a case, not least those whose fate depends on the decision of the jury. The cells below the Old Bailey have nothing to offer in the way of encouragement or cheer. They are dark, small, miserable places, little more than cubicles, closed with heavy wooden doors, with small windows protected by heavy iron bars. Those who enter them must, at once, experience a feeling of despair.

Upstairs in the large central hall, the lawyers engaged in the case, uncertain whether the jury will deliberate for minutes, hours or days, must remain close to the court room, and will pass the time as often as not pacing up and down, wondering, especially when hanging could be the outcome, whether there was anything they should have done which they omitted to do. In this case, it may be doubted whether anyone seriously considered that problem, despite the fact that there were many concerned who would have had good cause to do so.

Shortly before four o'clock, as the light was fading and afternoon was turning to evening, word went round the building, as in some mysterious way it always does, that the jury – after only fifty minutes' absence – were returning. Everyone rushed quickly to their places. The jury could not, they opined, have reached a verdict so quickly, in a case which had spread over five days; they must be returning for further directions from the judge on some aspect which was worrying them. The court was now so crowded that people were standing, packed like sardines, in the back. The atmosphere was electric.

There was the usual double knock on the door, and four aldermen entered carrying posies of carnations and anemones. They were followed by the judge, carrying the black cap, who returned their bow. He bowed to the court and the jury, who had already filed back from the jury room and assumed their places.

The Clerk of the Court, standing before his desk beneath the judge, turned towards the jury and asked, 'Do you find the prisoner, Alma Victoria Rattenbury, guilty or not guilty of murder?'

'Not guilty,' said the man on the front left nominated by the jury as their foreman.

'Do you find the prisoner, George Percy Stoner, guilty or not

204

guilty of murder?' asked the Clerk.

'Guilty,' said the foreman. But he added, 'We should like to add a rider to that: we recommend him to mercy.'

A graphic account was given by William Barkley writing in the *Daily Express*: 'Mrs Rattenbury had heard without emotion the jury foreman's verdict which set her free. Then came the foreman's words which condemned her young lover. She reeled. Her hands flew up in a quick gesture of shock, which might have been despair, might have been sympathy. She gasped. Her lips moved. [According to Margaret Lane in the *Daily Mail*, she cried, 'Oh no.'] She turned swiftly, with blank staring eyes, in the direction of the boy, who stood, unmoved and militarily erect, two paces from her. The wardress intercepted her and guided her, tottering, to the stairs which lead two ways from the dock.' Alma disappeared below. 'For a full minute Stoner stood there while the judge bowed his head over the court records, entering the sentence in a silence so still that the scratching of his pen could be heard. Women wept in the gallery. The two jurywomen, set and serious in countenance, averted their eyes as the judge's Clerk spread open the square foot of black cloth and placed it evenly over the white wig so that the judge could pronounce the death sentence.'

Margaret Lane took up the story in the *Daily Mail*: 'Brave as the boy had been throughout the trial, so uncannily brave that it had been scarcely possible to guess what resolution lay behind the outwardly calm face, he could not quite control his emotion at hearing the fatal words. His eyes dilated, staring at the Judge in a last supreme effort of self-control, his hands stirred vaguely from his sides, and grasped the edge of the dock, he swallowed painfully two or three times, and the knuckles of one hand began to tap with gentle monotony against the edge of the dock until the Judge's voice had ceased. Then he turned abruptly towards the stairway to the cells and was gone. Only a brief formality remained and for this Mrs. Rattenbury, weeping and incoherent, was supported back into court. There was a further charge: of being accessory after the fact. The Judge instructed the Jury to return a verdict of "Not Guilty". Her self-control gone, her eyes shadowed with exhaustion, and her white face smudged with tears this woman . . . hung limp and weeping in the strong grasp of the two wardresses who supported her. On their strength only – for her own had broken utterly – was she able to leave the dock and pass, what is ironically called a "free woman", for the last time down the steps of the Old Bailey.'

People in their thousands thronged the streets outside the Old Bailey. The police found it impossible to keep the road clear; too many wanted a cheap thrill. Inside, Alma was escorted to a room in a state of partial collapse. A doctor was fetched and she was given a bouquet of flowers, which Irene Riggs had sent in to her. A taxi was summoned and conducted to one of the doors. Alma appeared, accompanied by the doctor, entered the cab and was driven rapidly away, seen by only a handful of people. Stoner was taken back to the prison in custody to await execution.

CHAPTER 17

Aftermath

The taxi drove Alma to the home of her late husband's nephew, but some of the crowd, largely reporters, who had followed her congregated outside. Not unusually, the sympathy which her perilous situation had generated, whilst the trial continued and the shadow of the gallows fell over her, soon dissipated on her acquittal. She was free and the boy whom she had dominated, so the public had come to believe, was to lose his life. The police were called and they tried to clear the gathering away, but reporters in 1935 were no different from reporters today and a knot of them resolutely refused to be moved. Alma was made the more distressed by this and by the obvious and implacable ill-will which seemed to have arisen.

Another doctor was called and Alma was taken to a nursing home in Bayswater. It was reported that, as she left, one of those waiting outside called out that even if they took her to Bournemouth she would be followed there.

By the next day she seemed considerably better, but she evidently told Irene Riggs, who was of course again in attendance, that she wanted pink flowers at her funeral and wished to be dressed in pink in her coffin. Even making allowance for Alma's propensity for the dramatic this, understandably, occasioned Irene great disquiet. Alma carried a photograph of Stoner with her constantly and was urgent in her demands to be allowed to see him. She told her solicitor that no expense was to be spared in saving him. This, although it might be regarded as a small detail, may not have been without its greater significance. She had made no previous effort to provide funds for his defence, but had left him to the inadequate resources of the Poor Prisoners' Defence Act. Now that she was acquitted and he condemned, money was no object. It could have been a belated realization that she should have done more for someone she loved. It could equally have been indicative of the fact that she was enduring an intense sense of guilt that he was to be put to death for something for which she was partially or perhaps even wholly guilty.

Certainly, money was necessary now if he was to be helped at all. At the conclusion of the trial even the pittance available under the Poor Prisoners' Defence Act came to an end. That had been available only for his defence and there were no funds which could be used for post-trial activity. Stoner's father had been given permission to see his son and he told reporters that all the boy had said was that he was content since she had been set free.

Stoner's old grandfather had gone shopping in Bournemouth in the full expectation that his grandson would be acquitted. Quite why does not appear, other than that hope is never wholly absent. While he was out, news came to his family of Alma's acquittal. A *Daily Express* reporter arrived at the old fellow's home, and found the old man's son in the garden; the man asked the reporter for news of his nephew, George Stoner. When he was told, a search was made for the grandfather, who was brought home, heart-broken. When he had sufficiently recovered from the shock, a family conference was called. 'We must not leave the matter where it stands,' said the grandfather. 'We must do everything for an appeal.' His son, Stoner's uncle, told the *Express*, 'I would be willing to sell one of my two small houses to get the money together.'

The trial having concluded on the Friday, 31 May, no decision had been reached about an appeal by the following Monday, doubtless because money still had to be raised and decisions made by legal advisers. There was, however, a strong ground-swell of feeling that immediate steps must be taken to secure a reprieve for Stoner from the death sentence. It was believed that as a result of a nationwide petition, coupled with the jury's recommendation to mercy, the Home Secretary, who was then Sir John Gilmour, would be likely to recommend a reprieve. That would mean a life sentence for Stoner. Shoals of letters arrived at the family's home from all over the country.

Alma was still threatening suicide, but appeared slowly to be recovering, and spent some time reading through all the news-paper reports of the case, with a surprising degree of interest. That same night, Monday, 3 June, a friend took news to the

Matron that Alma was proposing to leave the nursing home. There was nothing which could be done to stop her and Alma, having packed, took herself with her friend to another nursing home in Devonshire Street.

She wrote a letter to Stoner, and one of her friends told the *Daily Express*: 'Mrs. Rattenbury never ceases to speak of Stoner. She took a photograph of him to the nursing home. She never seemed to be able to take her eyes off it. She cannot forget how she heard him found guilty of murdering her husband. She is very distressed but she is confident the worst will not happen to Stoner. "He is so young. I am sure he will be reprieved," Mrs. Rattenbury has said to me. She has gone into the question of how long he will have to stay in prison if the sentence is commuted to imprisonment for life. She knows a life sentence is twenty years and that the maximum remissions for good behaviour amount to about five years. "He would still be a young man when he is released," she exclaimed to me.'

By Wednesday the *Express* was reporting that Mrs Rattenbury, accompanied by a woman friend, had vanished from Bayswater. Well they might. On Tuesday morning, 4 June, she had travelled to Waterloo and taken the train to Bournemouth, leaving the train at Christchurch. She made her way to some marshland in one of the beauty spots of southern England, known as the Lakes. There she sat down and wrote a letter on an old envelope. Part of it read, after the date 4 June:

> Eight o'clock. After so much walking I have got here. Oh to see the swans and spring flowers. And how singular I should have chosen the spot Stoner said he nearly jumped out of the train once at. It was not intentional my coming here. I tossed a coin like Stoner always did and it came down Christchurch. It is beautiful here. What a lovely world we are in. It must be easier to be hanged than to have to do the job oneself, especially in these circumstances of being watched all the while.

She put the envelope back into her handbag and finished the cigarette she was smoking.

It so happened that William Mitchell, described by the press as a farmer, had been attending to a sick cow and as a result was in the vicinity of a tributary of the River Avon at a place known as the Three Arches Bend. He had noticed Alma walking across a field and thought she was picking flowers. He was surprised to see a woman there alone at 8.30 in the evening, so he continued to watch her. He saw her sit down and take off her fur coat. He looked round to see if there was anyone about who might be with her and when he turned back she had got up again. He saw her walk forwards with her arms swinging in a determined sort of way, a knife or dagger in her hand. She stood at the water's edge, amongst the irises and water lilies growing there, and plunged the weapon into her chest six times. Before the farmer could shout she had fallen into the water. He at once ran to her, but by then she was a distance from the bank. He tried to catch hold of her feet, but missed them, in the process almost falling into the river himself. He grabbed her fur coat and threw it towards her, calling to her to grab hold of it. Alma turned her head towards him and, so it was reported, gave a long cry which sounded like 'Oh!' before turning her head away again, ignoring the coat. Mitchell could not swim, and when he saw blood in the water he decided to rush off and get help. Alma Rattenbury had paid her price.

Meanwhile, arrangements had been made for an appeal to be lodged on behalf of Stoner. He did not know at once of Alma's death because no one was allowed to tell him. His solicitor broke the news when he visited him on the Thursday to discuss the appeal. Stoner cried like a child.

The inquest was conducted in a board room at Fairmile House, Bournemouth. It revealed that Alma had, indeed, stabbed herself six times, three of the wounds going straight into the heart. Death, the doctor who conducted the post-mortem said, was instantaneous, which is strange since she must have been alive up to the sixth stabbing. He considered she must have been dead when she entered the water, which made the farmer's belief that he heard a cry most improbable. When he was called to give evidence it was found, although it made no difference, that he was a cowman and not a farmer, and he said nothing about hearing a cry. A police officer produced her bag, which he found at the scene about four yards from the body. In it were a number of additional notes and letters whic'; the coroner proceeded to read. One read:

I want to make it perfectly clear that no one is responsible for any actions regarding the taking of my life. I made up my mind at Holloway to finish things should Stoner. ... It would only be a matter of time and opportunity, and every night is only prolonging the appalling agony of my mind.

Another read:

If I only thought it would help Stoner I would stay on. But it has been pointed out to me too vividly that I cannot help him. That is my death sentence.

Still another:

Thank God nothing stop me tonight. Am within five minutes of Christchurch now. God bless my children and look after them.

And another:

I tried this morning to throw myself under a train at Oxford Circus. Well; too many people about. Then under a Bus. Still too many people about. One must be alone to do anything like this. It is beautiful here and I am alone. Thank God for peace at last.

The verdict was 'that she died of self-inflicted injuries: not being of sound mind she killed herself'.

She died and was buried with that touch of theatre which had so often marked the life of Alma Rattenbury. Thousands of people arrived for the burial, mostly women. Irene sobbed, almost overcome with grief. Her favourite pink flowers predominated in the wreaths and sheaves of flowers. The crowd, estimated at over three thousand, swamped the churchyard, some of them leaning on the gravestones, others fighting for a better view. One wreath which came from Manchester bore the inscription: 'I am only sorry I did not offer you these flowers while you were still alive. You will understand, darling – J (who loved you).' A man wandered amongst the crowd obtaining signatures to the petition for Stoner's reprieve, which was receiving wide support, the local MP, Sir Henry Page Croft, having added his own.

By 15 June it contained 300,000 signatures but on 7 June 1935 great political events were occupying the minds of the English people and their representatives. Ramsay MacDonald's National Government resigned and the King invited Stanley Baldwin to form a new administration. It mattered little to Stoner and his supporters that Anthony Eden became Minister without Portfolio for League of Nations Affairs, but it was of some significance to them that the new Home Secretary was Sir John Simon.

On Saturday, 8 June, the clerk in the office of the solicitor representing Stoner went to see him with a copy of the notice of appeal, which Casswell had drafted. It is to be hoped that he had his client's authority to make the disclosure, but in his autobiography Casswell revealed a great deal about his instructions for the appeal. Stoner, he wrote, was in Pentonville Prison and when he was shown the notice of appeal he said, 'Yes, that's all right, but they don't know about the mallet.' The clerk told him that if, at last, he was prepared to speak, he should write what he had to say before the Monday morning.

On the Monday the clerk collected a letter from Stoner addressed to Casswell. In it he denied he had acted under the influence of cocaine or had anything to do with the killing. Casswell then disclosed what he described as the gist of the letter. Stoner began by saying that he had been misled and he had done this to help Mrs Rattenbury, that he would not have given the full story had she lived. 'I will start off by saying that I am perfectly innocent of the crime.'

He referred to the fetching of the mallet for an innocent purpose and said that on his return to the house he had put it in the coal-shed and then gone to bed. After about half an hour he had woken up and judged that Mrs Rattenbury would have gone to her room. He got up and was looking over the bannisters, as Irene Riggs had said, as she emerged from her door. He was, he said, looking to see whether the lights had been extinguished, because on occasions they had been left on. Then, having answered Irene's question, he went into Mrs Rattenbury's room. He found her in bed, in an apparently terrified state. She said, 'Hear him.' At that moment he himself heard a loud groan. She got out of bed and ran downstairs. He immediately dressed, all but his coat and waistcoat, and followed her, because he realized something was wrong. Downstairs in the drawing-room, he found Mr Rattenbury in the armchair with severe head injuries. Then, by accident, he came across the mallet on the floor, and he kicked it behind the sofa. Apparently Irene had not noticed it, and he did not want her to see it. Later on, when she had gone to telephone, he had hidden it in the garden. He then described how they had carried the old man into his bedroom and laid him on the bed, how he had motored to the doctor's house and afterwards to the nursing home. When he and the doctor arrived back at the house, Mrs Rattenbury was under the influence of drink; the doctor gave her morphia and put her to bed, but as soon as he had gone she came down again. That time Stoner carried her upstairs and put her to bed. In the morning he made a statement to Inspector Carter. If he had known then that Mrs Rattenbury had made any statements, he would have 'placed himself' in her position there and then. When she was arrested, he was terribly upset. He did everything that he thought would provide sufficient evidence against himself: that was why he had shown Miss Riggs where he had fetched the mallet from. Casswell disclosed no more.

Clearly, there was a great deal more that it was desirable to ascertain from Stoner. However, it would seem that he was not seen and questioned until he came up to London on the day of the appeal, because Casswell merely wrote that he saw him in the cells at the Royal Courts of Justice. Stoner then explained his presence on the landing, looking downstairs, in this way: 'I was trying to see if the old man had gone to bed so that I could go into Alma's room as usual.'

The appeal was heard by the Court of Criminal Appeal, as it was then called, on Tuesday, 18 June 1935. The Court consisted of the Lord Chief Justice (Lord Hewart), Mr Justice Swift and Mr Justice Lawrence. Stoner was again represented by Casswell. What occurred was predictable because it was a court over which Hewart presided and because of the established attitude of the appeal court – today called, not by any revolutionary change, the Court of Appeal (Criminal Division).

Gordon Hewart, history records, stands well placed to be one of the least satisfactory of the Lords Chief Justices of England – rude, arrogant, disputatious and with little of the milk of human kindness. His occupancy of that office had not been without its element of drama. As Attorney-General he had left the Prime Minister, Lloyd George, in no doubt that he expected the succession to the office, when Lord Reading, who was then the Chief, retired or died. Lloyd George, however, was anxious that Reading should become Viceroy of India, but for political reasons he was not anxious to lose Hewart as Attorney. Hewart, with much reluctance, agreed to a scheme under which A.T. Lawrence would become Chief, as Lord Trevethin, on the understanding that he would resign whenever required to do so. Reading became Viceroy, and Trevethin read in *The Times* one morning, whilst having his breakfast, that he himself had resigned. Hewart assumed office.

One of the problems with the Court of Criminal Appeal which appears to have been associated with it from its inception – certainly in the eyes of those who practise before it – is that one of its greatest concerns appears to be to reduce the ever increasing burden of work which it is called upon to perform. Thus the policy of the Court seems designed positively to discourage anyone from appealing, and to this end it has taken a highly legalistic approach to its duties. Stoner's appeal provided a good example. Before Casswell could even argue that Stoner wished to give his version and invite the Court to evaluate his story and perhaps order a fresh trial, he had to get permission from the Court to call him as a witness.

Casswell first argued that there should have been separate trials, a request to which Humphreys had refused to agree. It is questionble whether he was tactically wise in doing this, since there was no likelihood of success and it started him off on the wrong foot. He argued that the dilemma which Stoner and his legal advisers faced would have disappeared had they been tried separately, because Alma would have been tried first, being the first on the indictment, and if she had been acquitted, as in fact she had been, Stoner would have been free to tell his story; she could not be twice tried for the same offence. It was an attractive argument to place before laymen, but an affront to lawyers of the kind comprising the Court, implying, as it did, that in the result both of the accused might have got away.

Croom-Johnson, who appeared for the Crown, was not called on to reply. Hewart gave the appeal short shrift, trotting out many of the clichés which were then expected in that Court. Mr Justice Humphreys was a judge, he said, of great experience. This was undoubtedly true, but had the whole trial been properly analysed, as these pages have shown, he did a number of things which would not have been expected. 'It was apparent', Hewart said, 'that substantially the same difficulties confronted the defence, without reference to whether the cases were heard separately or together.' Precisely what that means is difficult to follow, but on any interpretation it is manifestly inaccurate.

As to calling Stoner as a witness to give his version, Hewart sought support from a judgment of Mr Justice Bray, in which he had said the Court would hear an appellant only in very exceptional circumstances, otherwise defendants would have to take their chance of not giving evidence before the trial jury. He said there were no exceptional circumstances in Stoner's case. 'Indeed,' he commented, 'the way in which the request that he should do so was presented appeared, when one examined it, to be almost cynical. It was desired that Stoner should now go into the witness box so that, after the death of Mrs Rattenbury, he might have an opportunity of swearing that which he was not prepared to swear while she was alive.'

A third argument, which equally might have been better omitted, that full weight was not given to the 'cocaine defence' was quickly dismissed, as was a suggestion that Mr Justice Humphreys had not properly appreciated the evidence. 'A man who was capable of believing that', said Hewart, 'was capable of believing anything.' It is just possible that there may have been quite a few lawyers about at that time who, on that basis, might well have believed everything. 'There is no need', concluded his Lordship, 'to reiterate the evidence of this sordid and squalid case.'

Hewart then trotted out another phrase which he constantly used and which reflected his common approach to such appeals: 'There is nothing at all in this appeal except that it arises out of a case of murder.'

The appeal was dismissed.

If the object of a court of appeal is to ensure that injustice does not occur, as indubitably it should be, what would these venerable gentlemen have lost, except time, in allowing Stoner to give his evidence? Moreover, if the circumstances in which he had placed himself were not exceptional, or very exceptional, what sort of circumstances were needed to make them so? One can imagine them saying to themselves, in whispered conversation across the benches, 'If we allow him to give evidence, we shall have everyone coming here and asking to do it.'

If it be correct – and who is to know? – that this very young man, infatuated and besotted by, and even under the domination of, a much older woman, had been unwilling, heroically, to endanger her, are the judiciary to be so remote from the realities of the world not to recognize the possibility of injustice when they see it? Stoner had not gone into the witness box and told a pack of lies. He had stood mute. The law of England gave him the right to do so. The justice of the question was whether or not he was guilty of murder. If there was any possible chance that he was not, how could anyone but the most insensitive autocrat stand aside and allow him to be hanged, because he had not observed what were regarded as the normal rules? This, together with many other cases in which similar attitudes have prevailed, reflects little credit on the system of justice of which the British are otherwise so rightly proud.

On Tuesday night, 26 June, reported the *Daily Mail*:

Stoner listened to the grating of the key in the door of the condemned cell at Pentonville Gaol, and watched the Governor, Commander Tabuteau, enter. He told him the new Home Secretary, Sir John Simon, had recommended a reprieve. Stoner's strange self-possession deserted him. He listened, almost unbelieving, to the Governor's words, and the long tension of weeks broken, sobbed unrestrainedly. He sat down, and buried his pale face in trembling hands, muttering a broken 'Thank you, Sir.'

Stoner served seven years in prison before being released on parole. His reprieve from the death sentence, and the substitution of imprisonment for life was granted to him barely three weeks after Alma had taken her life believing that Stoner would lose his.

CHAPTER 18
Was Justice Done?

Such then is the story of the Villa Madeira and those who resided in it, as they were affected by the tragic events of 24 March 1935.

It remains at least possible that the truth was to be found in the view, reflected in the verdict of the jury, that Rattenbury was murdered by George Stoner without the participation, knowledge or connivance of Alma. Upon any other basis, she could not have been acquitted whilst he was convicted. No one, however, is permitted to discover the secrets of the jury room, so it can never be known upon what basis they arrived at such verdicts. Were they satisfied that Stoner had gone to obtain the mallet from his grandmother, unbeknownst to Alma, entering her home for the purpose openly, and under the eyes of an independent witness? Did they believe that the frightful deed was done at a time when Alma was certainly in the house with her small son, she having not the slightest inkling of what was occurring when it happened? Did they assume that Stoner was left-handed and struck the blows from behind the chair, so that Rattenbury was surprised? Or did they assume that he was right-handed, as most people are, and achieved the impossible by hitting a violent and killing blow from behind to the left side of Rattenbury's head?

What, moreover, did they decide was the motivation for Stoner to have inflicted the terrible injuries? Was it, as the prosecution suggested, to get rid of the complacent Rattenbury, because he stood in the way of Stoner's and Alma's sexual activities, despite the fact that at no time had they lived with Rattenbury in the Villa Madeira in significantly different fashion from that which was likely to prevail had he not been there? Or was the motive, as Alma seemed to suggest, to cause sufficient injury to prevent Rattenbury going with Alma to Bridport the next day? At the risk of an indecorous pun, might they not have thought that that was, indeed, taking a sledgehammer to crack a nut? However infatuated, however jealous, however indignant a youth he may have been, could any sensible person believe that he, with his history and character, which no one ever disputed, would go to those lengths for such little purpose? Stoner had abundant confirmation from his own observation of Alma's assurance, as given to him and in evidence, that currently she had no sexual relations with her husband and had had none for over six and a half years. If any such desire remained, it could have been consummated with no less difficulty in the Villa Madeira than at Bridport. In their book *Tragedy in Three Voices*, Havers, Shankland and Barrett make much of information which they obtained from Mrs Kingham, who visited Alma in Holloway. Mrs Kingham claimed Alma told her, when asked why Stoner had done it, that 'he was angry because he had overheard Rattenbury telling her to make up to the man – presumably Mr Jenks at Bridport – who could arrange the finance for the projected block of flats, even expecting her to have an affair with him, if necessary'.

As a motive (which is what the authors of that book suggest it to have been) this seems even more improbable, if that were possible, than those motives already advanced. What splendid stuff it would have been to parade before the jury. This base and vile husband urging his spouse to prostitute herself so he could get the finance for his flats. What sympathy it would have aroused, not only for Stoner but for Alma as well. What is more, if Stoner heard it, so must Alma; why did she not mention it in evidence? Finally, does it have anything of the ring of truth that Rattenbury was urging her to seduce his sixty-or-so-year-old, happily married friend, the lord of the manor and a man of unquestionable probity, in return for a promise to finance her husband's flats project? As Lord Hewart would have put it, anyone who could believe that could believe anything. Did the jury believe that in the half to three-quarters of an hour between Alma's departure from her husband's presence in the sitting-room to the return of Irene to the house the assault occurred without Alma's knowledge? And that the blood had congealed to the extent, and in so short a time, as Irene described it when saw saw it?

In order to arrive at the verdict they reached, it would have been unnecessary for the jury to have believed that Stoner was under the influence of cocaine, and it must virtually be certain that they had rejected this suggestion. Indeed, there was no evidence before them on which they could have reached any other conclusion than that he did not take cocaine and clearly had not the remotest idea what it looked like.

Thus it has to be accepted that their verdict might conceivably have reflected a proper apportionment of the guilt and a proper reading of the true facts, but no one could be blamed for believing it more likely that they may have got it dreadfully wrong.

If proper care had been taken in investigating and presenting the case, might the verdict have been different? If so, the blame rests with the police, the Director of Public Prosecutions, the prosecuting counsel, to some extent the judge himself, and the absence at the time of requisite funds to ensure that someone of the stature of the advocate who defended Alma was available to defend Stoner. Casswell was excessively hampered by the instructions which he had received, and it might be said that it is unkind to criticize him on that account. On the other hand, certainly when it became clear at the beginning of the trial that Alma was intending to put the blame on Stoner, someone should have taken the responsibility of subjecting Stoner to a severe private cross-examination, and when the truth emerged, as undoubtedly it would have done, strong advice might well have persuaded him of the need to follow a different course from that which was chosen.

On closer investigation, and in the light of a full analysis of the content and conduct of the trial, does not a wholly different, albeit only a possible, scenario emerge?

On her own admission, Alma was distressed by the 'monotony' of her existence. There is, equally, no doubt that Rattenbury was in a state of considerable depression. Whether or not he actually read part of the book to Alma over tea, as she described, it is more than probable they had discussed the passage to which she drew attention. That passage outlined the frustrations of an old man, or one growing old, who sees his companion turn to others with greater virility and fewer years. It may have been true that Rattenbury did nothing to stop Alma's relationship with Stoner, but it would have been odd in a house that size had he not at least suspected what was occurring: it was far more likely that he was in no doubt at all.

In the course of his summing-up Travers Humphreys told the jury that Dr O'Donnell, 'who knew him well', had described Rattenbury as 'a very charming, quiet man, not at all of a violent nature'. Whether or not he was violent seemed hardly to arise since there could be no suggestion that he had hit himself three times on the head with a heavy mallet. Whether, however, anyone who had troubled to discover what had occurred in Canada, and the fashion in which he had treated his first wife, might have had cause to question whether he was so 'very charming' is a different matter. It is sometimes said that one of the penalties of old age is that a person's less attractive propensities tend to get worse.

There is little reason to doubt that a decisive factor in Alma's acquittal was the judge's observations to the jury, in summing up, that it would be very unfair to form any conclusion against the woman on the basis of a statement made in the circumstances which obtained on the morning of 25 March. He was referring to the statement which she had made after she was charged at 8.15 that morning when she had asserted that her husband dared her to kill him, that she picked up the mallet, and when he said, 'You've not got guts enough to do it' hit him with the mallet and hid it outside the house. Earlier when she awakened that morning she had said to Inspector Carter, 'I picked up the mallet, and he dared me to hit him. He said, "You have not got guts enough to do it." I hit him. Hid the mallet. He is not dead, is he? Are you the coroner?' This latter statement was the one which the judge found in Carter's notebook, but Carter had told no one about it because it was his view that she was not capable when she first awakened of making a statement. This view appears to have been accepted by everyone concerned in the trial. On the other hand, the first statement made shortly after 6.00 a.m. was virtually identical with the statement which she made at 8.15. If, as Carter believed, she fully understood what was occurring at 8.15 and virtually repeated the statement she had made at 6.00 a.m., it is difficult to see on what basis it was believed that the earlier statement was unreliable. Even allowing for the drug which had been injected, the jury ought perhaps to have been invited by someone, presumably the prosecutor, to consider the implications of her having made substantially the same statement twice, with an interval of something over two hours.

Is it possible that there had been an unpleasant argument that evening between Alma and Rattenbury, or that Rattenbury's depression had been such that the utter monotony of her life and the intolerable burden, as she believed, of having to live there with him overcame her? It seems inconceivable from what is known about her that Alma in anger or frustration and in her normal mind would have set about her husband with a mallet or any other instrument. It is no less inconceivable that a woman of intellect and intelligence would have conspired with Stoner, as the Crown suggested at the outset of the case, to rid herself of her husband without having contrived some plan which did not at once indubitably point to the guilt of herself or Stoner, or both.

Clearly, from the questions which Casswell put to her in cross-examination, he must have been told by Stoner that she was in the habit of taking drugs. Casswell regarded his instructions as placing a limit on what he could say to or about Alma, but he pressed her again, when she denied taking drugs, asking whether she was sure of that. The description which Stoner gave of the appearance of cocaine was an exact description of heroin. Moreover, Stoner's solicitor at the committal proceedings put it to Dr O'Donnell, on Stoner's instructions, that Alma was a drug addict. Taking those facts together, is it not possible that Alma was taking drugs and that one of them was heroin? In Canada there were a number of people who believed she had been on drugs and that this had originated from her contact with and experience of them during the war. Suppose, in her despair or frustration, following an altercation or even a discussion that made her miserable, she had walked from the sitting-room and taken some drug or other. On her return to the sitting-room she might, by then, have been high as a result of drug-taking, in a euphoric and far less controllable or normal state, and Rattenbury, having turned as usual to the bottle, may have gone on and on, moaning and complaining, to her increasing distress.

Might she not then have seized hold of or gone for the mallet and in a state of frenzy set about her husband, perhaps even shouting, 'You say you want to die. You tell me you want to die. You've lived too long anyway. Die, die, die' (to reconstruct a statement attributed to her by PC Bagwell) and, standing in front of him, using her right hand, have struck the blow on the left-hand side of his head which eventually killed him and, as his head fell forward, perhaps as she called out, 'Die, die, die,' struck him the lesser blows, more towards the back of his head? At a very early stage she had told both PC Bagwell and Inspector Mills, 'I did it with a mallet. He has lived too long.'

How would she have come by the mallet? There seems little reason to doubt that she had already asked Stoner to go and collect it. In the first place he would hardly have absented himself from the house, when he went to collect it, without getting her permission to go or at least telling her he was going to see his mother or grandmother. Even had he said nothing about the mallet, the likelihood would be that she would have seen him with it when he returned.

Casswell, when cross-examining her, again on obvious instructions, put it to her, though of course she denied it, that she had sent Stoner for the mallet. Moreover, as no one troubled to ascertain at the trial, Bournemouth that month had quite unusual weather, moderately warm – over 60° F – and it was not impossible that there was an idea of using the shelter as a wind shield to enable Rattenbury or Alma to sit in the sun.

The scenario would be more easily constructed if, on his return, Stoner had put the mallet down in the sitting-room or in the hallway. In his instructions for his appeal he told Casswell that he put it in the coal-shed. This was not marked on the plan produced at the trial. It is at least possible that, having seen the mallet put there, Alma had rushed in her drugged state to the coal-shed and retrieved it. It should be noted that no one described the actual state of the mallet and whether it had on it anything which looked like coal dust. It is a further matter for comment that, in any case, the mallet was never sent for forensic scientific examination.

Some support for accepting this course of events is given by the nature of the blows. The second and third blows were much more consistent with frenzy, it might be thought, than with any attempt to kill. Why, if Stoner was the assailant, would his blows have increased or progressively diminished in intensity? The likelihood, if his was the hand which wielded the mallet, is that each of the three blows would have been of equally devastating force. On the other hand, is it not more likely that Alma's strength may have been partially dissipated after the first vicious blow?

The consequence of taking heroin and many other drugs is that, after the initial sense of euphoria and over-excitement, there follows drowsiness, sometimes depression and often an appearance of drunkenness. How long this takes to develop depends on the quantity taken. Does it seem probable, if, as the Crown suggested and the jury believed, Stoner was the assailant, that he would not at once have gone to Alma and told her what he had done? Why on earth would he have thought it necessary, when they were both together in the house throughout, to have waited some time – well after Irene had returned and long enough for the blood to have congealed – before telling Alma what he had done?

If Alma had struck the blows in the manner suggested, Stoner may well have been both horrified at what she had done and desperate in his anxiety to protect her from it. In her euphoric state, he may have been unable to instil much sense into her and may have taken the mallet without telling her at all and hidden it in the garden – or that may have occurred later. By the time Irene returned Alma may have moved into or towards the second stage of the symptoms, and, when Stoner told her what had happened, what is more likely than that Irene and Stoner, with such help, if any, as they might have got from Alma, had endeavoured to put together some story which would help their beloved? The facts were so blatantly against Alma that they may have despaired and resolved to do no more than say as little as possible. The idea, as the prosecution case implied, that either Alma or Stoner – whichever was the assailant – could have been capable of ignoring the injured husband, intending to go to bed together and have intercourse as if nothing had occurred, really seems quite incredible. Moreover, is it not likely that one or the other or both would have told Irene what had occurred as soon as she returned, since it was obvious that at the latest they would have to do so the following morning? Is it really to be believed that they could have intended to put it off until then, and, if so, to what end? Is it not also possible that, as the effects of the drug wore off, Alma, in her depression, turned to alcohol to restore her sense of euphoria?

Initially Stoner said as little as possible to the police and, for that matter, to everyone else. It may slowly have dawned on him that one of them was bound to be held responsible, and the inevitable consequence of his belief that Alma was the love of his life – his first and only experience of that emotion – caused him readily to accept that he must shoulder all the blame and protect her. This may well have been his thought when he showed Irene on the Tuesday where he had obtained the mallet, and his journey to see Alma, which followed, may well have been made in the hope that the opportunity would present itself for him to convince her that this was the wise course. Is it plausible that, in the throes of his first love, Stoner, whose only desire was to protect Alma, would have stood calm and quiescent remarking only, 'You've got yourself into this mess by talking too much,' as Alma was taken to the police station to be charged? Would he have told Carter a story, when questioned on the Monday morning, which exculpated himself but did not clear Alma? Is it unreasonable to believe that Stoner, having refused to implicate Alma when she was alive, told the truth to his counsel on the eve of his appeal – that he was innocent and the first he knew of the injuries to Francis Rattenbury was when Alma told him of this in bed?

Alma's position until then may have been the reverse. Whatever her faults, and she was not without them, she was unlikely to be one to allow someone else to carry her burdens and shoulder her duty. When her solicitor, as he revealed later, was urging her to put the blame, where he believed it rested, on Stoner, she made it plain that this was unthinkable. The solicitor assumed this was valour and courage. It might have been, but equally it could have been her recognition that putting the blame, which was hers, on her eighteen-year-old lover, whom she had originally seduced, was such as would put her quite beyond the pale. Ultimately it was suggested to her, as her solicitor and her friends have confirmed, that whilst Stoner was a young man on his own – it was probably stressed that his very youth would probably save him from the gallows – she had the responsibility of two children who, if she were hanged, would be orphaned. At this point she may have decided to accept a version of events which was possibly hatched on Irene's return to the house on the night, but which she had then rejected, refusing at that stage to allow Stoner to take the blame, as in his immaturity and his besotted state he may have been urging her to do.

The press at the time, books subsequently written and, in particular, Tennyson Jesse's introduction to *Notable British Trials* would have had us believe that Alma's suicide was a measure of her inability to live now that she thought Stoner – with whom she was deeply in love – would inevitably die. Perhaps so, but did she really love him to that extent? If so, why were there periodic discussions in which she suggested – ostensibly on account of the difference between their ages – that their relationship must come to an end? Why did she use her financial resources from the outset to provide herself with the best possible team to defend her whilst leaving her beloved to such help as was available for the derisory fees allowed under the Poor Prisoners' Defence Act? Apart from the sexual relationship, which was so important to her, what could this talented, artistic, intelligent, experienced and at times calculating woman

224

really have had in common with the callow, uneducated, backward and immature Stoner, kind and devoted though he probably was?

The case for the prosecution contained a hint – it never
emerged as a bold assertion – that the visit which Stoner was
required to make to Dr O'Donnell in February arose because
Alma was laying the foundation for a subsequent story that he
was on cocaine. On analysis, that does not stand up. In the
first place, she made it plain that, following the visit, she did
no more about it, alleging that this was based on a belief that
he had stopped taking anything and was better. Secondly, it
became clear when she was in the witness box that her real
anxiety had been that he had something wrong with his head
– she meant his brain – and she had to be sure that no one
was around the house with her children who might be a danger
to them. The mention of cocaine may also have arisen because
Stoner knew she had recourse to it and she may have suspected
he was getting his hands on some of it.

What was the position of Dr O'Donnell in all of this? Clearly
he was not only their doctor but also a close friend of Alma
and Rattenbury. If, as seems evident from Stoner's instructions
at the time, despite his reluctance to allow Casswell to attack
her, Alma was having recourse to drugs, is it possible that
O'Donnell would not have known? He denied this in the witness
box, but did he have a special reason for doing so? It is clear
that he was throughout most protective of Alma. There is little
reason to doubt that his injection of morphia on the fateful night
must have involved an element of protecting her from police
questioning. Why else would anyone decide to render insensible,
in the presence of the police, the number-one suspect?

No satisfactory explanation was ever forthcoming from O'Donnell for Alma's periodic 'attacks', in respect of which he was
often called upon to visit her, although from the description
which each witness gave of them they had every appearance
of being drug-induced – and that drug was not alcohol, or certainly not alcohol alone.

The form and nature of the interview between O'Donnell and
Stoner itself had an element of farce about it. The doctor seems
to have dealt with him in a most perfunctory and cavalier fashion;
he gave him no advice; he did not examine him; he elicited
no symptoms from him which would have enabled him to build
up even a minimal clinical picture; rather he presented a picture
of a worthless and unnecessary interview. What was really the

truth about that visit it is difficult to imagine.

Drugs seem to have played a vital although undisclosed part in the story of the Villa Madeira, and it is for question whether they had not also assisted Alma when she ended the story, by plunging a dagger into herself no less than six times, before falling into the water, dead.

What occurred in the Villa Madeira must, therefore, remain in the realms of speculation. It is quite impossible, at this distance in time, to reach any positive conclusion about the truth of what happened there on the night of 24 March 1935, over fifty years ago. That the trial was far from satisfactory and did not provide a reliable investigation or a demonstrably just decision can hardly be denied. There remains, however, one person alone who can provide the answer: George Percy Stoner himself. He is still alive, over seventy years of age, and understandably unwilling to be interviewed, since he has long since established a new life for himself.

Perhaps the only reservation left in one's mind is that, in a case where he may well have suffered a major injustice, Stoner seems to have no wish to confirm the truth of what he told Casswell when preparing the appeal – which would provide the last opportunity to record for posterity that it was not his hand which struck the fearful blows which caused the death of Francis Rattenbury in the Villa Madeira.